To Study Deceit

Deceit is the worse disease in the world.
It has killed millions.

Beverly Thomas

authorHOUSE®

AuthorHouse™
1663 Liberty Drive
Bloomington, IN 47403
www.authorhouse.com
Phone: 1 (800) 839-8640

Image credit to Tyre Bowman

Published by AuthorHouse 12/21/2016

ISBN: 978-1-5246-5672-0 (sc)
ISBN: 978-1-5246-5671-3 (e)

Print information available on the last page.

Any people depicted in stock imagery provided by Thinkstock are models, and such images are being used for illustrative purposes only. Certain stock imagery © Thinkstock.

Scripture taken from the King James Version of the Bible.

This book is printed on acid-free paper.

TABLE OF CONTENTS

Acknowledgments ix

Introduction xi

PART 1
COURSE OBJECTIVES 1

Chapter 1   You Must Study *Deceit* 3

Chapter 2   The Works of the Devil 19

Chapter 3   How Demon Possession Affects People Part 1 40

Chapter 4   How Demon Possession Affects People Part 2 62

PART 2
COURSE TOPICS 87

Chapter 5   Where Is God? 89

Chapter 6   Do You Recognize Seducing Spirits Part 1 110

Chapter 7   Do You Recognize Seducing Spirits – Part 2
            My Brother Cain 125

PART 3
GRADING PLAN 143

Chapter 8   A Scheming Mother 145

Chapter 9   On the Run, Two Brothers 158

Chapter 10 There's No Place Like Home
            D. Thomas 176

PART 4

CLASS PARTICIPATION..201

Chapter 11 I Will, But I Don't Know How
                    [D. Johnson]..203

Chapter 12 The Devil's Man
                    The Antichrist, The False Christ........................219

PART 5

EXTRA CREDIT...247

Chapter 13 From Harlot To Bride...249

Chapter 14 Can Anything Good
                    Come Out Of Nazareth?..................................266

PART 6

FINAL EXAM..289

Chapter 15 Finally, Real Love...291

ABOUT THE AUTHOR

Reverend Beverly D. Thomas is a pastor, evangelist, television producer, writer and celebrated author. Reverend Thomas is the senior pastor of **A Passion For Christ Ministries** in Chicago, Illinois, which has been established for more than 19. The Gospel is spread through tapes, music, television, skits and literature all over the city, state and abroad. Pastor Thomas has taken three missionary journeys throughout South Africa, spreading the redemptive message of Jesus Christ. "**The Light Still Shines [PFC]**," broadcast is produced and directed by Rev. Thomas and is broadcasted weekly on **WJYS-62 television each Saturday morning.**

Through such ministries as *Cater-the-Word*, A Passion For Christ Ministries is reaching those persons who are unable to come out to the church. One of her greatest emphasis is on the youth, through Such programs as the *Teen Forum*, the youth are able to come and receive strength from leaders within the church as well as outside leaders who are invited to come and encourage the youth.

Visit www.apassionforchrist.net where you can listen to sermons, view our recent telecasts, read newsletters, request prayer and information, and much more. Please write me at passions@apassionforchrist.org.

You can purchase any of Reverend Thomas' books including e-books, at any store where books are sold, as well as on line.

ACKNOWLEDGMENTS

This book is dedicated to my Lord and Savior Jesus Christ who has redeemed me with His precious blood. I love you Jesus. A Passion For Christ Ministries – You all are my heart

A special note of thanks to everyone who typed, proofed, edited or contributed in any way toward the completion of this great work.

To my pastor, teacher and evangelist, Reverend Ernest Angley of Ernest Angley's Grace Cathedral, thank you for sharing your work with me and allowing me to use that work in my books.

"To Study Deceit" is a collection of sermons delivered to my congregation over several Sundays. At different points throughout this great work, you may feel like you are actually in the congregation. I pray that you will enjoy it.

The Sinner's Prayer is captured throughout the book.

God Bless You, is my prayer.

Yours with a Passion for Souls,

Reverend Beverly D. Thomas

Pastor, A Passion for Christ Ministries

INTRODUCTION

Deceit is the worse disease in the world.
It has killed millions.

PART 1

COURSE OBJECTIVES

CHAPTER 1

YOU MUST STUDY *DECEIT*

This is not a lesson for you to go and have Bible study with somebody else. But it is for you to recognize when deceit is in *your* life; when you are working in deceit. If you are around somebody that is deceitful, they will affect you in a tremendous way and you may not even know it. **Behold, I give unto you power to tread on serpents and scorpions, and over all the power of the enemy: and nothing shall by any means hurt you** (Luke 10:19). We are talking about to study deceit. When you study something, you are going to have some essential tools with you. You are going to have a notebook, a pen, Bible and if you can trust the author, you might have you a reliable concordance. There are a lot of people writing books, and concordance and Bibles and they are not saved. So, how can you really trust what they say? Again a notebook, and King James Version Bible, that is what we use here, printed in 1611. And the more of man that is in it [versions of Bibles], the more of God they take out. Our reference book for this study will be *"**The Deceit of Lucifer**[1]"* from our home church, in Akron, Ohio, written by Reverend Ernest Angley. **Behold I give unto you power** (Luke 10:19). We know this is red writing. So, we know this is Jesus talking to His people. He has given us power to tread on serpents and scorpions. **And over all the power of the enemy.** I want you to underline that, if your Bible is a workbook. **Over all the power of the enemy. And nothing shall by any means hurt you**. What a marvelous promise Jesus gave to His what? His Followers! But, if you notice with some Christians today, if you have a conversation

---

[1]   Reverend Ernest Angley, *The Deceit of Lucifer*, (Akron, Ohio: Winston Press, 1989).

3

with them, you would think Jesus never got out of the grave. They complain about every little thing, every problem. Some people, who do not have Christianity but they will take Jesus say, "I don't want to be a Christian, it seems like you all have more problems than those of us who are unsaved." They complain about everything. Some pray Lord, Lord, Lord, and soon as God moves for them, they forget who made the provision for them. For example, we pray, "Lord we are all in this studio apartment." Then God moves you into a one bedroom. Then you start complaining about that. These are Christians, God's people. The Lord is trying to teach us to be thankful for what we have. And if you are honest in your own heart; if you are for real with yourself, you will realize that when you had less, you were a better person. To study demonology is to study deceit. And the Bible clearly tells us **to study to shew thyself approved unto God, a workman that needeth not to be ashamed, rightly dividing the word of truth** (2 Timothy 2:15)**.** Yes, study to shew thyself approve unto God. A workman, a worker. Now some of you are going to trip over that because you are lazy. To get anything out of God you have to be motivated. You have to do something. So when you study something you might go to different authors on that same subject. It is like some of our children in their classroom studies. They might have African American history. And we have Rosa Parks, and we have other Afro-American heroes. And so maybe you might go to the internet and there are different authors who have put pen to parchment and wrote something about this particular one. Well, it is the same thing with the Word of God.

NOW IS MADE MANIFEST

You have study His word. In Paul's writing, Jesus said ***Even* the mystery which hath been hid from ages and from generations, but now is made manifest to his saints: To whom God would make known what *is* the riches of the glory of this mystery**

among the Gentiles; which is Christ in you, the hope of glory: Whom we preach, warning every man, and teaching every man in all wisdom; that we may present every man perfect in Christ Jesus (Colossians 1:26-28). But in this final hour, those of us who are seeking, through prayer, fasting and living in the word, those mysteries are going to be unlocked to our minds. So, to study demonology is to study deceit, and to study deceit is to study yourself. Yes! What does it mean to deceive? It means to ensnare, to make a person believe what is not true. And the enemy is busy with that and so are a lot of these false doctrine churches. If in these churches, these people tell you that nobody can live free from sin. That is deceit. They beat Jesus to death and you think that you can be a whore and shack up, and watch all sorts of pornography, and all this other kind of stuff and say a little simple prayer and go to Heaven? It's sad but most churches today preach that no one can live free from sin. How horrible! Oh God, help us! That is false doctrine. Listen to it again, it says to make a person believe what is not true. To think that you can lie and you are still going to heaven. To think you can smoke? And it tells you right on the package, that this causes cancer. To study deceit. Really it is studying yourself in most cases. Deceit is the devil's business. It is his business. If you have a business, you know you work harder than anybody else. You get there before your employees, often times. If you are a good worker, you will often still be there when everybody leaves. When it is their day off, you fill in. You are thinking about how to grow and succeed; you are formulating a lot of plans. Well that is the way the devil is. But his business is you. Getting you to trip over the word of God.

THE DECEIT OF LUCIFER

Deceit means to delude and mislead. *Deceit is a lie*. It is a dishonest action or a trick. *A deceitful person intends to deceive*. To be deceptive is to be false. Apt to lie or to cheat. If you are deceivable, you can be deceived. So, that leads to the one big question. Can you be deceived? To study deceit. We have a lot of examples. We are going to start in the life of Samson. Judges 13:1, says **And the children of Israel did evil again in the sight of the Lord**. Now underline that if your Bible is a workbook. If you know anything about the Children of Israel, they were always in and out with God. They were always making God false promises. Have you made promises to God that you have not kept? The Bible is so plain when you allow the Holy Spirit to lead, guide and teach you. It tells us in that first verse in Chapter 13 of Judges, **And the Children of Israel did evil again**. So here they are back in trouble again. In my mind's eye, when I read that statement that tells me a lot of information before I go any further. So it says, **the Children of Israel did evil again in the sight of the Lord**. So let me break that down. What does that tell me? That lets me know they were unfaithful. It lets me know they were apt to lie. They were apt to deceive. And it also lets me know that at some point or time in their lives, as a group of people, they had to humble themselves in order to be delivered. So that one sentence is telling me a lot. So they knew the way to God. It says, the Children of Israel did evil again. The word "Again" means one more time. So that means previously handled deceit. That means that previously and one time before they knew how to humble themselves so God could come to their defense. And it says again they find themselves in the same rut. I do not know what you got out of that, but I was like "Oh man, again!" It is not like getting in trouble with your momma or your daddy. *This is God*! It says, Judges 13:1 **In the sight of the Lord; and the Lord delivered them into the hand of the Philistines forty years**. Now notice this, God is so consistent. So the Philistines were their enemies. Right! **Let God be true, but every man a liar** (Romans 3:4). **Jesus Christ the same yesterday, and to day, and for ever** (Hebrews 13:8). Have you forsaken God? Thereby being turned over to the hands of your enemies. An enemy does not always have to be people. It could just be hard times. You just can't get out. You just can't make it. Your ends cannot even communicate, let alone ends meet. You are unlikeable. You are unapproachable. Those are hard times. Kids, husbands, friends, and you are not getting along with nobody. Nobody can get along with you; because the Lord has turned you over to the devices of the devil. It is right here in the word of God. Thank God! I did not write it. It says that the Lord delivered them into the hands of the Philistines. The Philistines were their enemies. Sickness is an enemy to us. Oppression, depression, struggling and not having enough is an enemy to us. **But my God *shall* supply all your need according to his riches in glory by Christ Jesus** (Philippians 4:19)**.**

PERFECT PEACE

The Lord *promised* to keep us in perfect peace. **Thou wilt keep him in perfect peace, whose mind is stayed on thee: because he trusteth in thee** (Isaiah 26:3)**.** Jesus said He would make us the lender and not the borrower. He said He would make us the head and not the tail. But, if you find yourself in opposition of the word, you will tie His hands on your behalf. To study deceit. We always want to find out their deficiency. Well, I can tell you what was going on with them. You give your opinion by saying, "They should have never got married." And you still have not been married once. But, like Jesus, I want to go. "Where is your husband, bring him here." You will get that one later. Why did Jesus call the woman at the well, those men she had been with her husbands? They had laid with her. And I am not talking about a ring on your finger either. Neighbor, I know you got that one. I love you neighbor. Judges 13:2,5 say, **And there was a certain man of Zorah, of the family of the Danites, whose name was Manoah; and his wife was barren, and bare not. For, lo, thou shalt conceive, and bear a son; and no razor shall come on his head: for the child shall be a Nazarite unto**

God from the womb: and he shall begin to deliver Israel out of the hand of the Philistines. Underline that if your Bible is a workbook. God works the same way today, neighbor. He changes not. The Lord is not going to give you all the blessing of your life at once. You could not even bare it. You fast. You pray. You face persecutions and you get *just a little bit more faith*. You fast and you pray and you study the word. And He gives you *a little bit more* temperance. You fast and you pray and you cry out to God. And He gives you *a little bit more* long suffering. That is the way it works. The Lord gives you a little bit of wisdom. A little bit of knowledge. And as you really work with that and you really use that measure, *then* He gives you a little bit more. And I thank God for that because what kind of creatures would we be? I don't care how close you are to God, you are not going to get it all on this side of heaven. I heard this one false doctrine pastor say he had ten gifts. When the Bible says it is only nine. How could people still have been sitting in that congregation? That means they are false. To stay in false doctrine. You know in your mind, you say, "I thought it was only nine." And some of you are still giving them your money. You are still giving them your holy tithes.

FOR REAL

Judges 13:5,6(a) says **For, lo, thou shalt conceive, and bear a son; and no razor shall come on his head: for the child shall be a Nazarite unto God from the womb: and he shall begin to deliver Israel out of the hand of the Philistines. Then the woman came and told her husband.** But this is where a lot of people miss it. They feel that awkwardness. The weirdness, the uncomfortableness in the fact that God's hand might be on their life. Who in the world, in their right mind would call themselves to be a pastor? I mean on a crystal clear day. Who would say, "I want to be a pastor." I am not talking about reality TV. I am talking about for real. You have the reality that the same people you are leading everyday day are going to lie on you. You have been with those people in the midnight hour, when a loved one was sick or near death. You have been down to juvenile court for their children so many times until you've lost count. You may have even bailed some of them out of jail. You helped some of them. You have kept them from being homeless. And they team up with the weak ones in the congregation. And they start talking about they are going to oust you. I am not talking about what I heard. I am talking about what I know. They go around, just like little serpents whispering in the ears of people who are not in there with God like they should, which makes them susceptible to deceit. So, since they are not in there with God; they do not recognize when something false is coming their way. How can you recognize the truth – how can you tell when something is false? You have to first know the truth about it; in order to recognize that it is false. But, if you do God's word; you are going to accept everything that is coming and going. The battle is on! The battle is on! Churches and houses of God are not being destroyed on the outside but from the inside out. Yes! You are not going to let a person come in off the street and sit on your nice blue couch. You are going to clear your throat and offer them to sit on your father's chairs and not sit on this side. And you should feel the same way about the enemy coming on your turf. The devil intercedes. He comes in through just one thought. And he marinades your mind with your favorite kind of thing. It may be sexual, monetary, power, whatever that is. He preys on your weaknesses and she uses your personality. He preys on your self-doubt.

AND ENTICED

Let no man say when he is tempted, I am tempted of God: for God cannot be tempted with evil, neither tempteth he any man: But every man is tempted, when he is drawn away of

his own lust, and enticed. Then when lust hath conceived, it bringeth forth sin: and sin, when it is finished, bringeth forth death. Do no err, my beloved brethren (James 1:13-16). Lust is not always sex, but most of the time it is. We are talking about studying deceit. Notice this, how in the 16th chapter of Judges, there was a man called Samson, who God had chosen to destroy God's enemies. At one time, what an anointing Samson had possessed. He was consecrated before God and the sign of his consecration was his uncut hair. Knowing that as long as his locks were not shaved. He would have superhuman powers. It is the same promise that the Lord makes to us. That you can take it. With Jesus, you can make it. **But they that wait upon the Lord shall renew their strength; they shall mount up with wings as eagles; they shall run, and not be weary; and they shall walk, and not faint** (Isaiah 40:31). None of your enemies will be able to stand before you. **Thou prepares a table before me in the presence of mine enemies** (Psalm 23:5). The Lord said **When a man's ways please the Lord, he maketh even his enemies to be at peace with him** (Proverbs 16:7). They might want to do something but the Lord will change their mind. That is if you are living right. These are all the promises of God. This is what He promised you. If you live a life free of deceit. Righteousness, Holiness, Purity and living right. These are the things that belong to you. But you cannot play around with sin. You cannot be two faced. Jesus is not working off Mardi Gras time. They sell masks that have two faces. You have been down to Mardi Gras, some of you. Where they have those beads around their neck and they don't have on some *other stuff.* Everything is dangling. More than the food makes you fat. You are down their visiting them wizards and witches. And you just turn yourself loose; and just the time the devil moves in. There you are on the floor. They are throwing down beads. And you look up and see the senior deacon on the deacon board. There he is and both your eyes meet. Somebody is always watching. Samson was playing with deceit. He had an opportunity to really serve God's people. He had an opportunity, the people had gotten in trouble once again. They were crying out. It's the same way in this final hour. People are looking for the real Jesus to stand up. They come into the houses that are supposed to be of God. And the people in the churches are still performing magical acts. They have turned the houses of God into a circus. They have turned God's pulpit to a profane pulpit. They have turned His pulpit from things that are Holy; from things that are righteous into a man-made pulpit. They have turned His holy pulpit into a satisfaction store.

LIKE A DRUNKEN MAN

Mine heart within me is broken because of the prophets; all my bones shake; I am like a drunken man, and like a man whom wine hath overcome, because of the Lord, and because of the words of his holiness. For the land is full of adulterers; for because of swearing the land mourneth; the pleasant places of the wilderness are dried up, and their course is evil, and their force is not right. For both prophet and priest are profane; *yea, in my house have I found their wickedness, saith the Lord* (Jeremiah 23:9-11). They say, "My sermons are for sale. I'll say what you want me to." Most pastors preach a *watered-down* gospel; there's no conviction, no reproof, no rebuke. People are at ease. Not here! It can't be bought or bargained out. It can't be weaseled out. Because the Lord is the captain of this ship [speaking of her congregation]. Jesus has landed many of thousands of holy souls. Samson told Delilah the secret of his heart. And he betrayed God. Not only did Samson betray God but he betrayed himself. And when you fail God, you not only fail people connected to your life, you fail some of very own loved ones. We are talking about studying deceit. You fail yourself. You fail God and then you have to crawl to get back with God. That devil is right there to let you know, "God doesn't love you; God doesn't want to be bothered with you no more." Then you just keep trying over and over again. The more you fail God the harder it is get back with God and just think of all that you lose. So many don't find their way back.

What did Samson do? He told Delilah a lie. You can search this in the 16th Chapter of Judges. **And she** [Delilah] **said unto him, How canst thou say, I love thee, when thine heart is not with me? Thou hast mocked me these three times, and hast not told me wherein thy great strength lieth. And it came to pass, when she pressed him daily with her words, and urged him, so that his soul was vexed unto death; That he told her all his heart, and said unto her, There hath not come a razor upon mine heard; for I have been a Nazarite unto God from my mother's womb: if I be shaven, then my strength will go from me, and I shall become weak, and be like any other man. And when Delilah saw that he had told her all his heart, she sent and called for the lords of the Philistines, saying, Come up this once, for he hath shewed me all his heart. Then the lords of the Philistines came up unto her, and brought money in their hand** (Judges 16:15-18).

IF YOU LOVE ME

A young man tells you, "If you love me, lay with me now." You say, "No!" But, you let him keep rubbing on you. You have such low self-esteem. You feel like life is going to pass you by. How is your life going to pass you by? You only get one virginity. And you cannot go to the pawn shop and get a new one. You cannot trade nothing in for it. Once it is gone! It's gone baby! It's just like one of those rare things in life. Once it is gone, it is gone. It is like your first house, you cannot ever go back and apply for first time buyer promotions. That doesn't qualify for you. It's like when I was growing up. They had a baby shower for the first baby. They are having a baby shower for all the children. And your virginity is one of those things. It is just one time. So you should save yourself. Did you know young men are to be virgins too instead, of testing the waters. The waters might get a little rough when you get in it and you get carried off with the current. In the beginning, the waters look so calm. Then you get in up above your head. You do know what I am talking about. Men you have to make good choices in life because somethings you will spend the rest of your life trying to correct that BIG mistake. To study deceit. If a man loves you, he is going to treat you like a lady. He is going to treat you like a lady and he's going to give you a contract [proposal and marriage].

YOU CAN'T BUY LOVE

Samson decides he is going to tell Delilah some lies. And I am bringing this out again because I want you to think about it. Samson was so deceived, but he just kept on playing with her [playing with sin]. Now, get this today. To study deceit. You can't buy love. You can't make people like you. You can't use your body to be liked by – people like you or they don't. It is grown people still in clicks from high school. It is grown people, listen to what I am telling you today, they are still playing the same games they played in high school. Here you are, in your fifties and you are still talking about *boy catch a girl, kiss a girl*. Some of you are too young, but some you around my age, you know what boy catch a girl, kiss a girl was. Wasn't that boy catch a girl? They tag you and your *it*. You will get that one when you get to the house. But, I have been it [*fast tail*] before and some of you up in here have been it before too. Lying to Delilah. Samson was just telling her all kind of lies. But notice this. At first, it was just a fun thing. How many things have caused you harm that started out being just fun? Bullying somebody, talking down to somebody, treating somebody, it just seems like it was a fun thing, but you just didn't know the end result. Notice this, it was a fun thing. But Samson was to learn that there was nothing funny about being under the tree of forbidden fruit. The devil just kept on assuring Samson, "You are not going to tell her everything. You are not going to go all the way." And sex isn't sex until you go all the way. You got little sensors in your lips. Can I help you? You are doing all that deep passionate kissing. To study deceit. "You are not going to give your whole heart. Why, you didn't tell all the other women," you tell yourself. The devil was playing on Samson. "When the Philistines tried to take you, what did you do? You rose up and carried the gates of the city off to the top of a hill, Samson. You are fly. You are too cool to get caught. You are the number one player," the enemy whispered. Just like the devil plays on you. "You got two phones. If the girlfriend wants to search this phone, you got the disposable in your jacket." You always have an answer but when God riseth up, what will you say? Somebody is always watching. Remember when the Lord spoke to Job? **Gird up now thy loins like a man; for I will demand of thee, and answer thou me** (Job 38:3)**.**

LUST AND LOVE

Who wants to remember a lie? Not only do you have to remember the lie, but you have to keep the lie in order. Who wants to be under that kind of stress? But the truth, you don't have to remember it because it's the truth. Right? And notice this, this is the way the devil does, Delilah just whined, and again you can read it in Judges 16. She just whined, and whined, and whined, and whined, and this is what the devil does. If you love me. That wasn't really love that they really had for one another. She wanted money and he wanted *something* from her. That has not changed at all today. Not even here in 2016. Yeah, I know, you didn't even see that coming. Many today are confused about lust and loved. Lust destroys. But love edifies. Real love builds up. Real love includes respect honor and protect. If you love me, you won't lie to me. But Samson did lie to Delilah, again and again. And he never thought he would go all the way and reveal that which the Lord said was sacred; that holy covenant between him and the Lord. Notice that. Real love is what? Respect and honor.

If you love your children, you are not going to make a difference in them or call them degrading names or talk down to them. Not if you love your children. If you love your wife, you learn sometimes, even if she is wrong, how to just keep that thought to yourself, because the price is going to be too great. And the same thing with the woman. Because you know this little disagreement that you might be having right now, it is just for a moment. But the repercussions are going too far out last the disagreement. And now the edge between you is getting bigger and bigger. Just because you had to say what was on your mind and give your opinion. But you have got to study deceit. *Right* in the eyes of God is not the same *right* as in the eyes of people. The Lord says in Isaiah, **For as the heavens are higher than the earth, so are my ways higher than your ways, and my thoughts than your thoughts** (Isaiah 55:9). And you may think being strong is telling people your opinions and doing things the way you want to do it. But strength is really in suppression. Strength is really having self-control. And what a powerful thing that is! Even though you may be angry, the Bible says don't go to bed on your wrath. Be angry and sin not. Even though someone has said something to hurt you, you have studied deceit enough to know that even though you're mad, it is not going to help both of you to hurt one another in the long run. Young girls and young men, you have to honor your body and respect your own body and respect who you are. Have something about yourself! So many of the wrong things happen when people have low self-esteem. They are easily taken in. They will easily be tricked by money and love and sex and what people can promise them. And the *sugar daddies*, and *cougars*, all those other things. You have heard of those things. Do not play with me. Are you a cougar?

HIS SOUL WAS VEXED

Samson told Delilah if he were bound with new ropes that were never occupied, he would be as other men. She did. Samson however, broke the ropes as though they had been threads. When he heard Delilah cry the Philistines be upon thee Samson, He grew a little bit more creative with the next lie. Finally, his soul was vexed unto death and Samson told Delilah all his heart. *She wore him down* to the place where *he did not care.* And that what's the devil wants to do to each one of you. Write that statement down. She wore him down to the place where he did not care. And sometimes families can do that too. They say, "You fasting again? What kind of church is that? It that in the Bible?" This kind come not but by prayer, fasting and living in the word. Isn't that what they did under the Old Testament did when desperate people wanted to see how God would move for them? They proclaimed a fast to afflict their souls. Even the animal fasted. Because they needed to hear from God. It always amazes me, when Godly people are fasting and people call me. But, when you were out in the streets drinking and going from lounge to lounge, where was the concern? And here were are afflicting our souls to get more power from God. And you want to call me? We have got things mixed up! We have got things mixed up! But notice, I want you to write it down and this week ponder it in your prayer time, "She wore him down to the place where he did not care." Think about Samson, the Philistines came, they burned his eyes out. Now he finds himself down in the dungeon. Delilah just wore him out, begging him every day. But, finally Samson came to place where all he wanted was a little peace. So, he sold the Lord out for a *little peace*; some of you have sold him for a *little piece*... To study deceit. Because you gave over to their whining and crying. Why is your child spoiled rotten? "Oh Momma! Momma! Momma! Momma can I? Momma can I? Gone on boy!" So, now you are at the morgue that night. In our house when we were growing up with my momma, Louise, if she said "No" that was it. And then if we tried that on our daddy, he *always* said, "What did your momma say?" And that was it. Do you have those kind of principles in your home? Does your child put a wedge between you and the husband or between you and the wife?

"Momma, daddy said I can't have this." And you say, "Gone on, you can have it." And you don't realize what you are doing. Now you are causing differences. I notice this down through the years. A minister might say something out here [in the congregation] to one of your kids, and after they come out from the meeting, they start acting like they are crying. And you come over and rub them. What you should say is, "You got in trouble. You deal with it." And see what that is teaching them is to rise up against authority – that what your good leaders say really doesn't count. It really doesn't matter. And you do the same thing with God. Didn't Jesus say that what you do to the least of thee, you also do it to whom?

WE LEARNED TO HONOR GOD

When we were coming up, we respected authority because we respected our parents. Authority and respect came in the house. We learned to honor God by honoring our parents. My momma fixed my daddy's plate off the top. It didn't matter if he didn't come until the next night. That plate was waiting. All the kids had chores assigned to us. We had responsibilities. And that has a lot to do with who we are today. People and children coming up today don't respect God because they don't even respect their parents. *I thought God and my momma, Louise were like almost equal.* Almost. I thought God and Louise were like almost equal. I didn't want God to get me if He whipped anything like my momma did. I just didn't want God to get me if He whipped anything like Louise did? She was punching on that key machine [at work] and then just come home with that robotic arm. It just seemed like her arm was anointed with more strength. The closer she got to house. It seemed like it got faster and faster because she knew she was coming home to whip me. My mother was a key punch operator for IBM for over 30 something years. It just seemed like that arm would just start going around. It just seemed like it was spelling my name. B-E-V-E-R-L- and by the time

17

she got to the Y, she was ready. So, we didn't have a lot of trouble respecting God in our home because we respected our parents. See how it works? And Jesus said through the Old Testament, He said teach this from generation to generation; how to respect your elders. Don't talk about holiness people or people going to church. Keep your mouth off of them. Right? But, people today are doing everything but that. Some folks are doing everything but that!

A SPECIAL MISSION

Samson at one time, God had been so proud of him. God had spent so much time and invested so much for a special mission for him to help his people. How disappointed God must have been. After Samson told Delilah all his heart. He was so deceived that he placed his head on her lap. Now that can be another series, "And fell asleep." We could have a new series, "And fell asleep." The series before that could be head on lap. And then the one after that could be fell asleep. It is in the word. I am not making these things up. A sleep that ended in destruction. That is in the "Deceit of Lucifer." Samson the Philistines are upon you cried Delilah for the fourth time. Samson got up. He shook himself. But the power of God would not work. To study deceit. The Bible says Samson got up and shook himself and would go out as he did at other times. But he did not realize that God was not with him anymore. I challenge you to go back and study it. This is a book you need to study (*The Deceit of Lucifer*). I remember when we had introduced this book one time and a pastor came by and got a book. And he did it so quick, I guess he thought that one of his parishioners or somebody out there, may have seen him come in here to a lady pastor's church, of all places. But he came in to buy this book. He came in got and got the book and went out the door. No one told me but I believe he was a pastor. That makes me laugh every time I remember it.

CHAPTER 2

THE WORKS OF THE DEVIL

You have to know your enemy. You have to know who is fighting against you. How can you fight a good fight if you don't know who your enemy is? How can you tell if something is false, except you first know the truth about it? There are so many things going on in many of the churches today. And it is false doctrine. But because the people of God, the people who are called of God, they have not studied the Word, they been blinded by deceit. They have not studied the word. **Study to shew thyself approved unto God, a workman that needeth not to be ashamed, rightly dividing the word of truth** (2 Timothy 2:15). Many people have not taken the time to still away with the Lord. The Bible encourages us, prophetically to study. You need to study. You must study. Going to church once a week is simply not enough. You have dedicated, diligent prayer time. You have to be an avid Bible reader. You have to be an avid person who is in there with God. In the Pauline epistles, it tells us to pray without seizing. No, that does not mean walking around praying in tongues. And so many people, they are deceived about the Baptism of the Holy Ghost, believing that they can turn it off, they can turn it on whenever they get ready. My child, that is not the Baptism of the Holy Ghost, if you can speak in your "prayer tongue" whenever you get ready. If YOU can turn it on and off then YOU, not the Holy Spirit is the one who is in control. It is not the Baptism of the Holy Ghost as was demonstrated on the Day of Pentecost. Many, many people, have been deceived because they would not accept truth. They did not study the word of the Lord. Everybody receives the Baptism of the Holy Ghost in the same manner. The same way as those people did on the Day of Pentecost. The Holy Ghost will not speak through a liar. The Holy Ghost will not use a practicing homosexual to perform

His marvelous gifts. Hear me today. The Lord only uses the pure in heart. **Blessed are the pure in heart: for they shall see God** (Matthew 5:8)**. I will therefore that men pray every where, lifting up holy hands, without wrath and doubting** (I Timothy 2:8)**.** You can't lift up holy hands if you have a heart full of degradation and abomination. You have to know who you are fighting against. And the enemy, I want you to right this down, he is playing with you. Your enemy is playing on you. He is playing on two key elements that exist in your life. That if you don't know about yourself. He will use those two things against you. He is playing on your ***weaknesses***. Your ***personality***, he knows who you are.

IF

If you are saved today, you use to belong to him. Everybody that was born since the fall of Adam came into the world needing a savior. Nobody since the creation of Eve, were born in the image of the Almighty God. We, who are born again and have the blood of Jesus on our souls, came into the image of God by the blood that stained the old rugged cross. How much false doctrine does just that sentence alone expose? But people they are lost and they are deceived about salvation. How many people in the year of 2015 died deceived about salvation, with lying on their tongues and unforgiveness in their hearts? They had the obituaries all made out. Only to rest and open their eyes to a hell, a consuming fire. A fire that will not be quenched. And now they realize the truth about Jesus the Christ and holy living. But, it is too late and they can't do anything about it. If you are having trouble in your life, don't miss one. The devil again, work on your ***personality*** and your ***weaknesses***. These are the two things he uses against you. Your personality is who you are. If you are easily hurt, he is always there enticing you with hurt feelings. "Somebody don't like you." If you didn't grow up with enough love, you are always looking for love in all the wrong places. Your weakness, that low self-esteem and how you think about yourself. Personality and the kind of person you are. He knows you. But, you don't even know who you are fighting.

HE WILL WAIT A LIFETIME

You don't know your enemy. He is skilled. Your enemy has ambassadors and lieutenants. He has captains in his army. He is patient. *He will wait a whole life time to get you*. So throughout this series, we will be talking about your personality and weaknesses. We all have a personality and we all have weaknesses. Some of you didn't grow up with enough love. Love in the home. You don't even know how to love yourself. You think sex is love. But, it is not. You think buying stuff is love. From one relationship to another, but you need to be healed up from the inside out. You have to know your enemy; who's attacking you. The devil has you thinking you are going crazy; he wants you to kill yourself, knowing for sure that you will end up in Hell. He is right there. You are never alone. You are never alone. I want you to read the book of Ephesians. That is going to be a great book during this time. **For we wrestle not against flesh and blood, but against principalities, against powers, against the rulers of the darkness of this world, against spiritual wickedness in high places** (Ephesians 6:12)**.** Stand! But, you can't stand. Stand on what? If you don't know the truth, what can you stand on? You have to be a person that loves truth. I'm giving you some bountiful tools. You have to be a person who *loves* truth. Not understands the truth. It is not enough. Not receives the truth. It is not enough. You have to love it and then cover yourself with that truth on a daily basis. Because most truth that is going forth will be to expose what's really going on with you. Often times, you are the hindrance in your life. Did you know that? You are the one that is defeating *you*. So many have become their own worst enemy.

STAND

Wherefore take unto you the whole armour of God, that ye may be able to withstand in the evil day, and having done all, to stand. Stand therefore, having your loins girt about with truth, and having on the breastplate of righteousness; And your feet shod with the preparation of the gospel of peace; Above all, taking the shield of faith, wherewith ye shall be able to quench all the fiery darts of the wicked. And take the helmet of salvation, and the sword of the Spirit, which is the word of God: Praying always with all prayer and supplication in the Spirit, and watching thereunto with all perseverance and supplication for all saints (Ephesians 6:13-18). Multitudes have been defeated by the deceit of Lucifer because they didn't *recognize* him. They didn't recognize his scheme and his plan. So many didn't recognize him because the person that the devil uses might be close to you; maybe a companion or loved one. The person that the enemy uses might be your child; the one you brought into this world; maybe the one you almost lost your life for to bring into this world. But, the enemy will use that person. The enemy will use your best friend against you. The enemy will use your father; will use your mother. The devil will use somebody who is promising you all kinds of love and affection to draw you out of a truth-teaching ministry. You never hook up with anybody who does not believe what you believe in. It is an all-out battle.

WE ARE NOT IGNORANT

The fight is on. **Lest Satan should get an advantage of us: for we are not ignorant of his devices** (2 Corinthians 2:11). **And a man's foes shall be they of his own household** (Matthew 10:36). Jesus said **Think not that I am come to send peace on earth: I came not to send peace, but a sword. For I am come to set a**

man at variance against his father, and the daughter against her mother, and the daughter in law against her mother in law (Matthew 10:34-35)**.** You say you are engaged to somebody. You must sit down and find out what they believe. You have given your life, some of you; you have been ostracized. You have stood against your family and your friends. And here comes Cinderella, with her glass slipper and here comes somebody who is just going to *turn into a pumpkin at midnight. The midnight in your life is just ahead neighbor.* Don't be fooled. Think about it. Holy, Lord, God Almighty! They will turn into a pumpkin when? In the midnight of your life. When you really need him. Poof! Just turn into a pumpkin and now he or she is gone. And have left you there with all the fragments that are left behind. You don't want to hook up with somebody who has a problem with you giving to Jesus, going to a blood-bought church, fasting and spending time in prayer. Wrong story. These are the things you have to get worked out in your life.

BEFORE MARRIAGE

There are many decisions that must be made prior to engagement; prior to marriage. There must be a discussion about finances, religion, children, and sex. During my nearly 20 years as a pastor, these are the causes of rift in most marriages. People do not recognize when the devil is really coming against them. So many are not able to identify with the tactic that the enemy uses. So these are the things that I want you to look up, because we are having a study session. I want you to look up the word: *recognize.* And I want you to look up the word: *tactic.*

THE ANTICHRIST

People must be schooled in the ways of Lucifer and his demons. In fact, many people believe that the idea of a devil on planet earth today is just a myth. But he is a real person. Jesus declared, **I beheld Satan as lightning fall from heaven** (Luke 10:18)**.** The Antichrist, I know you have heard about him. He is on earth *right now*. We believe that the Antichrist was born in the latter part of 1968. And his *forerunner is in place* in a very high place in government. The spirit of the Antichrist is already here, but he cannot be revealed until the Church is gone. When the Church is removed, [Rapture] then the Antichrist will rush in. Remember, in the trinity of the Godhead we have the Father, the Son and the Holy Ghost. In the Antigod head are the devil, which is the Antigod; the Antichrist, which is the Beast; and the Antispirit, which is the False Prophet. The Holy Ghost works in the interest of Christ. He is not working to glorify Himself, but the Father and the Son. In that day, the Antispirit will be working to glorify the Antichrist and the devil. He will deceive men with the great miracles he is able to perform and tell those who dwell on the earth to make an image of the Beast. **And he had power to give life unto the image of the beast, that the image of the beast should both speak, and cause that as many as would not worship the image of the beast should be killed. And he causeth all, both small and great, rich and poor, free and bond, to receive a mark in their right hand, or in their foreheads** (Revelation 13:15,16).[2] Those who do not accept the teachings of Christ, this will be their fate. It will be the worst time on planet earth. Have you considered this? **Blessed is he that readeth, and they that hear the words of this prophecy, and keep those things which are written therein: for the time is at hand** (Revelation 1:3)**. Behold, I come quickly:**

---

[2]   Angley, Ernest. *Raptured.* Akron, Ohio. Winston Press. 1950.

blessed is he that keepeth the sayings of the prophecy of this book (Revelation 22:7).

THE FORERUNNER

He that loveth father or mother more than me is not worthy of me: and he that loveth son or daughter more than me is not worthy of me. And he that taketh not his cross, and followeth after me, is not worthy of me. He that findeth his life shall lose it: and he that loseth his life for my sake shall find it (Matthew 10:39). Wasn't John the Baptist the forerunner of Jesus? What was his [John the Baptist] mission? To prepare to way for Jesus. Jesus was born of a woman. And so was the Antichrist. He was born of a woman who was not a virgin. And like John the Baptist, is a forerunner. The forerunner in the world today. Again, the Antichrist is on the earth today and his forerunner is in a high political office in the world. And he is making the way for the Antichrist. People simply have not been schooled in the ways of Lucifer and his demons. In fact, many believe the ideal of a personal devil alive on planet earth is just a myth. That is exactly what Satan wants you to think. He would delight if he could destroy you. And some of you, he is *working hard* to destroy you. Some of you, it's by suicide. But remember what the Bible teaches, "Thou shall not kill," including yourself. The enemy has done and is doing everything in his power to send you to hell. And you got to recognize it. You have got to wake up. You have to realize it. Sin is enticing. It feels good. It makes you feel strong. Sin makes you feel like you have super human strength, but it's all just plain old deceit. Sin makes you feel loved. Sin makes you feel wanted. Sin makes you feel like, "Oh, my God, you are just the greatest thing in the world." It is only momentary. The gifts of God, it says that the Lord will give you things that will bless you and won't cause sorrow. It won't cause hurt and heartache. What the Lord gives you will edify and build you up. You have to ask yourself, "Is it clean? Is it

Holy? Do you have to be alone in a dark room? Does it cause you to be separated from the ministry? Does it cause you to be separated from purity and holiness?" If it does, then it can't be of God. The Bible says **He was in the world, and the world was made by him, and the world knew him not. He came unto his own, and his own received him not. But as many as received him, to them gave he power to become the sons of God, even to them that believe on his name: Which were born, not of blood, nor of the will of the flesh, nor of the will of man, but of God** (I John 1:10-13).

You have got to understand what you are up against. Some you have been defeated in your prayer life. You were not aware that the devil and his demons were hindering you. As part of your mind was drawn in by seducing spirits and you didn't even know it. Some of you are devil oppressed and some even possessed and you are wondering what is wrong with you. Why all the pressure tearing at your mind and your emotions; your thought life? You are unhappy. You are discontented. Those are demons both around you and in your soul. You have been victimized by Lucifer. Never have there been a time where there have been so many doctrines of devils. There are so many false doctrines. So many churches, so many denominations. There has never been a time, like the time we now live in. Never has there been time where there are so many doctrines of devils as is on planet earth now. And the Lord said it would be so. When? In last days, and so we are in the last days. You have to learn what the deceiving and seducing spirits of Lucifer have done in the past. And so you will know what he is trying to do today. You may say, "What does that mean?" You have to study that Word and you have to study until you know the spirit of God, spirit of man and spirit of the devil and then be able to separate the spirits. You have got to be able to dissect God's and know what He means right at that point that you are studying. This is possible for the children of

God in this last and final hour. You have got to be able to discern in it in your own life, first. Some people are good at throwing the word on other people. How does it fit my life? Where am I in the scheme of this whole scripture? You can search the scriptures for in them you think you have eternal life. Search the scriptures. He said that if you sought me diligently, I will be found of you. That is what His word declares. If you are lost today. Then you are not looking in the right place. If you don't have peace today. Your mind is not upon Him. Then your thoughts are not upon the Lord. Because He said, "Take my yoke upon you, learn of me." The Lord said to give Him your burden. The Lord said to take His burden because His burden is light. The burden of the Lord is easy; it's a burden for lost humanity. So if you are burden down today, you are in the wrong army.

The deceit of Lucifer enters into the hearts of people in many, many different ways; as you can find in the word of God. God put information in His book, called the Bible. He wanted you to have it. The question is: Are you using it? Are you using it? Are you using everything that the Lord has given you, today?

SINCE THE FALL OF ADAM

We are studying about the works of Lucifer. How many devils/demons can a soul contain? And everybody who has been born since Adam, you have a living, eternal soul. We believe that Adam was the first man with a soul. We are not saying, Adam of course, science has proved that Adam was not the first man. We believe that there were pre-historic men. But we know emphatically that Adam was the first man with a soul. And that soul came from the breath of God. And since God is eternal. Your soul is eternal. That is the real you partner and you will not die. **Where their worm dieth not, and the fire is not quenched** (Mark 9:44). No! Flesh and blood cannot enter into heaven. **Now this I say, brethren, that flesh and blood**

27

cannot inherit the kingdom of God; neither doth corruption inherit incorruption (I Corinthians 15:50). But, that real you it is going somewhere. It is going somewhere. **And they came over unto the other side of the sea, into the country of Gadarenes. And when he was come out the ship, immediately there met him out of the tombs a man with an unclean spirit** (Mark 5:1-2). A devil possessed man. **Who had his dwelling among the tombs; and no man could bind him, no, not with chains; Because that he had been often bound with fetters and chains, and the chains had been plucked asunder** (Mark 5:3-4). But look at the strength that the devil gave this man. The devil supplies his people with wisdom and knowledge. The devil can slay you and make you fall down. The devil can make you feel something. There is this false demonic laugh that is going around, people say in the churches. But you search the scriptures. You should be able to find evidence of what Jesus is like. You should find evidence of the characteristics of the Holy Spirit. You should be able to know about God. All in the Bible. You show me at any time when Jesus was in the temple and the word was going forth and people just broke out and started laughing. But, you got to study deceit. A lot of people who are deceived, most of them will not come out of it. Because it is so strong. It is so strong. And if you are in deceit today you have got to cry out from the bottom of your heart to be free; only the truth will bring you out. You have got to promise the Lord that once He sets you free; you will stay free. That is the reason why some of you are playing around with the thought of suicide. That's the reason why there is so much hatred. That is the reason why some of you have trouble in your mind because you are devil bound. That devil is in you. Devil possession. Some people who to church and claim to be children of God are devil oppressed because we know true children of God cannot be devil possessed. The children of God can be oppressed but not possessed; you can't have God and the devil in the same your temple [body]. But you have got to *hold on to the* *truth*, every single day. Every moment you have left. You have to cry out. And I believe those chains will fall and your eyes will be opened to the greatness of God. The chains of the enemy. The chains of oppression. The chains of fear. Fear has torment.

LEGION

Mark 5:9 says, **And he asked him, what is thy name: And he answered, saying My name is Legion: for we are many.** And I want you to look up the word: *legion*. And it goes on to say; **And he answered, saying, My name is Legion: for we are many. And he besought him much that he would not send them away out of the country. Now there was there nigh unto the mountain a great herd of swine feeding. And all the devils besought him saying, Send us into the swine, that we may enter into them. And forthwith Jesus gave them leave. And the unclean spirits went out and entered into the swine** (Mark 5:9-13). But the devils did not drown only the swine. **And the heard ran violently down a steep place into the sea, (there were about two thousand)** (Mark 5:13). That is what I want you to see. Underline that if your Bible is a work book. So that one man had two thousand devils in his soul. Now your soul, remember, came from the breath of God it is the real you. **And the Lord God formed man of the dust of the ground, and breathed into his nostrils the breath of life; and man became a living soul** (Genesis 2:7). You will never die. Your soul can hold *all of heaven* or it can hold *all of hell*.

WHO IS TALKING TO YOU?

Demons of the mind have intelligence. Notice this. Demons of the mind have intelligence. This is prophetic. This is great because it is coming from God. And this is the answer to some of your questions about your life. *Why am I unhappy? Why do I want to cut myself? Why do I want to pull my hair out? Why do I want to make myself bleed? Why am I interested in such violent movies? Why do I just can't get rest unless I am drinking? I am hooked on pain killers. I love violence.* Demons of the mind have intelligence and talk to people just like human beings. I would challenge you to write that down. They talk to people just like human beings. If you saw the devil in his true form, it will scare you. But when your momma come and say, "You are ugly, you are no good." When your husband comes and says, "You can't please me; don't pay your tithes; don't give to the ministry." Come on somebody isn't that what happened to Adam. Eve said, "Look, look, look, I bit the apple [forbidden fruit] and I am still alive." But it cost Adam his soul. You have got to know the truth about God. You have got to know the truth about His word. And you have got to know *the truth about yourself.* If you have weaknesses, if you have apprehensions; face them. You have uncertainties. That is okay. But God cannot deal with you until you first get yourself in a position to say, "I am hooked on porn; *I need some help."* If you are hooked on porn, based on God's word, you don't have the blood on your soul. Porn is filthy and you couldn't have God in your soul with the filth in your spirit. James says, **Let no man say when he is tempted, I am tempted of God: for God cannot be tempted with evil, neither tempteth he any man: But every man is tempted, when he is drawn away of his own lust, and enticed. Then when lust hath conceived, it bringeth forth sin: and sin, when it is finished, bringeth forth death** (James 1:13-15).

LUST OF THE FLESH

For all that is in the world, the lust of the flesh, and the lust of the eyes, and the pride of life, is not of the Father, but is of the world (I John 2:16). **If we say that we have fellowship with him, and walk in darkness, we lie, and do not the truth: But if we**

walk in the light, as he is in the light, we have fellowship one with another, and the blood of Jesus Christ his Son cleanseth us from all sin. If we say that have no sin, [that we have never sinned] **we deceive ourselves, and the truth is not in us. If we confess our sins, he is faithful and just to forgive us out sins, and to cleanse us from all unrighteousness. If we say that we have not sinned** [never sinned]**, we make him a liar and his word is not in us** (I John 1:6-10)**.** You are on the right track now. It doesn't matter what you have or the situation you are in, or how long you have been in that situation. It does not matter if doctors say you are going to die with this or die with that. Are you ready to accept truth? Then, you can be free. Yes! Now, some people try to pick apart the messages to fit their sinful [selfish, deceitful] lives. But, these messages come from the Lord. They just find you out. I don't follow people around. God knows all. The Lord teaches us through His word, you have to be the first partaker. Smokers and liars will not be in heaven. It doesn't matter what others are talking about; it doesn't matter how long their robe is and how long their veil is. It doesn't matter how long their train is or how expensive their garment is. ***Only the pure in heart*** shall see God. It will be no other way. We are almost at the end of this great time in our life; it is the final sweep for souls. What a shame it would be not to make it with God. People who are not living right. Many of them are devil possessed. They hear voices. They hear them in their mind. But they believe that the voices are their own thoughts; their own ideas. Part of that person's mind if not all of the mind is being directed by demonic powers. Only the truth brings the happiness of God, only the truth brings joy-the greatness of the Lord into your life. So you have got to think about this. You have to take a person's message for yourself. If you are discontented, if you are indifferent, if you are a person who loves gossip; you know there are gossiping devils. It is lying devils. People can't stop lying. Cursing demons that inhibit the soul. Only the truth, you can't go around it. If you are going to be free, you are going to be free *God's way*. Yes! But it so hard for people to accept that demonic spirits can be in their mind and that they are talking to them. And because people don't think right and are not using the blood of Jesus. The Children of God. They reached for the things that were to have been left untouched. Saying words that damage; do things not in harmony with the Holy Scriptures and God himself. We are talking about Lucifer himself today. I want to discuss some of the forms that the devil takes.

FACE YOUR FEARS

You have to face yourself and find out what manner of person you are. You have to write that down. You have to face yourself and find what manner of person you are. Then you have to get rid of all deceit and never forget that the devil cunningly seeks to reflect your image in his personal mirror of distortion and perversion. He wants to take that image that you like so much that is wrong; the enemy wants to take your thoughts that are perverted and shine them before you say, "You are some great wonder." Yes, you are not! Think about actually looking into a soul that is bound by devils, maybe thousands of devils. To see those devilish eyes, ears, and teeth is absolutely terrifying. But we can use the word as our safety today. We don't have to leave out of here with any fears. All we have to do is just love the Lord with our whole heart soul and mind. To love Him with all that we have, asking him to clean us, to make us what He wants us to be. Would you agree with that today? You want the Lord to make you? You want to be better in your life? You want to be different? Deceiving demons operate undercover with a deceiving light. And multitudes are in hell because of it. This is one of the devil's favorite tactics. And I told you to look up the word tactic. He successfully beguiled people with it for thousands of years. So he doesn't feel any need of any improvement. However, the devil's demons don't always appear as light. Sometimes they appear in the darkness as two big horse eyes lit with fire starring directly at you.

DEMON SPIRITS

Demons appear in many different forms because a wide variety of demon spirits exist. There are demons that affect the soul. Demons that affect the mind. Demons that afflict the body. Some scoff at the thought of sick spirits. Blind devils and deaf and mute devils but Jesus taught about them all when he was here on earth. All of this is in the word of God that we are studying here today. And I think it is marvelous in our ears that the Lord has provided a way for us to study about the deceit of Lucifer. The Lord dealt with demonic power in a direct way. In Mark 9:25, you can write it down, **When Jesus saw that the people came running together, he rebuked the foul spirit, saying unto him, Thou dumb spirit, I charge thee, come out of him, and enter no more into him.** The bulk of Jesus' ministry was the healing ministry and in that ministry people got healed of cancer and all kinds of deadly diseases. The Lord healed me of cancer two times. Oh my God! People with AIDS and HIV they can be healed. But the ministry has to be sold out. It has to be solidified by the Word of God. It has to hold on to truth. The truth has to be its allegiance on the wall. It has to be its mission statement. The truth has to be what is spoken through the Sunday school teacher. The blood truth has to be what is sung through the songs. The truth has to be given when people open up the door. The truth has to work on those who are working with the children. Then people can come in and be free. There are many different kinds of demons that can destroy completely so you must open your eyes to the deceit in this final hour. Never before has there been such a crucial battle as so many demon's fighting mankind as now. So many demonic angels were held in captivity until now – because this is the final hour and the great war is on for your soul. The great war between God and the devil is raging and you are *right in the middle*. There is a great war going on right now. And maybe you can't see it. Sometimes you can feel that demonic power around you. Sometimes you can be happy one moment and then you go around somebody that is complaining and before you know it you got that complaint on your tongue. Sometimes you can be happy and full of joy and you sit down and watch the wrong things on TV. When you get up, you have that lust spirit just raging in you. So, you have got to watch what your eyes take in. You have to watch what you allow to come into your ears. You have got to watch what you allow to even to come into your home because you are responsible for what happens under your roof. You are responsible. You are responsible for that.

The devil is doing everything within his power to see that you fail. He is tempting you with anything and everything that he possibly can. But this is to study deceit. To study deceit. And we have keep ourselves together. We have to keep our lives pure and clean; no matter what the world is doing. We have got to keep ourselves whole. We have to let the Lord know that every tomorrow we have left, we want His divine will. We want the truth, no matter if that truth exposes us. If it tears us down, then we know the Lord will build us up. If it exposes our weaknesses then we can say, "Lord, it's me Lord, I am standing in the need of prayer." If it shows me that I am arrogant, that is okay. "Lord, knock me down and build me back up in grace. Build me back up in truth," but you got to make it to heaven. No matter what is going on in your life, you have got to make it to heaven. And you are not going to make it in heaven without knowing your enemy.

I HAVE UNCOVERED SATAN IN THE PAST

Thus saith the Lord: Just as I uncovered Satan in the past, I am uncovering him in this the final hour of the Gentiles. I will reveal to my Children his works, his plans. Lucifer is planning to destroy you, my Children, saith the Lord. Lucifer knows that he has but a limited time to destroy you. He knows that I am giving you my greatness, my power to defeat him, to trample his demons underfoot: but he is seeking to destroy you. He is seeking to deceive you. He will deceive you in your prayer life; he will deceive you with my Word. He will deceive you in your walk. He will deceive you with unrighteousness and make you believe it is all right. He will deceive you with lies and half-truths. He will deceive you in so-called visions and dreams. He will deceive you in your sleep and when you are awake unless you yield to my Spirit day and night. He is seeking to destroy you, to destroy your happiness, your peace of mind. He is seeking to destroy the holiness of mind that is yours in your life.[3]

ONE SEED OF DECEIT AFTER ANOTHER

Devil possession is not the result of just one little sin. It comes about sowing one seed of deceit after another or allowing someone else to sow them into you, for you, or through you. Just telling lies and causing mischief, and causing confusion. Now only are you on the road to being devil possessed but in this final hour, you are on the road to blaspheming against the Holy Ghost. It is a late hour. It is a crucial hour. This is not the hour to keep playing church. You better get in God and stay with God. My nephew delivered a wonderful message not long ago. He said you have to yield. But, that is not good enough, you have to *stay yielded*. You have got to get in God and stay in God. You have to get in grace and stay in grace. You have got to get

---

3   Angley, *The Deceit of Lucifer.*

in salvation and stay in salvation. Some of you, you are coming into the end of God's mercy in your life. You are in and out. You are in and out with salvation. You are in and out with love. You and in and out with grace. But, God long suffering it starts way over here. But, it ends. It's going to come to an end, one day in your life. And the Bible says, **For the wages of sin is death; but the Gift of God is eternal life** (Roman 6:23). The Word says in Leviticus 11:44, **And ye shall be holy; for I am holy.** He says in the writing by Peter that Jesus gave us an example. We never saw Jesus curse. And we never saw Him smoking. We saw our Lord holding up the blood stained banner. Not only did Jesus lift up the blood stain banner, but that banner was drawn from His side. They pierced Him in His side. And because they pierced Jesus in His side, we must! We must live free from all sin! It's not an option! It's a commandment from the Almighty God. John 15:22 says, **If I had not come and spoken unto them, they had not had sin: but now they have no cloke for their sin.**

Devil possession is not the result of just one little sin. It comes about by sowing one seed of deceit after the other or allowing someone to sow them inside of you. Who you hang around with, they are influencing you. How many young girls lost their virginity because their girlfriend had a baby? And there you are alone because the father is gone? Have some integrity about yourself. Have self-worth in yourself. Everybody is not doing it because nobody would be in heaven. But people are in heaven, because the Lord gave His life so people could go to heaven. If the evil seeds are not killed out, you will reap an evil harvest. The first seed of deceit affects a person's heart. The same way the first drink affects an alcoholic. Seeds of deceive have put souls on the road to destruction. While for most, the first drink does not make one an alcoholic, but after the first, second, third, fourth and so and so on. There are those who become alcoholics with the initial [very first] drink. Lucifer has the person addicted. In like manner, the more you deceive, the more you lie, the more you sin, the more you give yourself over to the devil. The more, and more, and more, and more; until he completely has you. The more you give over to anger, eventually you are going to hate.

UNDERCOVER

Lucifer works undercover. He may even be in the form of a handsome man or a beautiful girl. Sometimes the enemy can even appear as a lovely woman but when his disguise is stripped off, he is still yet an ugly demon or the devil himself? Oh my God! Again, we know that demons can come in different forms. But a demon has a head the size of a man. But, no hair. This is how a demon looks in the soul. Maybe you never heard about this neighbor but it is right. A demon, now think about this, hundreds of thousands of them can live inside your soul. A demon has a head the size of a man, but no hair. He has leery eyes that glitter with satanic power. That is just something to think about. And more and more and more inhibiting your soul. What about demons that take on the appearance of wolves? Have you ever thought about that? The writer of this one article, whom I love so much. He says "I remember one particular woman who had deceived others and was playing the role of the hypocrite. I told her how deceived and disgusting she was in the eyes of God and that she didn't have just a few devils but many; God had numbered them." Now, notice this. This man who is giving this illustration, he is God's holy prophet. He's a holy prophet. I don't' know how many people I can really say that about today. But, I've tried him and I know he is. He's God's holy prophet. This pastor has the true gift of discernment. And through the gift of discernment, he is able to see good spirits and bad spirits. He can see angels. And through the gift of discernment he can take on the mind. He knows what God is thinking at any time. He has the mind of Christ. Notice him saying here, again the woman wanted to be delivered. "When I prayed for her," he said, "the devils came in the forms of wolves.

Suddenly, it was like a mad house. Demons surrounded the two of us." Now you got to think about how that could have been a mad house. This wonderful pastor, through the gift of discernment, saw the demons. The lady crying out for deliverance, did not see them. Just their influence -- just their presence affected all the people that were around. Just like inside our church today, it is warm [speaking to her congregation]. But when you go outside, it's freezing cold and all of us will be affected. Some people will be affected greatly because they don't have on enough attire. Some don't have their hands covered. Some don't have their head covered. So when we got out, we all will be affected. But some at greater degrees than others. But we will all be affected. This lady wanted to be delivered. "Again," this pastor stated, "when I prayed for her, the devils came out in the forms of wolves. Suddenly, it was like a mad house. Demons surrounded the two of us. Snaring and growling with their tongues, licking out, as the struggled to get back into her soul." They [the demons that had been cast out] struggled to get back in. So, you got to know your enemy. If you get free, stay free. If you are free, stay free. You have got to run for your soul. Now, I just took you to the word of God, Mark Chapter 5, about the man who had over 2000 demons in him. I just read to you another scripture that said when Jesus got there, He cast out the dumb and death spirit. So this is all Bible what I am telling you. I told you I would give you scripture for everything I show you. There were trying get back inside her soul.

When the unclean spirit is gone out of a man, he walketh through dry places, seeking rest, and findeth none. Then he saith, I will return into my house from whence I came out; and when he is come, he findeth it empty, swept and garnished. Then goeth he, and taketh with himself seven other spirits more wicked than himself, and they enter in and well there: and the last state of that man is worse than the first (Matthew 12:43-45). The Bible declares not only do they come back with a force but seven times greater because they found a house [the soul] empty and missing the precious blood of Jesus Christ. While the soul had been swept clean, the blood was still missing [the person had not sealed the soul with the blood; the soul was clean but not protected]. Haven't you noticed some people who have failed God? They were worse than before. The pastor continues by saying, "They were limited at how close they could come to us. It was as if we were encircled with the blood of Christ, and that blood protected us. I had no idea what to expect because I had never before witnessed anything like those demons. I just knew God was with me."[4] How was He with this prophet? By the same blood of His son, Jesus! How is He keeping me today? By the power that is in the blood! Why am I healed? Because of the power that is in the blood. How *can* you and *must* you live free from sin? By the power that is in the blood. You can't do it on your own. But, it is power! It is wonder working power in the Blood of the Lamb!

---

4   Angley, *The Deceit of Lucifer.*

CHAPTER 3

HOW DEMON POSSESSION AFFECTS PEOPLE
PART 1

Neighbor, when you think about reality TV and all that is going on in the world today, how everybody and everything is coming out; don't you think it's time for the people of God to rise up and to come out. People must be aware of the manifestation of the devil. People must be awakened to the power of God in this final hour. And the Lord will not let souls to be hindered in any way. People need to be awaken for the hour is far spent. The days are so dark and the night is far spent. The enemy is coming from under every rock possible. He is coming out of corners. The enemy is doing everything that he can to get you to turn away from God. The devil owns many pulpits across America; they belong to him. Many of the so called prophets and evangelists and those who say they are full of God; they are simply full of the spirit of the devil.

GREAT VICTORY OR TOTAL DEFEAT

You must be wise in the truths of the Lord and His ways. There must not be any disobedience in your heart in this hour. There must not be any half-truths, or Lucifer will possess you. You are in the hour of *great victory* or *total defeat*. You are in the hour that the greatness of the Lord is being poured out. But Lucifer is sending for his spirit throughout the whole world. He is seeking to destroy the promises of God from your heart and he seeks to destroy the visions of this end-time hour. Lucifer knows the word has gone forth in heaven that he is to be destroyed, that his destruction will shortly come. We must arise and let it be yes, yes, yes to our God day and night, crying for the holiness of your God, crying for the protection of the blood of the Son of the Living God, crying for purity so you will be without spot or wrinkle, and so we can do the whole will of the Lord in this our final hour;[5] *the final sweep of souls.*

THE NIGHT COMETH

And neighbor, it is our responsibility. Did you know that? When Jesus saved you, at that point, lost humanity; the whole wide world, became your responsibility and my responsibility. And neighbor we have to do all that we can because time will soon be no more. John 9:4 says, **I must work the works of him that sent me, while it is day: the night cometh, when no man can work**. I am going to be talking about different things and I just want to talk about Godly people. Some Godly people have been oppressed by the devil. Let me clarify that because the alcoholic says he is saved today. The devil possessed they are saved. Those shacking up together; they say they are saved. But those who are saved; living free from **all** sin. Their hearts are pure and they have accepted the blood of Jesus on their souls. Some of them have handicaps. Some of them are blind. Some of them are halt. Some of them are lame. Some of them are deaf. But yet, they are true children, men and women of God. Those are not the ones that I will be alluding to. I want you to understand that children of God can be oppressed but they cannot be possessed by the devil. It should be made clear that demon *possession* is different from demon *oppression*. A person can't be a child of God and be devil *possessed*, but children of God can be *oppressed* by demon spirits.

I want to give honor to all of the physicians, and the psychologist, and the psychiatrist, and all of those in the healthcare industry who

---

[5]   Angley, *The Deceit of Lucifer, 358-359.*

do all they can to help people. There are some very good doctors but there is none like God.

POSSESS(ION)

I have a few words for you today. And the first one is *possessed*. I want you to write this one down neighbor. *Possess* is the word I want you to write down. It means to seize of to take. To occupy or hold. To have as belonging to one. To have as property; to own; possess. And so today, we are going to start in Romans 1:21, you know this is one of Paul's writings. And if your Bible is a workbook, you should write these scriptures down. This book that I am using so much during this time, you need to have it in your catalog, *"The Deceit of Lucifer."*[6] It tells you so many different things. It is from our Pastor, our dear pastor who founded this church. **Because that, when they knew God,** (see they had the knowledge of God. You see the Lord, God through His son Jesus Christ, made an attempt to introduce Himself to them) **they glorified him not as God** (as being the one and true living God)**, neither were thankful; but became vain in their imaginations, and their foolish heart was darkened. Professing themselves to be wise, they became fools, And changed the glory of the uncorruptible God into an image made like to corruptible man, and to birds, and fourfooted beasts, and creeping things** (Romans 1:22-23)**.** That's what they wanted. Instead of honoring the true and living God, they made themselves God. Some people believe that they are God. Other believe that they can take the place of God. Some people believe we are little Gods. But there's no Bible for it; there is no scripture to back that up. **Wherefore God also gave them up to uncleanness through the lust of their own hearts, to dishonor their own**

[6] Ibid

bodies between themselves (Romans 1:24). So since they didn't want to honor God, He turned them completely over. He turned their minds over to a reprobate mind, an unsaved mind, an unholy mind, a disgusting mind, a lascivious mind, a mind taken over by the works of the flesh. He gave them over because the people did not want to yield to truth. And that is the step that starts people onto blaspheming against the Holy Ghost, the one sin that even God can't forgive. And that's the spirit that put people on the path to be devil possession. When people will not yield to the truth of the Almighty God, there's nothing He can do.

GOD GAVE THEM UP

Wherefore God also gave them up to uncleanness through the lust of their own hearts, to dishonour their own bodies between themselves (Romans 1:24). **Who changed the truth of God into a lie, and worshipped and served the creature more than the Creator, who is blessed forever. Amen.** (Romans 1:25).

LET NOT SIN REIGN

This is so rich. **Let not sin therefore reign in your mortal body, that ye should obey it in the lusts thereof. Neither yield ye your members *as* instruments of unrighteousness unto sin: but yield yourselves unto God, as those that are alive from the dead, and your members as instruments of righteousness unto God** (Romans 6:12-13). See you are dead in trespasses and sin, when Jesus washes you clean through that blood, you become alive. You become alive! **Neighbor yield ye your members as instruments of unrighteousness unto sin: but yield yourselves** (verse 13). So this sounds like this is something you can do. It is a part you can do in righteousness. It's a part you play in holiness. It is a part that you play in living free from *all* sin. While you [within your own power] may not have the power to stop cursing; to get free of addiction but if you yield to God, through the power of His son Jesus, you will be free. You can do it! And you must! **For sin shall not have dominion over you: for ye are not under the law, but under grace** (Romans 6:14)**.** So where does that leave false doctrine? That says that no one can live free from sin. The Word of God states that sin shall not have dominion over me —over you. Did you read it? **For sin shall not have dominion over you; for ye are not under the law.** We are under grace! Under the law, my Lord and my God, some of the things that happened to me when I was in the world of sin, I would have been stoned to death. But when Jesus came, He gave His shed blood for me to be free from *all* sin. **When his disciples heard it, they were exceedingly amazed, saying, Who then can be saved? But Jesus beheld them, and said unto them, With men this is impossible; but with God all things are possible** (Matthew 19:25-26)**.** In the flesh, it is impossible. In disobedience, it is impossible. In lust and lasciviousness, it is impossible. But, with a pure heart, through the shed blood of Jesus Christ, through perfect obedience, all things are possible! **What then? Shall we sin, because we are not under the law, but under grace? God forbid** (Romans 6:15)**.** God forbid! Shall we keep sinning when they beat Him to death for our freedom? God forbid! Shall we keep lying and having a heart full of unforgiveness? God forbid! Shall priest and prophets, and profane pulpits purchased by false leaders, teachers and preachers -- shall we keep on going? God forbid! **God forbid: yea, let God be true, but every man a liar; as it is written, That thou mightiest be justified in thy sayings, and mightiest overcome when thou art judged** (Romans 3:4)**.** Those who say you cannot live free from all sin; *they are liars*. And *all* liars shall have their part in the lake of fire. **What then? shall we sin, because we are not under the law, but under grace? God forbid** (Roman 6:15)**.** That is what I say, God forbid! **Know ye not, that to whom ye yield yourselves servants** to obey, his servants ye are to whom ye obey; whether of sin unto death, or of obedience unto righteousness? But God be thanked, that ye were servants of sin, but ye have obeyed from the heart that form of doctrine that was delivered unto you (Romans 6:16-17). Thank God I say, for the truth. Thank God for the delivering power of Jesus Christ! **For it is the power of God unto salvation to every one that believeth** (Romans 1:16). Though your sins be as scarlet, you can be as white as snow. You can be free from sin! And you must live free from all sin!

WE WANT LIES!

Now go, write it before them in a table, and note it in a book, that it may be for the time to come for ever and ever: That this is a rebellious people, lying children, children that will not hear the law of the Lord: Which say to the seers, See not; and to the prophets, Prophesy not unto us right things, speak unto us smooth things, prophesy deceits (Isaiah 30:8-10). That's what people want in the churches today. "Don't tell us the truth. We want lies. We want deceit. We want to go a church that fits our whoring lifestyle. We want to go to a church where we can go to the boat and then come rest in our seats and feel good. Prophesy deceit!"

TO STUDY DECEIT

I am going to take you now to that book that I told you that you *need to get*. And we are just going to make our through. To study demonology is to study deceit. What does it mean to deceive? It means to *ensnare, to make a person believe what is not true*. Deceit is the devil's business and truth is God's business. Deceit means *to delude, to mislead*. Deceit *is a lie, dishonest action or trick*. A deceitful person intends to deceive. *To be deceptive is to be false. Apt to lie*

45

or to cheat. And so we have to ask the profound question today, can you be deceived? Can you be deceived? 2 Peter 2:4 says, **For if God spared not the angels that sinned, but cast them down to hell, and delivered them into chains of darkness, to be reserved unto judgment**. Angelic beings, holy beings that God made and yet, Lucifer was able to deceive them. And he can't deceive you? I'm just asking. And God cast them out of heaven. Now if God cast angels out of heaven because a seed of deceit entered their heart and produced a disobedient harvest, God will cast you into hell for the same thing. Now we are living in a day, we are living in a time where so-called saints of God smoke. They can fornicate. They can whore hop. They can gamble. They can curse. They can fight. They cannot pay titles. And they are still going to heaven? But we just read here that angels, angelic beings that God created, they had a seed of deceit in them and He kicked them out of His heaven. Now it's God's heaven and the requirements to get there all belong to Him. With all deceit gone, you have to face yourself and find out what manner of person who you are. Never forget that the devil cunningly seeks to reflect your image in his own personal mirror of distortion and perversion. You must be able to recognize the works of the devil. Write that down. You must be able to recognize the works of the devil. You have to first recognize him where? In you. What are you using as your measuring rod? You spirit? Not! You have to use the word of God. You have to take every manifestation, every vision, everything has to be taken to word. If there is one particle or variance, then you must throw it *all* out. You must throw it out.

DO YOU ACT LIKE THE DEVIL?

Now people who are devil possessed act up and act out. They act a certain way. And some of these characteristics or these traits that we might be talking about today. So, you shouldn't be acting like a devil?

Should you? How does demon possession affect people? When a person is possessed by the devil, how do they act? Previously, I told you that demons can appear in all different forms. Sometimes they appear in the darkness as two big "horse-eyes" lit with fire. A demon can have a head the size of a man's but with no hair. His eyes can leer and glitter with satanic power. So think about this or 10, 20, 500 or 1000s of these demons living in your soul. Your soul is a living entity and can hold all of heaven or all of hell. It will never die. Even though you flesh will go back down to the earth. The real you, which is your soul, came from the breath of God, it is going to live on forever *either* in heaven *or* hell. Everybody planning on going to heaven, has got to be living a sin free life. There's no if, ands, or buts about it. Living free it has to be or you are not going to heaven.

DEMONIC KNOWLEDGE

How does demon possession affect people? When the devil possesses a soul that person becomes whatever the demon is. For example, there are murdering devils who desire to kill. They [the murdering demons] will capitalize on every opportunity to take a person over enough to kill another. You read of hideous crimes and think that is inhuman. Indeed, it is! You read about the devil using people to cut a baby out of the mother's womb. The lady dies but with such precision, with demonic knowledge, demonic wisdom, the devil imputes within that person skillfully how to cut that baby out of that woman, without killing the child. While the woman dies, the baby lives. It is demonic knowledge. It is demonic wisdoms. It's inhuman! To take another person's life, it's inhuman; it's not natural! To rape your child, to rape a woman, it is inhuman. It is not natural. The murderer is operated by a demon or demons. Just as the Holy Spirit possesses a child of God, evil spirits possess and control ungodly people who give completely over to them.

POSSESSED WITH A DEVIL

Matthew 9th chapter says that Jesus cast out demons. **They brought to him a dumb man possessed with a devil** (Matthew 9:32)**.** And when the devil was cast out the dumb spake. Now notice, we talked about this in part three. How does demon possession affect people? Now remember earlier I mentioned to you that there are some dumb people who are godly people. I mentioned that there are some blind people who are godly people. Matthew 9:32 says, **they brought to him a dumb man possessed**. The scripture plainly states that this man was possessed with a devil! This devil is living in them; inhibited inside that person. That devil or demon have come in and made that person's soul their home. The devil is living on inside of you when you are devil possessed. How would you feel if you could look in the soul of a human being and see hundreds, upon hundreds of demons, hundreds of little heads the size of a man, glaring eyes, with teeth and claws, just hanging on? Thousands upon thousands! If you could see those leeches masked on the mind, through the spirit of discernment. True prophets, with the gift of discernment, can see them. Note, just because a person cannot speak does not mean that he or she is devil possessed. But, in this case, *the Bible says he was possessed*. He not only had a dumb spirit but an unclean spirit as well in his soul. When the demon went out of his soul, the dumb spirit, although not a spirit of the soul, went out also and the man started talking. These things are plainly in the Bible. They are plainly in the Bible about devil possession. They are plainly in the Bible about adultery. They are plainly in the Bible about shacking up. Why come so-called pastors and leaders are not preaching about from the pulpits? Because it is a man-made pulpit. Because it is a profane pulpit. It's a pulpit that has been bought with less than thirty pieces of silver. They sold my Lord for thirty pieces of silver. It says in Matthew 12:22, **Then was brought unto him one possessed with a devil, blind and dumb: and he healed him, insomuch that the blind and the dumb both**

spake and saw. Now this man had an unclean spirit along with a blind spirit. Certainly, not all blind people, like was said before, have unclean spirits. Some wonderful, godly people are blind and dumb. This man, however, the Bible tells us, was devil possessed. When he received salvation, the Lord delivered him from the spirits that bound his eyes and his tongue. You were no longer full of lust. You no longer looked at women with incestuous eyes; wanting to have them at every opportunity. You could look at them with their clothes on and not with their clothes off. Every thought on your heart, every imagination of your heart was not evil continually when you got saved. But if you say you are saved and you are still battling with your old ways those are foul winds, resurrection of the old man. Even people who are devil possessed, they will say that they are saved.

I AM SAVED

Listen to this one conversation that a young man had with a true prophet of God.[7] It says a man came to the healing line of a revival service, he had a blind spirit. One eye was out. "Are you born again?" the man of God asked. "Yes!" However, he was not. Everybody says they're saved. You can ask the alcoholic. "Well, I am saved, I know God, I know God." You can ask people who shack up. "I am saved, I know God." You can ask the people who don't pay tithes and they have been taught about it. "I know God, I know God, I know God." How can a person who don't pay tithes know God? The Bible says he is a thief and a robber. And if you steal, isn't that one of the works of the flesh? How can you be going to heaven? Smoking cigarettes and blunts and lacing them with cocaine and talking about you know God. He say's know ye not that they your body is the temple

---

7   Ernest Angley, "The Sins of Witchcraft," *The Power of the Holy Ghost Magazine*, Feb. 2003.

of the Holy Ghost. Cursing. Curse words, blaspheme the name of the Almighty God. And you are his child? No! He says you do the works of your father, the devil. So here is this man, and he is having a conversation with the prophet of God. He was devil possessed, and the Lord was going to uncover that devil. And see by teaching about the deceit of Lucifer, the devil is going to be after you. He's going to be after you. But, souls are going to be saved. He's [the devil] going to rise up in people. People are going to give you a hard time, but somebody is going to be set free. The devil is going to stir up strife and discord. The truth stirs up the hornet's nest. It makes people angry. So called Christians, they get angry. They are talking about I am harming the children of God. How am I harming the children of God when the Bible says few that be that find it? How am I harming the children of God when the Lord says to blow the trumpet in Zion. The Almighty God says to warn His people and tell them that destruction is coming? How am I harming the people, by telling them to flee the wrath to come? These pastors, these leaders, these adulterous and fornicating pastors, these pulpits that have been purchase by the money of men. They are telling people, "Howdy! Howdy! Everything is alright. But, they are going to hell! They are going to hell and taking people with them.

UGANDA, EAST AFRICA

Now listen to this. This prophet wants to share this astounding story with us today and it's real. The prophet goes on to say, "I have an astounding story to tell you. If it doesn't shake you, there is not much shake in you. I came in contact with a most unusual family in Jinja, Uganda, East Africa." This prophet is telling us about an incident that happened to him in Africa, when he was dealing with devils. There was a time in third world countries such as Africa, where witchcraft, voodoo, and sacrificing children, sacrificing of others was common. Oh my God! It was so profound. But, don't you know that other countries are now sending missionaries to these *United States of America* because we have lost our way. We have lost our way. We are no longer a Christian nation. Our President, the President of the United States [our president at the time of this writing – Barack Obama], has already said, we are no longer a Christian nation. So listen to the prophet's experience. I am moved every time I read it. The man of God says, "Just before the service as I was moving to the platform, I was met by a wild boy, fourteen years old, who had to be physically restrained." Mark the 5th chapter talks about a man bound with "legion." Take note of the power and the strength that devil gives people. Listen to it again. "Just before the service, I was moving to the platform," the prophet says. "I was met a by a wild boy, fourteen years old, who had to be physically restrained." Doesn't that sound like the man recorded in Mark 5th chapter who was in the tombs who cutting himself and nobody could bound him? Have you ever been on the psych ward? I have. Have you ever been there to visit a family member or friend? I have. And they have to be kept in physical restraints. They have them wrapped up in a white jacket where their arms be wrapped around them. Because they are so strong. They are so powerful. Those demonic spirits. Those devils in their souls give them strength. The pastor goes on to say, "He was one of those awful cases, jerking this way and that way. People were trying to hold him until his parents could get him prayed for. Night and day they hadn't been able to do anything with him."

REAL TALK

This is real talk. Do you have a child on drugs and alcohol? Those devils will drive you crazy. Some of you, you don't know what your kids are doing. They are sneaking their girlfriend and boyfriend in the house. *They've got you down to a science.* They know you go to bed at seven-thirty or eight o'clock. They know you can't keep your eyes open past nine. Your child will steal your car right from under your nose while you're sleeping. Notice this, People were trying to hold him until his parents could get him to get prayed for. "The boy was possessed by evil spirits that had taken him over and attached themselves to him when he was only three," the man of God explained. "From then until he was fourteen, the devils controlled him. I prayed for him, and when I touched him, he came to normal. It was an instant miracle."[8] The Bible says, Train up a child in the way he should go: and when he is old, he will not depart from it (Proverbs 22:6). **Withhold not correction from the child** (Proverbs 89:23). What can you do with a twelve-year-old boy, whom you have never disciplined? Twelve year-old girls are having their menstrual cycles and having babies, intercourse, oral sex, doing all sorts of ungodly acts. By sixteen, seventeen, some of them are high priced call girls. See those devils have grown up in them. Those demonic spirits will grow up in these kids. Some of you let your kids talk back to you. And you let them tell you *what they are going to do*. Three and four years old, cursing. When they have got you locked up in the room somewhere treating you like a dog. I am not talking about something I heard but I am talking about something I know. Down through these eighteen years as being a pastor – PFC [Passion for Christ] has been my university. Your children know what you are up to; that you have a boyfriend in the back and that it is the third man that has been in your house this week. And now they are of the age, and what do they tell you? "You can't tell me nothing, because you were in there with your best friend's man and now all of sudden want to be a parent?" This young man, he got devil possessed when he was three. From that time, until he was fourteen, those devils controlled him. Now this is something we have to take notice of. We must set parameters. We have to set constraints, restraints. We must set the standers in our home. "You can't do everything. You can't come and go as you please. Not up in here."

---

8   Angley, *The Sins of Witchcraft*

MOMMA'S HOUSE BURNED DOWN

It was a blessing in disguise when my momma's house burned down. She's in heaven and doesn't mind me telling you the story. One of my other kids. You say man, she has a lot of kids. *"Not anymore, they are all grown and gone."* I couldn't do the things for myself that I am able to do now when I had little bitty kids because I had to make sure a coat stayed on their backs and shoes on their feet. I had to make sure all of them had gloves and hats, but *they're on their own now*. But, before my momma's house burned down, one of my kids was living there, and you would have thought it was a hard rock hotel. You don't hear me! When the fire was settled and they [the insurance company] built it back up, I moved in. Oh glory! We have a new house. That child of mines took over the whole house. You had to wave a flag before you went up to that part of the house because there was no telling what you might have seen. *That fire was a blessing in disguise*. They had good insurance. The house was in great need of many repairs anyway. We got a brand new house and peace, and joy, and happiness came right along with it because I brought it, when I moved in. You don't hear me! Everything is howdy, howdy at your house. Everybody saved in your house. You don't hear me! All your girls pretty little angels at your house. You don't hear me! All your sons, they doing all they can at your house. But, I had the devil and his first cousin with me. He had some twins. Went down there and had a spiritual IVF. Spiritually, those demons were popping out. Talking about rabbits can have babies. What about them devils? That's what I am talking about up in the house where I was living in. And I had five aliens. Phew! I had five teenagers living with me at once. People criticized us. They talked about us. "Why yall doing all this? Why yall doing all that?" We were just simply trying to keep them [our children] alive, one more day; one more week, one more month, one more year. For one more day, for one more month, for maybe two more weeks. We had some long days, but we knew the weeks would be short. We had some long days, but we knew the years would be short; we knew sooner or later they would be out on their own. But, if we didn't show them the way, they would be lost. But, my Lord and my God, we still lost one. We can lift our heads up in gratitude that God kept us. We can lift our heads up honoring the Lord because we never came down. We never bowed. We never succumb to their wishes and what they wanted. And every one of them, if they could be honest today, they would tell you. "Momma, I wish I would have listened. Daddy, I wish I would have listened. I wish I would have stayed in school. I wish, I would have saved my money. I wish, I would have kept myself until my wedding night." If they were to be truthful, they would say it today. We are talking about to study deceit.

THE DEVILS MASTERED MY LIFE

Now back to this great incident as told by our pastor, "From then until he was fourteen, the devils controlled him." Our pastor said, "And when I touched him, he came to normal. It was an instant miracle. At that time, I didn't know the story behind it, but, I thought it was strange the way his deliverance came. Peace had settled down on him like the sun came out of a storm. He stopped struggling. No longer did he have that terrible insane look. The father later told me that after I prayed for the boy he immediately changed. No more attacks of the devil. He was doing well. It was marvelous to see him now," concluded our pastor. But notice this, notice this, listen as you find out what caused the son to be devil possessed. It was the daddy's fault. "The father had been a witch doctor. *That is one of the reasons my child was under the influence of the spirits,* the father said; *the devils mastered my life, and they mastered my son's life. They took possession over the life of my child,"* the father admitted.

I WENT BACK ON GOD

The father had once known the Lord, but he back slid and he went away from God. So you don't think your kids are effected when you go out and party every weekend? You don't think your kids will be effected when they hear you gossip on the phone? You don't think your kids will be effected when your teenage girl hears that you get married to somebody who don't even believe what you believe? You don't think your children are observing your actions? You don't think your son is taking mental notes of you bringing women in every night? You don't think they're watching that? You don't think they're watching that? Oh, you are so foolish!

The devil told him that he could not live unless he accepted the devils of witchcraft--and he believed it. The devil has power to kill those not protected by the blood of Jesus. And they will kill. The father went on to tell how he received this power from the devil. So, the devil was telling the father of the son, who was devil possessed, "You cannot live without my power!" Just like the devil is telling some of our young people today. "Kill your momma! Stab her while she is sleep! Take her car, while she is sleep. Go in her purse and get money. Get high and keep on getting high." The devil gives his people power but, it is bad, false power. He will give you wisdom but it's foolish wisdom. He will give you knowledge, but it's the knowledge that leads to your own destruction. The father went on to tell how he received power from the devil. He said, notice this, *"When I turned myself over to the devil."* He didn't say he was forced. He didn't say he was forced. This is a hard subject but I am going to keep on going. The father continued with his confession, *"When I turned myself over to the devil,* he said, *I was taken into a round grass hut. Seven witch doctors were around me. They started charming.* The witch doctors were dancing, rattling gourds. They actually call up devils that way."

DEVIL POSSESSED PEOPLE SEE DEMONS

This is Bible. How many people have come into our ministry and said, "Reverend Thomas, before I got saved, I use to see horses and demons dancing around me in circle." Listen to it. You may be saying, "Reverend Thomas give me some Bible. Reverend Thomas give me scripture." Wasn't that what Saul trying to do – to call up Samuel from the dead? But, he didn't call up Samuel. He called up a *familiar spirit.* He called up a devil. He didn't call up Samuel. Samuel wouldn't have never came back from heaven. He called up a demon who looked like a dead loved one; who could talk like your dead loved one. It's a familiar spirit. What is a familiar spirit? It's a spirit of the devil that mimics a person who once lived or is still living, a spirit that is familiar with that person. This familiar spirit can impersonate a person so closely that even family members can't tell the difference in the voice and appearance. Familiar spirit makes themselves look exactly like the ones they're imitating; and when they speak, even their voice can sound the same.[9] Because of false doctrine, people are being fooled all day long. Calling these 1-900 -numbers, going up to séance. You are not calling up your great granny The Bible says the dead know not what the living are doing. They are not coming back to talk to you! They are dead. But, the devil will play on your heart strings and send you back a demon who will look like your deceased mother, father, sister, brother or child; they will talk like them and walk like them. You ought to thank God for your deliverance if you believed in that mess.

Saul went right down there to the Witch of Endor. It's Bible. How is that any different than what we are studying about today? Defeated Saul wanted to call up Samuel. Samuel was in heaven. He [Samuel]

---

[9] Angley, *The Deceit of Lucifer*

did not come back to talk to Saul about nothing. But, he [the devil] did have a demon who could walk like Samuel and talk like him.

THIS IS NOT MAKE BELIEVE

The man of God said that the witch doctors were dancing, rattling gourds. They actually call up devils that way. Again this is not make believe. Our pastor continued his conversation with the man who had been a witchdoctor, "The witch doctor charm the spirits--the devils--when they want them to come upon themselves in a great way and take them over, or when they want someone killed or manipulated in some manner. *The spirits came mightily upon me*, the father said, *upon my head*. This demonic power, these devils had taken him over, possessed him completely. *I became transformed that night*. Listen to it. *After this, I was taken out an open air, and the witch doctors sacrificed some goats*. Doesn't the devil counterfeit what Jesus does? Didn't He [Jesus] tell people to sacrifice animals that did not have spot or blemish. Here they are sacrificing, it's just a counterfeit. *I returned to the hut*, the man continued telling our pastor. *Later, I was taken out in the cold hours of the morning to a pool stream of water to bathe. After sacrificing more goats, I had to carry parts of their organs on my head back to the pool. This was to signify that the spirits agreed that I should be working along with the witch doctors*. Now remember, this man had backslidden from God. That's the reason the devil was able to take possession of him and his son. I would write that down. This man had backslidden from God; he knew God but this went away from the pure, true and holy ways of our God. That's the reason the devil was able to take possession of him. This is Bible. The Bible says the Lord will come; that Jesus will save you and heal you. Those spirits will be cast out. Those spirits will come back around again to see if you have got any honey; to see if you got old time salvation in your soul. The Bible says those devils, if you still don't have Jesus in your heart, will come back again with more demon, seven times worse. What does that mean? If you are with God, *stay with God*. Usually when people go back on the Lord, they end up worse than if they had never known the Lord. Count on it. In other words, they are a greater whore than they were before; some even go right back on alcohol. The addiction is stronger than it was before they knew God.

WHEN THEY KNEW GOD, THEY GLORIFIED HIM NOT

The Bible says, **Because that, when they knew God, they glorified him not as God, neither were thankful; but became vain in their imaginations, and their foolish heart was darkened. Professing themselves to be wise, they became fools, And changed the glory of the uncorruptible God into an image made like to corruptible man, and to birds, and fourfooted beats, and creeping things** (Romans 1:21-23). They once knew God but turned away. And the Lord turned them over to a reprobate mind. **Wherefore God also gave them up to uncleanness through the lusts of their own hearts, to dishonour their own bodies between themselves: Who changed the truth of God into a lie, and worshipped and served the creature more than the Creator, who is blessed for ever. For this cause God gave them up unto vile affections: for even their women did change the natural use into that which is against nature: And likewise also the men, leaving the natural use of the woman, burned in their lust one toward another; men with men and working that which is unseemly, and receiving in themselves that recompense of their error which was meet** (Romans 1:24-27). Some of you lived some degrading lives. You were in gross sins; you couldn't help yourself. But, now the services are too long [speaking to her congregation]. The messages are too tight. You better cry out. The Lord said the day you hear *My* voice. And if you are not hearing His voice today you better cry out until you do. This is the final sweep of souls. It almost over.

COLD HOURS OF THE MORNING

This man who was delivered from demon possession continued and said, *"I was taken out in the cold hours of the morning to a pool or stream of water to bathe. After sacrificing more goats, I had to carry parts of their organs on my head back to the pool. This was to signify that the spirits agreed that I should be working along with the witch doctors."* Now remember, this man had backslidden on God. That's the reason the devil was able to take him over and possess him so completely. Jesus warned people of the dangers of devil possession and the state of a person who goes away from God. You can write it down, Matthew 12:43-44 says, **When the unclean spirit is gone out of a man, he walketh through dry places, seeking rest, and findeth none. Then he saith, I will return into my house from whence I came out; and when he is come, he findeth it empty, swept, and garnished.** Don't find no blood. Don't find no love. Don't find no holiness. Don't find no righteousness. Don't find no consecration. Don't find no obedience. Those devils decide we are going back in that soul again; there's no blood there. **Then goeth he, and taketh with himself seven other spirits more wicked than himself, and they enter in and dwell** (live, abide) **there: and the last state of that man is worse than the first. Even so shall it be also unto this wicked generation** (Matthew 12:45)**.** The devils can be cast out of a person. But if the person does not take Jesus into his heart and soul, the devils will return. The devils can be cast out of a person, but if they don't live right. If they don't take Jesus in, the devils will return and they will be worst. Without Jesus, the soul is empty. No matter what a man puts in. As far as the devils are concerned, the house is not furnished. As noted in today's lesson, those devils had gone out of the father years ago when he found Jesus. But then when he went away from God, he was taken over by the devils in a greater, darker way. His story fits right with the scripture in Matthew. The devils took full possession of him. Don't play around with God. Serve Him with your whole heart and mind.

THAT DEVILISH SPIRIT

Why is there so much violence? And we are going to see more and more and more violence. Because of the spirit of the Antichrist; that devilish spirit that we were reading about today. It is covering the whole earth now. And things that you never thought you would see or hear in your lifetime, they are coming right into our living room through TV and the internet. You can get raw porn right on your computer, neighbor. And people feel as if they haven't done anything wrong because they didn't go outside to a whorehouse. But, they turned right on to the channel.

Get in your Bible, read, fast and pray. The devil is really battling now. He is really loose in the world. And the enemy wants you to get use to sex on TV and drinking and drugging. Some of you, you watch pornography don't you. But, you had that problem before. You got to get a hold of God, before there is no help for you. You know if the Lord can't reach your mind, He can't help you. That pornography comes straight from hell.

TODAY IS YOUR DAY OF FREEDOM

This is your day to be free, if you want to be free. This is your hour to be what God wants you to be. Some of you have those cursing demons in you. You just curse, curse, curse. Hypocrisy deceit, lying; God knows all about you. But, you can be free today. And those of you with children. You better be careful. They are watching everything you do. They are watching everything you say. They watching everything you do and everything you say! You shouldn't be performing no sex acts or doing none of that stuff in front of your kids. You should not be doing it. And you can hate me if you want to. But, you won't get into heaven like that.

I thank the Lord for giving me the strength to deliver my soul this day. The enemy was really busy. Neighbor, the fight is on. People are going to fight you because this message. How sad it will be if you are not ready for the fight. *But the fight is on now.*

CHAPTER 4

HOW DEMON POSSESSION AFFECTS PEOPLE
PART 2

One of the great realities that we have to face the Christian world is that so many Christians do not believe that the devil is real. They don't believe in demons. They believe that it is God's will for them to be sick. Well none of that is truth. I had cancer. How was that God's will? God doesn't get any glory out of you being sick. Matter of fact, as I searched the scriptures, Jesus' ministry was one of healing the soul, mind and body of mankind. He had the greatest healing ministry I ever heard of. Our Lord was raising people from the dead. So, Jesus has nothing to do with sickness, sin or death. Even though there are some very godly people, as I mentioned before, who are dumb, deaf, blind, or lame. Some of God's people are oppressed. But, a true child of God cannot be possessed; two spirits can't possess the same body. So, if a person is possessed, that means Jesus is not there; the precious blood is not on their souls. Light and darkness can't dwell in the same place.

THIS IS A BOLD STATEMENT

How does demon possession affect people? When the devil possesses a soul that person becomes whatever the demon is. That is a bold statement. When the devil possesses a soul that person become whatever the demon is. For example, there are murdering devils[10]. Here in the wild, wild west [Chicago], you can get shot just by sitting in front of your house or in your car. If you are on the

---

[10] Angley, *The Deceit of Lucifer*

porch, if you are in the house, you can get shot and lose your life. If you are driving down the expressway, they can shoot you. See, these people are devil possessed with murdering devils. There are sex devils. People who are possessed with sex. All they think about is sex. It leads them to perversion, rape and watching porn. People are addicts. People who are on drugs, they are devil possessed. People who are alcoholics, they are devil possessed. People who curse, they have cursing demons. People who lie habitually, they have lying spirits, lying devils, live on the inside of their souls. Those possessed with these murdering devils look to capitalize on every opportunity to take a person over to kill another person. Demons live in their soul. And those demons are not going to let that person get any peace until they get that next drink or have sex, even if that means raping someone. The same thing applies with a murdering devil. Those devils are not going to let that person find rest until they kill again. And then the urge subsides momentarily but then it comes back and will not be quenched until the act is fulfilled. People who are addicted to pornography, are in devil bondage.

DEVIL BONDAGE

That is devil bondage! And for a moment you feel satisfied that you have watched pornography. And some of so-called Christian people say that they are saved but yet they have an addiction. There is no Bible for it that. Jesus came to heal, deliver and save *the whole man*. So to say that you are addicted to porn, or that you are an alcoholic, or that you are addicted to some drug and yet you say that you belong to God, it's not Biblical. That's false doctrine. How can you be addicted to something that is against the will of God? How can you be sho-nuff hooked on something that is against the will of God and still be of God? There is no Bible for it. But, in the Bible, in the word of God, we see very plainly the works of Jesus. When Jesus found a person that was devil bound, those devils were cast out. When Jesus found the woman that was caught in adultery, He set her free. Jesus didn't stop there; He reminded her how to stay free. *Go away and sin no more.* There are miles and miles of churches that teach that nobody can live free from sin; that all religions will be accepted in Heaven. It's false doctrine. There's no truth to it. If you couldn't live free from sin, why did they beat Jesus to death? Why did they pierce Him in His side? Why did they take my Lord from hall to hall and keep Him up all night long? Why did Jesus wrap Himself in a wrapper of flesh and come down and say, "**I, Lo, I come (in the volume of the book it is written of me,) to do thy will, O God** (Hebrews 10:7)?" Jesus came to seek and to save that which *was* lost. **For the Son of man is come to save that which was lost** (Matthew 18:11). My Lord did not die for people to make *living as a sinner* a lifestyle. I'm not a sinner saved by grace. I *was once* a sinner but now I'm saved and *grace did it.*

SINNER OR SAVED

You can't be a *sinner and be saved* at the same time. But, the churches are polluted with this false doctrine; it's oozing from them like a person who has bled out. And so many of God's people, listen, they have their wills made out, how they want things to happen at their funeral but they aren't ready to die—not ready for heaven. They have been lying, playing cards, gambling, been out at the boat, living with somebody that is not their Biblical spouse. They are going to heaven? Not so! Dying, deceived about salvation. And God is forced to send them to hell because there is no place for them to go. *It's heaven or hell.* Matthew 9:32-33 says, **As they went out, behold, they brought to him a dumb man possessed with a devil. And when the devil was cast out, the dumb spake: and the multitudes marveled, saying, It was never so seen in Israel.**

Jesus cast out demons. And every blood bought church where the truth is being preached, *there will be signs, wonders, miracles, and healings following*. People *will* be delivered. People *will* be set free. If the head [pastor or person in charge] is not right, then the congregation will be contaminated with false doctrine. Oh my, if the pulpit is purchased by man. They can tell you what to preach about. They can tell you what not to talk about. It is a *profane pulpit*. The Lord talked about this in the Jeremiah's day. **Mine heart within me is broken because of the prophets; all my bones shake; I am like a drunken man, and like a man whom wine hath overcome, because of the Lord, and because of the words of his holiness. For the land is full of adulterers; for because of swearing the land mourneth; the pleasant places of the wilderness are dried up, and their course is evil, and their force is not right. For both prophet and priest are profane; yea, in my house have I found their wickedness, saith the Lord** (Jeremiah 23:9-11)**.** These are pulpits made by man.

A DUMB MAN POSSESSED

Matthew 9:32 says, **They brought to him a dumb man possessed with a devil.** Now notice this, this is profound. Because again, we know that there are godly people who love God and are blind. So, it doesn't mean that they have sinned. The Bible says, they brought to *him a dumb man possessed with a devil*. So we know the man that was *dumb* and *devil possessed*. Can you see it? It says, and when the devils were cast out, the man began to talk. So that's why we know he was possessed by a dumb devil. In this case, because the Bible tells us, he was devil bound. Matthew 12:22 says, **Then was brought unto him** (Jesus) **one possessed with a devil, blind, and dumb.** Notice this, it says, right in the beginning of the scripture. The Bible is plain. It lets us know that the man was devil possessed.

65

He was **blind, and dumb: and he** (Jesus) **healed him, insomuch that the blind and dumb both spake and saw.** This man had an unclean spirit along with a blind spirit.

THE DEVIL WILL TAKE OVER THE CHURCH...IF

The devil will take over your church if you are not careful, if you are double minded. If you are worried about people, if you are worried about the board, and if you worried about the bishop, or if you are worried about the deacons, if you are worried about the Levites, you are in trouble. If man put you in, then man can put you out. And when you compromise like that, you just open up your church for disaster. And some of these people that we encounter, and some of these people that we come in contact with, well see, we will only have one chance to reach them. And you are responsible; pastor; evangelist; Sunday school teacher. Man, how many concepts and teachings do I use today that I learned when I was in Sunday school all those years ago? And just like good qualities grow up in you, bad qualities grow up in you as well. It does not matter what people think about you. You must do what's right. Jesus Christ brought each and every one of you; His blood was spilled as the purchase price for our redemption. Jesus paid it all and we owe Him all. That's a great statement but it's true. Let it marinate over in your mind! Jesus blood brought our redemption. There is no way you can to come God on your own. It's not even in your mind to approach God! Since the fall of Adam, everybody born needed to be saved [needed a Savior and that Savior is Jesus Christ]. **Neither is there salvation in any other: for there is none other name under heaven given among men, whereby we must be saved** (Acts 4:12).

AN ENCOUNTER WITH A WITCH DOCTOR

I want to continue with my pastor's account of his encounter with a witch doctor in Jinja, Uganda, East Africa. This is so profound. The man of God continued, "I prayed for him, and when I touched him, he came to normal. It was an instant miracle. At that time I didn't know the story behind it, but I thought it was strange the way his deliverance came. Peace had settled down on him like the sum coming out of a storm. He stopped struggling. No longer did he have the terrible insane look. The father had been a witch doctor. That is one of the reasons why the child was under the influence of the spirit. The father said, the devils mastered my life. He completely gave himself over to the devil, but at one time he had knew God." Listen to what I am telling you today. It's the quickest way to get possessed by the devil. To know God, and then go the way of the devil. Because to go the way of the devil is to no longer acknowledge God in your life or in your home. You let your child come in and have sex under your roof and you are just glad they are home. Turn your house to a whore stable. I didn't' say horse, I said whore. You are just so glad that Johnny here. "Oh, Oh, Johnnies here" and so are all his whores walking around necked in your house. The house you are paying the mortgage on.

A BLESSING IN DISGUISE

I will tell you when my parent's house burnt down, it was a blessing in disguise. A whole lot of whoring stopped there on Euclid. So, I know your home is a palace. So, let me share my story with you. It's sad, what our parents and grandparents go through in this day and time. It's just sad. But, all you have got to do is rise up and be the parent you say you are. The parents you tell all your friends you are. I am not getting too many Hallelujahs but that's alright. The father said, the devils mastered his life. They mastered his son's life.

They took possession over the life of my child. The father had once known the Lord, but he back slide and went away from God. The devil told him that he could not live unless he accepted the devils of witchcraft. And he believe it. People believe what the devils more than believe what God say. "Oh, you are not going to get pregnant?" That's not the devil? "No, that's not the devil Reverend, that's that handsome boy. You know I am a freshman and he a senior. He's on the football field." That's the devil! You hear me. There's a lot of them in the churches and on all these boards; deacon, mother, willing worker, willing helper, communion board. Whores! Whores! Whores! Embezzlers, thievery, cheating, perverts. The father said that he had once known the Lord. It's true. Some of these churches ought to be ashamed of themselves calling themselves houses of worship. Everything is going on in the church. Listen to some of these programs that are on TV, where the man is on the down low. Where did he say he met his partner? In the church. The church got a big coach bus in the back. Where does it go, especially in the summer? To the casino. People sexting and texting in the church. Come on! I've seen pastors in the back chewing gum, on the phone, right in the church on TV. The man be preaching his heart out. Sweating and losing weight, and right behind them. People talking in the back, chewing, on the phone. I can't even hear the message because I'm watching, and there is no order. I'm so attracted to what is not happening, that I can't really hear what he is saying. "Get your house together first, then come back and tell me something about God!" Right! You wouldn't be on TV. What I want you to get out of this is that the father had once been with God. The father went on to tell our pastor his story. He said how he got power from the devil. When I turned myself over to the devil, he said, I was taken in a round grass hut. Seven witch doctors were around me and they started charming. What I like about this part here is, we have had a few people come to our ministry. And this is how I knew they were devil possessed. They said, they could see little things [devils] marching around their head. Those are devils.

THEY CAN SEE DEVILS

People who are devil possessed, hear voices and can see demons. They can hear them. See the demons, just like Jesus and the Holy Spirit, he [the enemy] uses your voice. But, if you are not living close enough to God to discern who is talking to you, you will think the thought of the devil is your thought. So, listen to that again. I am a witness to this. It says here, "I turned myself over to the devil completely he said. I was taken to a round grass hut. Seven witch doctors were around me. They started chanting." I have witnessed this for myself, in counseling people, in talking to people. People who are devil possessed can see demons. They can see demons. And we have people in our church who have been delivered who have experienced it, and who have told me, "Reverend, sometimes, I can see things marching around me in my mind." Those are demons. "The witch doctors were dancing, rattling gourds. They actually call up devils this way. This is not make believe. This is real. The witch doctors charm the spirits (the devils). When they want them to come upon themselves in a great way and take them over. The demonic power, these devils, had taken him over and possessed him completely. He says, I became transformed that night, this father says." So, if you haven't been following me, we started reading because we are studying about deceit, how does demon possession affects people?

LIKE FATHER, LIKE SON

We are studying about a father whose son was devil possessed. So, now we are going back in his life to find out what happened to him that caused his son to be bound. "Reverend Thomas, present day application, give me Bible?" Why is your child acting the way he's acting? Why is your child acting the way she's acting? Maybe, she is a high price call girl because of the many men you had. Just go back. That's all we are doing. We are just going back in the daddy's life. Maybe your kid's don't like you now because, in your old age, because of the way you treated them when they were younger. Calling them all kind of names; they aren't any good. But, see you forgot that one day you would get old and they would get grown. I remember some things from when I was real young. I remember hearing my momma cry from the depths of her soul. And it wasn't over God. And I would never forget it. So, don't say what your kids won't remember. So don't say what your kids don't know what you're doing in the house or in your room. Have enough respect for yourself, and your child. Don't do *grown up things*, say *grown up things*, in the presence of others. It will cripple them. And it will be your fault. So notice how the devil uses things that the Lord uses. In the Old Testament they would sacrifice animals unto the Lord. So this father was saying when the devils took him over, they gave him power. They started sacrificing goats. Remember, this is what I want you to keep in mind. This man had backslidden from God. That's the reason the devil was able to take possession of him. Jesus warned people of devil possession in Matthew 12:43-45. This is a good memory verse. Matthew 12:43 says, **When an unclean man spirit go out of a man, he walketh through dry places, seeking rest and findeth none**.

STAY FREE

When the Lord sets you completely free and you say the sinner's prayer, you've got to get Jesus in your heart and start living right. You can't leave your house [soul] that once belong to the devil unoccupied. That's what this sentence mean. Read to it again. When an unclean spirit go out of a man. The Bible says how can any man be good unless Christ be in him. When you repent, you acknowledge before the Lord that you are lost and that you need Him to be your Savior. You acknowledge that you have trampled the blood of Jesus underfoot and that you want to be free. When you say that with your whole heart, soul and mind, you are made free. That Blood of Jesus is applied by the Holy Spirit and no one can break that seal but you by committing willful sin. It says, he walketh through dry places. You've got to keep the Lord in your heart. You got to keep salvation burning on the coals of your heart. And then said, so he goeth and findeth none. You repent but maybe you don't get Jesus in. Those same devils come back and see. Some people don't get Jesus all the way in. They get a form but no power. **Having a form of godliness, but denying the power thereof: from such turn away** (2 Timothy 3:5)**.** They get a resemblance but not the full thing. If you are new in Jesus, II Corinthians 5:17 says, **Therefore if any man be in Christ, he is a new creature: old things are passed away; behold, all thing are become new.** So, you say the sinner's prayer. Those devils come back around but now you have Jesus in your heart. If the blood is there, the enemy won't be able to do anything with you unless you fail God.

MY OLD MAN

The *old man* is always waiting in the corridor saying, "Do you need me? Did you call?" That *old man* of unforgiveness, that *old man* addicted to porn, that *old man* of hate, that *old man* that's watching other women, that *old man* of watching other men, that *old man* of sleeping around, that *old man* of not doing what's right. He's always waiting in the vestibule. "Did you call me?" I see your heart is broken. "Did you need me?" You husband, your wife, they didn't treat you right. "Did you need me?" You feeling lonely. "Did you need me?" The devil will never leave you along; you have to learn how to fight and use the blood. The Lord asked the devil one day, **Whence comest thou? Then Satan answered the Lord, and said, From going to and fro in the earth, and from walking up and down in it** (Job 1:7). Your old is always waiting to open up the door. "Let me get that door for you." So, it says that the devils come back to see if you have Jesus in your heart. Do you have Jesus in your soul? If Jesus is not there, **then he saith, I will return into my house from whence I came out** (Matthew 12:44). Notice how bold the devil is. I'm going back home where I was at. And **when he is come, he findeth it empty, swept and garnished** (Matthew 12:44). No blood. Repenting is not just about saying sorry. **Then goeth he, and taketh with himself seven other spirits more wicked than himself, and they enter in and dwell there; and the last state of that man is worse than the first. Even so shall it be also unto this wicked generation** (Matthew 12:45).

THE DEVILS CAN BE CAST OUT

The devils can be cast out of person, but if that person does not take Jesus into his heart and soul the devils will return. The devils will come back greater. Have you ever seen a person that once knew the Lord and they went back on God? And you will be like, "Man, they are worse now than before they started going to church. They act like they are not saved." Maybe they are no longer saved. How can you be tired in these services where you are learning how to fight the devil and make it to Rapture ground? How can you be sleep in this hour? Itching has to cease. I said that because some people start scratching when I say, "Now for the word of God." That's what I said. Some people, they just start scratching when I say, "And now for the Word of God. They just start scratching. You know how they play that violin. They start walking. Their bladder is weak. Come on, pastors. You know what I am saying. Everybody has to go to the bathroom on the whole row. But, while we are singing. Everybody is like, "Wow that song was the bomb." All that singing and good testimony is just an appetizer for the Word of the living God – the main course. The devils can be cast out. Some people get saved and they act like that not saved which makes you question their salvation experience. When they first come to the ministry, they are late and we have to teach them. When they first came, we had to teach them about tithe. They were paying tithe. When they first came to the ministry before salvation, they use to lie to me all the time. Some of them are still lying now and they will end up in hell for it. Some were impatient and not kind. Everything and everybody got on their nerves. You don't think you get on other people nerves. Really? You are always running your mouth. Just always got to complain. You wake up complaining. You don't have a praise on your tongue for nobody. Haven't seen your wife all day, you won't even say hello to her. Haven't seen your kids (they bad), you haven't seen them all day long. Haven't seen your husband all day. Haven't even thought about talking to him. You take too much upon you. You assume that you should have made it home. No good words, no kiss on the cheek. How people treat one another is really something.

POSSESSED BECAUSE OF MY FATHER

We are going back in the life of the father who son was taking over by devils and see what happen to him. He is saying not only was his son devil possessed but the witch doctors also required that he kill his daughter. This great article continues and says, "After a period of time, the spirits demanded that I sacrifice my daughter, that I loved most. She was five years old, and the most beautiful child that we had. They demanded that I sacrifice her so they could use me in a greater way." You see how the devil works and how he tries to counterfeit what the Lord does? What does the Bible say, that if you don't hate mother and father [their ungodly influence], then you are not worthy to be His disciple. In this sense, it is a very literal sense of this father killing his child. But, the Lord demands the same from us *spiritually*. Your first responsibility is to God. He is to be first in your life each day, even over your loved ones. "If you can't separate the influence they have over you, if you can't separate what you owe the Lord, based on what you think you owe them, then you can't be My disciple," the Lord is saying. This father, the devil told him to literally kill that daughter you love so much. What does the Bible tell us? That a man's foes are those in his own household. The witch doctors demanded that this father actually kill the daughter and we will give you more power. The father continues speaking to the author, "They demanded that I sacrifice her so they could use me in a greater way. I was promised more power if I would sacrifice my daughter to the devil." Jesus is the total opposite. We get more power when we put Him first. We get more power when we deny *self*. They get more power by feeding self. You see what I mean? And it hasn't changed. The devil always wants the best out of you; out of your health and mind. "I handed my daughter over to the spirits. The witch doctor knew how to handle her. They took all her blood, put it into a pot, dried it and crushed it into powder and put it into different medicine. After sacrificing my daughter, I went through another process. I met witch doctors. They slaughtered a goat. The spirit of devils came upon me mightily. And I ran out of the hut. I received a greater, evil anointing." But, notice this. The more he sacrificed, the more of the devils power he got.

THE WAY TO REAL POWER

Matthew 17:21 says, **Howbeit this kind goeth not out but by prayer and fasting** and *living in the word*. In Matthew 17th chapter, A lady brought her son. The disciples didn't have enough power to help the lady's son. They needed more power. You see how the devil does it? The more the father sacrificed, the more power he got from the devil. The more we sacrifice unto the Lord, the power we will receive. Galatians 5:22-23 say, **But the fruit of the Spirit is love, joy, peace, longsuffering, gentleness, goodness, faith, Meekness, temperance: against such there is no law.** Ephesians 6:10-13 say, **Finally, my brethren, be strong in the Lord, and in the power of his might. Put on the whole armour of God, that ye may be able to stand against the wiles of the devil. For we wrestle not against flesh and blood, but against principalities, against powers, against the rulers of the darkness of this world, against spiritual wickedness in high places. Wherefore take unto you the whole armour of God, that ye may be able to withstand in the evil day, and having done all, to stand.** See the power that the Lord gives to us. See how it works. You see with the Lord, we will never get more power being selfish. Selfless but not selfish. The devil does the total opposite of what the Lord does. The devil tells you not to give; to always think about yourself. The Lord says give more. The devil tells you to hold your body.

GOOD LOVE

The Lord says give your husband good love. Men are supposed to give good love to their wives. Want to come in smelling like Rudolph and it is summer. It's not even Christmas. Don't want to shave. Don't want to put on that nice cologne that your wife loves. Saying, "Here I am baby!" "Here you are?" You need to go back out and try it again. Men should give their wives good love. Not what guy wants all the time but satisfy his wife. She wants her hand held for a few seconds. She wants you to look into her eyes. Maybe she wants flowers. Maybe she wants a soft drink. Not a stale one that you forgot to put in the refrigerator. Maybe she wants you to vacuum the rug that will put her in the mood. Women want good love. Women are to do the same for their husbands.

EVIL, GREATER ANOINTING

Let's continue. This father received an evil, greater anointing. When the devil takes over a person, he has the mind as well. And that's why the first symptom of a person leaving God happens in their mind. It might be very subtle. The first sign of a person being devil possessed is noticed in the mind. It may be very subtle. That's why the devil tries to kill people's mind through Alzheimer's and mental illness. He tries to make the people of God, their minds weak through doubt and unbelief. The Lord promised to keep us in perfect peace as long as our minds are **stayed** [constant] on Him. It's periodically? No, stayed. You have to watch what you watch on TV, what kind of music you listen to. Look closer when something is advised as "Christian." Some much of it is worldly. Christian rock, study the history of rock. How many people went out and did some dangerous stuff after listening to rock music. I am telling you nothing new. Christian rock, so much of it, blasphemes our God.

CHARM THE SPIRITS

"Those who give themselves over to the devil can charm the spirits to come to them in a great way to do the great works that they want. Now they have the same power as the devil," this father stated. More deadly, devilish power was given to the father. He continues his story. He talks about how he ran out of the hut not knowing where he was going. He was cast down by the spirit. Then the witch doctor brought him blood mingled with human flesh. After that he was taken almost unconscious to the hut. For some time, he stayed in the hut. He says, "For some time, I had a greater evil anointing. The witch doctors took me to the market place. I was dirty, I was filthy. Witch doctors don't bath." They say the witch doctors don't bath. A lot of people who are devil possessed like to expose their breast and other parts of their bodies.

NO MAN COULD TAME HIM

In Mark the 5th Chapter, there was a man who was devil bound. **And when he was come out of the ship, immediately there met him out of the tombs a man with an unclean spirit, Who had his dwelling among the tombs; and no man could bind him, no, not with chains: Because that he had been often bound with fetters and chains, and the chains had been plucked asunder by him, and the fetters broken in pieces: neither could any man tame him. And always, night and day, he was in the mountains, and in the tombs, crying, and cutting himself with stones** (Mark 5: 2-5)**.** When he came to himself, the Bible says, he was sitting there in his right mind and he was clothed. **And they come to Jesus, and see him that was possessed with the devil, and had the legion, sitting, and clothed, and in his right mind** (verse 15). And when those boys in 19th chapter of Acts, acted like they had God, the devil whipped them out their what? Their clothes and they were what? Naked. **And the evil spirit answered and said, Jesus I know, and Paul I know; but who are ye? And the man in whom the evil spirit was leaped on them, and overcame them, and prevailed against them, so that they fled out of that house naked and wounded** (verses 15-16)**.** The devil hates the body. Every Impulsive thing he can do to get people to degrade the bodies, he does. In the sixties, the hippies gave over to the devil. Not caring how they looked or how they smelled. They wouldn't clean up. This man was dirty. It really behooves you also if you want to know about the day and time we live in.

THE YEAR 1968

Study about the year of 1968 when Antichrist was born. The world changed. The *New York Times*, and all those famous magazines talked about the year of 1968. I believe the Antichrist was born, and is now on the earth now. The flower child. The whole thing about that was that they were just having sex with one another. They were having sex everywhere. Everybody was nude and having orgies. Those were devils. Just getting you to degrade yourself. A lot of young girls don't feel comfortable unless their breast are exposed. They crave attention that is not good. It is disgusting to me. I don't want to see no part of you. Do you hear me? Cover yourself up. You can't fall down. You can't sit down. You can't lay down. You can't roll over. If you catch on fire, you can't stop drop and roll because of your stuff is going to be hanging out. You have to laugh at how the devil, gets people to make fools of themselves; he is something else. But, the Lord wants us to be wise and know about the things that the devil is doing in this final hour. I hope you will join me next week, as we go more and more and more.

NO LONGER A CHRISTIAN NATION

Missionaries are now coming back to the United States because we are no longer a Christian nation. Our former President said it. Did you know that? He said, "We are no longer a Christian nation." Did you question your salvation while studying this chapter? The way you act; the way you don't forgive; the way you don't show love. How are you handling truth today? Why go all this way? Why make such a sacrifice? You have ask yourself, where do you stand with God? Where are you at regarding His greatness? Where are you in the scheme of witchcraft and voodism? Where are in the scheme of adultery and fornication? Where are you at in terms of pornography? Where are you at today, in terms of lying and being seduced? Where are you, where are you at today? Only you can answer this question. But, here's another opportunity, for you to give your heart over to the Lord.

Say the sinner's prayer and get Jesus into your heart. And everybody saying, **"Oh God! Oh God! Please forgive me for sinning against you. But, I have come home. Never to leave you again. Lord, I've found myself, in this lesson today. What a profound teaching! And I accept it all. Every accusation that you brought to me, it is true indeed! But, oh God! Don't leave me like this. Don't leave me wretched and undone. But, by faith and the blood. By faith in your blood, save my soul! Save my soul! Save my soul! Save me Lord! Save me, Lord! And if you meant that you can leave here with a clean house."** It's not empty but that blood is there. If you meant it. That blood is there. That blood is there. That blood is there. That blood is there. If you meant what you said, that blood is there. That blood is there. That blood is on your soul. That blood is there. No matter what temptation comes upon you. That blood is there. Temptation is not bad. Yielding is a sin. No matter what happens in your life, if you stay with God; God will stay with you. You're free! You're free! You might still have problems, but you're free. You are free! By the power that is in the blood. Who has the power to set you free? Jesus! Who has the power to set you free? Jesus! Who has the power to keep you free? Jesus! Jesus our king!

Are you ready? Let's go!

NOTES

DJG

NOTES

DJG

NOTES

DJG

NOTES

DJG

QUIZZES

SHARON HUMMER - PERSONAL TESTIMONY

My name is Sharon Hummer and I want to share a magnificent Miracle that God gave me through the blood of His Son, Jesus.

On May 11, 2011, I had to see my gynecologist for an emergency and from there he referred me to have a CT-scan on my abdomen. Later I got the results that there was a tumor on my left kidney that seemed highly suspicious of cancer.

My Gynecologist referred me to an Urologist. I spoke to the Urologist later that day he said from what he saw on the scan the tumor was cancer. I was afraid. I had never had cancer, and cancer runs in my family. Many things were going through my mind.

One month later, I had an appointment to see another Urologist who spoke to me about all the things to expect when you have kidney cancer. He begin to show me the image of the tumor on my kidney and said the discoloration/darkness in the tumor was cancer for sure.

He said once the tumor is removed, they will test to see if the cancer had spread anywhere else in my body. He also talked about me going on dialysis. I felt so overwhelmed and afraid. I talked to Jesus a lot I asked Him to help me to use my faith. I knew He could heal me but did I have the right amount of faith, was the question to myself.

I got prayer from Reverend Thomas and then I went for another appointment to see the Surgeon in Urology. He discussed with me the complications that happen with removing a cancerous tumor; that I will lose a lot of blood and need a blood transfusion.

On the day of the surgery, Jesus helped me to not be afraid. I had the tumor removed. The surgeon spoke to my family that was there, he said that there was no sign of cancer at all. So I did not have to have dialysis. I later looked over my report of my surgery and I did not have blood transfusion like the surgeon said. One doctor mocked and said, "You can pray and hope it go way." That's what I did and JESUS heard my prayer and HEALED ME of CANCER. JESUS helped me understand that it does not matter if cancer runs in my family. If I live holy before him, ALL generational curses have to stop with me and I can have a miracle. I still have my miracle today. Three doctors said "Yes" to cancer but Jesus said, "With His blood stripes I am healed."

PART 2

COURSE TOPICS

CHAPTER 5

WHERE IS GOD?

Have you ever been in a church and you leave out scratching your head wondering, "Where is God?" People, when asked, will ramble on about the singing; how good so and so looked. Many will comment on how well the first lady was dressed, the songs that were sung or how elegant the place was put together but I want to know about the Word. What were you taught? Were you encouraged to be a better Christian? The problem of unforgiveness that you had in your heart, did anything come across the pulpit to help you? You've been sick for a long time. Did you hear any words of faith to encourage you to stretch out your hand and be made well? Where's God?

ABSENCE

One word I want you to look up today is *absence*. **Absence** is *the state of being away, not being present[11]*. So we are talking about in His own house. In the Lord's own building, that was supposedly purchased by the blood of Jesus Christ. The Lord, He is not in many of the churches today. The pastor's name is on the outside. Somebody has a collar on. Whether it's a man or woman. They have the furniture arranged. They have people in the pulpit. In my early days as a minister, we use to call those people "pulpit furniture." Just people in the pulpit, but they never had an opportunity to do anything but be seen. Maybe once a year, we would be allowed to say the opening scripture. We [A Passion For Christ Ministries], come from a very big church, in Akron, Ohio. Our pastor travels all over the world. He has one of the greatest missionary

---

[11] Dictionary.com

ministries that I have ever seen. I have travelled to Africa with our home church a number of times. So, it's not about the building or the size of the congregation. It's not about the place. Where is God? Absent! People say absence makes the heart grow fonder but not in this case. We are in a terrible shape as a nation; as the body of Christ, in our homes, in our marriages, and in our communities. My Lord, in my community, as I've told you before, I am in the middle of the wild, wild, west, here in Chicago[12]. It's the wild-wild-west. But through His grace, through the love of God, He has kept us yet one more day. **Absence**, again it is *the state of being away or not being present.* Now what you have to keep in mind as we continue our study of deceit today is the building is there and the people are coming in. The people are building more and more churches; just demolishing one building and building bigger ones. Some churches are getting so big that they have to shuttle the people in from some garage, located away from the sanctuary. The place is so massive. Big or small, the question remains, will you find God in there?

HERESY

The next word I want you to write down is **heresy**. *It is belief and opposition to sound choice.* Do you notice how people want to blame God for all the bad stuff? Why did God allow someone to be born a homosexual, blind, sick, deaf? Well, that person doesn't know the Word of the Lord. The Bible is plain in the fact that when Adam fell the *curse* came on *the entire world.* So why blame God for that? Others ask, "Why is the Lord letting all these murders take place and letting all these bad things happen in the world?" Well, it's right there

---

[12] At the time of this writing, Chicago has over 625 people shot & killed; 3288 people shot & wounded and 3931 people shot for a total of 698 homicides [various articles].

in Genesis. Didn't the Lord tell Cain if he didn't humble himself that sin lieth at the door? See that was the first murder. God was there to warn Cain, "Boy, don't do that!" But he didn't heed the warning but proceeded to kill his brother, Abel because of jealousy and deceit. **Doth a fountain send forth at the same place sweet water and bitter? Can the fig tree, my brethren, bear olive berries? either a vine, figs? so can no fountain both yield salt water and fresh. But if ye have bitter envying and strife in your hearts, glory not, and lie not against the truth** (James 3:11-12,14). The Bible said yield not to temptation, for yielding is a sin. James 1:2-4 say, **My brethren, count it all joy when ye fall into divers temptations; Knowing this, that the trying of your faith worketh patience. But let patience have her perfect work, that ye may be perfect and entire, wanting nothing.** To be tempted is not a sin. The sin comes in when you yield to the temptation of the devil. So, Cain yielded to the anger that was in his heart, but the fruit of that anger led to murder. **He that committeth sin is of the devil; for the devil sinneth from the beginning. For this purpose the Son of God was manifested, that he might destroy the works of the devil** (1 John 3:8). **Let no man say when he is tempted, I am tempted of God: for God cannot be tempted with evil, neither tempteth he any man: But every man is tempted, when he is drawn away of his own lust, and enticed. Then when lust hath conceived, it bringeth forth sin: and sin, when it is finished, bringeth forth death. Do not err, my beloved brethren** (James 1:13-16).

BLINDED LEADERSHIP

The Bible says that when leadership hasn't studied the Word of the Lord, you cause God's people to err. A lot of stuff that is happening in the churches now, people are just following poor, blinded leadership. They are just fanatics. They are all on the bus speaking in tongues. Talking about they see, they see, they see. And God's people are eating it up. They love this mess. It's that what he said in Jeremiah? He said, "My people, they love this mess." Jeremiah 5:31 says, **The prophets prophesy falsely, and the priests bear rule by their means; and my people *love to have it* so: and what will ye do in the end thereof?** Everybody is a prophet. But, The Lord said, through Jeremiah, both prophets and priest are profane. In Ezekiel the 8th Chapter, the Lord told Jeremiah there is a hole in the wall. But dig in, you see the abomination that *my people do*. Where's God? The church as a whole is lost. Oh God, help us!

FALSE DOCTRINE CAN BE FOUND

This is an hour of information and you're going to *have to know* what information is of God and what is not. You're going to *have to know* what to accept what to reject. God wants false doctrine exposed for what it is. He wants false doctrine to be exposed and brought out in the front because multitudes have been destroyed by it. And multiples will burn in hell for all eternity because of false doctrine. So many pulpits have everything *but* God in them. And the people are dying lost. False doctrine can be found very prevalent in the Christian world today. *Heresy*, I gave that word to you a few minutes ago. Again *it is the belief in opposition to sound truth*. Meaning it is simply false. Paul was a heretic before he was saved. He believed that Christ was an imposter. He was a heretic and he endorsed heresy. False doctrine is a heresy and so much of that is going on now in pulpits across America. It's an opposition to the truth. The truth is the Gospel of Jesus Christ. And now in this final hour, it's a lot of heresy in the Christian world. And we have to study to show ourselves approved unto God, a workman that need not be ashamed, rightly dividing the word of truth. *And how can you know something is false if you don't know the truth about it?* If all you have been taught is false doctrine -- nobody can ever live free from sin -- then you are going to be lost. And you will be damned and go to hell. For the Bible says for the wages of sin is death. But, the gift of God is eternal life through Jesus Christ our Lord. If all you've been taught is that when you willfully sin, you have got to do is keep on repenting, then you are going to die lost. Hebrews 10:26 says, **For it we sin willfully after that we have received the knowledge of the truth, there remaineth no more sacrifice for sins.** There remain no more sacrifice when the truth has been given to us, over and over again. You won't find one speck of sin in Heaven. You won't find any liars, or back bitters there. There will be no smokers. You won't find anyone who has an addiction. You won't find them in God's Heaven. The shaker uppers, those whore mongers; you won't find them in the Kingdom of God. Where is God? He's in the same place that He's always been. In the hearts of true believers, pure in hear who are a living pure, and holy and living free from all sin. Matthew 5:8 says, **Blessed are the pure in heart: for they shall see God**. Hebrews 12:14 says, **Follow peace with all mean, and holiness, without which no man shall see the Lord.**

WHEN GOD IS ABSENT

Any pulpit where God is absent is of the devil. Those who live according to false teaching and doctrines, they are captains to Satan. Yet, they claim they are children of God. They claim to be of God. Yet, they are not of God. Because false doctrine is not of God. It's so simple! How can they be of God? Jesus said you are of your father the devil. You do the works of the devil. He says for this cause, in 1 John 3:8-9 say, **He that committeth sin is of the devil; for the devil sinneth from the beginning. For this purpose the Son of God was manifested, that he might destroy the works of the devil. Whosoever is born of God doth not commit sin; for his seed remaineth in him: and he cannot sin, because he is born of God.** For this cause, the son of God was manifest, so that He might destroy the works of the devil. He says you will not sin because the seed of God remaineth in you. Right? So many churches teach nobody can live free from sin. They say Jesus knows our thoughts. He knows we are weak; Jesus knows we are of flesh. That's why Jesus died and shed His blood for you and me. Where is God? Those pulpits without God were created by Satan himself. He is the master of deceit and he has a doctrine of his own. Now false teachings of the Holy Bible always deny the power that is in the blood. These profane pulpits, they always deny the blood in one way or the other. False doctrine denies that no one can live free from sin. "My Lord and my God, Reverend Thomas I can't come to your church, you have to live *too good* [holy and pure]. I can't come to your church you got to be too perfect! You mean to tell me; you don't even tell not even one lie?" All liars are going to have their part in the lake of fire. "You never got mad and a curse word slipped out?" Where did it slip from, your heart. The Bible declares that from the abundance of the heart, the mouth speaketh. It slipped out from your heart. No! No! Where is God? Where is God? Some pulpits where God is absent they will tell you: we know that the blood can destroy sin, but we are always going to be a sinner. We are talking about to study deceit. We know that the blood can destroy sin, but we always a sinner? We are going to always be a sinner. You know they say, "I thank God for His power. I thank God for His Son, Jesus Christ, and I just thank the Lord." They say, "I am not what I use to be. I am not what I should be. But, I sure thank God that I am not what I to be. Because I use to curse you out." All that garbage equals *nothing*. You were nothing then in sin, and if you believe that mess, you'll end up in hell with *"they say."* James say, how can you consider yourself Holy and you can't even keep your own tongue in check. **Even so the tongue is a little member, and boasteth great things. Behold, how great a matter a little fire kindleth! And the tongue is a fire, a world of iniquity: so is the tongue among our members, that it defileth the whole body, and setteth on fire the course of nature; and it is set on fire of hell. But the tongue can no man tame; it is an**

unruly evil, full of deadly poison (James 3:5-6, 8)**.** James explains that if you keep your tongue, you will keep your whole body intact. In the churches across America, they are throwing the Lord out and putting the lock on the door. So many don't want him in their church because you must live holy if He is to stay in a place; you have to be consecrated and dedicated. To have God in the church means man has to come down off of his pulpit and put God back on the thrown. Where is He at today? People are getting swindled and cheated thinking that they can get a miracle in such a place.

WHERE ARE THE MIRACLES?

There will be no miracles happening without the preaching of the Gospel. There is no healing, no deliverance, and nobody is being set free! Give me some Bible Reverend! Gideon said, "**Oh my Lord, if the Lord be with us, why then is all this befallen us? and where be all his miracles which our fathers told us of, saying, Did not the Lord bring us up from Egypt? but the Lord hath forsaken us, and delivered us into the hands of the Midianites** (Judges 6:13)**.** The God of miracles lives! He lives! The Lord will honor faith wherever it's truly displayed but you can't keep a miracle and stay in in false doctrine and sin. So many of the pulpits have become so degraded; many of them have been purchased by man. Pastors are told what to preach, what to say, and *what not* to say. The pulpits have become so defiled. God cannot even stay in the place if He wanted to. Our God couldn't move in such a place if He wanted to; sin and unrighteousness ties the hands of God. Where's God?

WHO CAN LIFT UP HOLY HANDS?

The God of miracles is where He has always been, high and lifted up. Who can praise the Lord? Only those with Holy hands and a clean heart. You will find him there! You will find him by the meek and the lowly. You will find our Lord amongst the common folks; those who the world church have rejected. You will find Him there. You will find the Healer around those where people have been rejected and cast down. You will find Him around those where people have been talked about and pushed aside. Look among them and you will find God. They are already low, so they just become humble. You understand what I am telling you? When you are in fear for your life; when you are fear of not being able to make restitution -- when you are in fear of not paying your bills. When you think maybe you might get evicted humility is easily found. So don't tell me you can't humble yourself, Ahab. Don't tell me you can't humble yourself, Ahab! You can humble yourself if you have to and you get in the doctor and they say the big C word (Cancer). You can humble yourself. Then, for the first time for so many, God will come first in their lives. While God has nothing to do with *sin* or *sickness*, He will take advantage of any opportunity afforded Him to manifest Himself. It will then be up to the individual to accept or reject His calling. "I've been calling Him! I've been calling Him! I've been calling Him! They say, "God is the reason why my momma is dead!" Is He really? What about the life she led? They say, "God took my daddy from me."

MURDERED AT WILL

You know they were saying all this stuff when my son got murdered. "God had another plan for his life." Another plan for his life? No! Daniel, died because he wanted to die because he wouldn't listen. **Children, obey your parents in the Lord: for this is right. Honour thy father and mother; (which is the first commandment with promise;) That it may be well with thee, and thou mayest live long on the earth** (Ephesians 6:1-3)**.** Some of you think that is tight. But, you need to grow up in God. Where is God? He's with mature people. He's with people who have already been weaned off milk. You have got to let some people go. You will be a better Christian if you just let some people go. They aren't doing anything but bringing you down; they are no good for you. You don't hear me?

YOUR PAST

Jesus paid for all **past** sins; He didn't pay for you to keep on sinning. People say, "I got Jesus for that." Stop lying to yourself! Stop lying on God. Give God a break. You already know before you go out you are going to steal. Lying on your timecard. You know you took forty-five minutes and all you had was thirty minutes for lunch. That is stealing. You are going to call and tell somebody to punch you in when you aren't there. That is for somebody. That is a firing for insubordination and they will block your unemployment. When you are saved, old things are passed away, behold all things become new. **Therefore if any man be in Christ, he is a new creature: old things are passed away; behold, all things are become new** (2 Corinthians 5:17)**.** Therefore, those who in are Christ, the Bible says, are not doing the same things they use to do before salvation. If person claims to be saved and yet still are exercising the works of the flesh, they never got saved. They are not saved. The Lord told us that when you are born again, that *old man* is gone. He is no longer on the throne; that one that wants to fight and give people a black eye. He is not on the throne anymore.

IT'S GOD'S FAULT!

Many people have blamed God for the problems and sorrows of this human race for the last six thousand years. God **could have** known, but He chose not to know. Some are convinced that, "Well, God knew that Adam was going to fail. And that's all we have to do is keep on repenting." Don't be foolish! All you have to do is study the Bible. People must study the Word. God has the power to know and He has the power not to know. He trusted Adam when He created him and placed him in the garden. God trusted Adam to name those animals and those animals are still named that way today. The Lord wanted a relationship with the man and woman that He made. God the Father, God the Son and God the Holy Ghost desired a close relationship with us. The Lord wants a relationship with you, neighbor. What kind of God would He be if you were to come to Him, pouring your heart out saying, "Lord, please forgive me," and He looks into your tomorrows and says, "No, I am not going to forgive you today, because I looked into your tomorrow and saw that you are not going to be any good." Our God is not like that; He trusts you like *you must trust* Him. Hebrews 11:6 says **But without faith it is impossible to please him: for he that cometh to God must believe that he is, and that he is a rewarder of them that diligently seek him**. Our precious Lord doesn't look into your tomorrows regarding salvation. *He takes you at your word*. When you come to Jesus, He takes you at your word at that very point. When you say, "Father, forgive me Lord, I am lost." You get a brand new chance at life. However, some say they wish they could start over but they would start over doing the same things that got them into trouble before. The sincere hearted ones who come before the cross will say, "Lord, I am lost and I need a savior. Lord, Oh, the wretched man that I am! Dear Lord please take the coals from off the altar, and set my tongue on fire that I might talk right, that I might walk right. That I might live right!" Glory to God, neighbor, you become new that instant. You are new through and through. There are no more curse words in your body. You don't want to curse nobody out because the old man has been cast out and the Holy Ghost now lives inside. Oh Hallelujah! The bed he use to sleep on, now grace stays there. And the lock that is on the door, mercy got the key.

GOD KNEW

Don't let people preach that false doctrine to you. "Well, God knew we were all going to be sinners." No! He trusted Adam. Come on! Why would God ask Adam where he was? God expected Adam to be in the same spot where He left him. Why would God, who can know all things be going around saying, "Adam, where are thou?" He would have known Adam failed. The Lord didn't know Adam failed until at that point. He trusted Adam; they had a relationship. It was only when He went to call Adam that the Lord knew that Adam wasn't in his place. He was like, "Uh-Oh, something has changed! Things are not like they use to be," the Lord must have thought. Just think, Adam and Eve use to look right into the face of God. God would come down in the form of a man, because He can do anything. Jesus is God in the flesh and He came down. Adam and Eve looked Him right in His face. Had they continued in holiness and true righteousness, they would have had such a wonderful fellowship and this earth would be Eden. God was just coming down to be with the man and woman He had made as He often did. Something was different and it wasn't on the Father's part. God is still God. He still came down in the cool of the day but the man and the woman He made, they weren't in their place. The Lord started perusing the kingdom of earth that He had made for them with His holy eye sight. The animals were where they should have been. The sun, the moon and the stars were still rotating and in place. They hadn't moved.

The Lord began to say, "Adam, where are you? Adam you are not in your spot. Where are you?" That's when the Lord knew Adam had failed. God *can* know and *not* know because He is God. It's important that you understand how God works because so many false doctrine people are preaching that God knew that Adam was going to fall and that Jesus would have to come to earth and die.

This doctrine has sent so many right to the pits of hell. Count on it. A lot of people are boldly preaching that God knew He was going to have to send His only Son to come down here and be beat to death. They are preaching, "God knew Adam was going to fall." He did not know because He didn't want to know because He's God. "Give me Bible, Reverend." It says that when you go to hell that He will never remember you again. It is just posted throughout the Psalms that when the Lord locks you up, He will never remember you again. **For, behold, I create new heavens and a new earth: and the former shall not be remembered, nor come into mind** (Isaiah 65: 17). **Therefore, behold, I, even I, will utterly forget you, and I will forsake you, and the city that I gave you and your fathers, and cast you out of my presence** (Jeremiah 23:39). Our Lord boldly stated that He would cast your sins in the sea of forgetfulness to *never remember* them again. **I, even I, am he that blotteth out thy transgressions for mine own sake, and will not remember thy sins** (Isaiah 43:25).

PASS BY AND FELLOWSHIP

You've got to ask, "Where is God in your life?" Where is He at in your life? Have you made Him a room on the wall, so that the Holy Spirit can come in as He passes by and fellowship with you? Have you made Him that room in your soul; in your heart; in your mind? That the Father can just come by anytime. **Nevertheless I tell you the truth; It is expedient for you that I go away: for if I go not away, the Comforter will not come unto you; but if I depart, I will send him unto you. And when he is come, he will reprove the world of sin, and of righteousness, and of judgment: of sin, because they believe not on me** (John 16:7-9). **And I will pray the Father, and he shall give you another Comforter, that he may abide with you for ever; Even the Spirit of truth; whom the world**

cannot receive, because it seeth him not, neither knoweth him: but ye know him; for he dwelleth with you [salvation]**, and shall be in you** [Holy Ghost baptism]**. I will not leave you comfortless: I will come to you** (John 14:16-18). Again, I feel the need to repeat somethings here. God could have known about Adam, but the great God of the universe chose not to know. He wanted the man and woman that He made to be perfect and to have perfect trust in Him. Therefore, being a just God that He is, He had to trust them too. Don't you trust your companion? Do you call them fifty times a day saying, "Where are you at? I'm still at work!" If you don't trust somebody, don't marry them. If you don't trust them, don't marry them. Don't marry them! If you don't trust them, do not marry them. Neighbor, I've married so many people and if I had known they were going to turn out like they did, I wouldn't have married them. ***I want to know*** if you are going to do right; if you are going to continue to live for God and love one another. ***I want to know*** if couples are talking about having a baby, I want to know if they are going to be Holy enough to raise them in holiness. They say, "Reverend we love each other, Reverend this is the one." What am I going to say? "No, that is your life mate?" Don't you know, they are not listening to anyone at that time? Count on it. I just go, "Alright baby, alright, I am going to be praying for you." And then comes the war.

THE TASMANIAN DEVIL

What is that name of the cartoon? *Tasmanian Devil.*[13] Some of you are too young for this. When I was coming up, the *Tasmanian Devil*, when he came around, you knew he was coming because all this dust was kicking up, the wind. So, when he started coming around, he just swirling around and bringing up dust. As he twirled around,

---

[13] "Tasmanian Devil (Looney Tunes)" Wikipedia, the free encyclopedia.

all this wind is just moving. I can just see it now. I would tell my ministers, "Here they come. I can see that dust following them." Some of them will go from one minister to another seeing if they can find one that will go along with their foolishness. They don't want you to tell them the truth. They will say, "I know, I know, I know, Reverend don't say that part." See, they try and shut me up when I get the part they don't want to hear about. It's deceit. One couple said I made them to get married. I made you to get married? No, I told you that if you are going to keep whoring then you need to make the marriage bed right. That's what I said. You let your flesh choose. Flesh has a loud voice. You've heard it before, haven't you? "Oh, baby!" Flesh be like, "Oh me! Oh my! Oh my!" And then when sin is finished, the only thing you can say is, "Oh me, Oh me, Oh my!" Right? James 1:15 says, **Then when lust hath conceived, it bringeth forth sin: and sin, when it is finished, bringeth forth death.**

SEX, MONEY & RELIGION

So if you don't trust each other now, that is a ***good sign*** not to get married. You should talk about *everything* before you get married. You should talk about money. You should talk about sex. If you want to know if we are going to get it on or are we going to be playing games. You should talk about your religious beliefs. Now these are the things people fight about in counseling. They fight about money, sex and religion. You must have these matters **settled** prior to marriage, I will assure you. We are talking about to study deceit. That is what we are talking about. Talk about these things before you get married. You say, "I am paying my tithes now and I'm going to make a pledge. When I say *I do*, I am going to still pay my tithes and continue to give a pledge and a love offering and because you are going to be with me, *we will* be able to give more. Do you understand that? I go to church and I go to Sunday school. I go when they go visiting. So when we go and get married I'm still going to be going to church. I go to Sunday school and when the Pastor go out, I go." You have to lay it all out up front *before marriage*.

THERE SHOULD BE NO SURPRISES

There should be no surprises. You have to lay it out. It might be four and a quarter. Those very important matters – discuss them now. These are the things you need to talk about. These are the things that people fight over. You let them know, "I pray and I love God! Now, if you don't believe in what I believe in, number one, it's going to be a problem." Everybody is saved now! Everybody loves God. Everybody believes in Jesus *until you marry them*!" Then all of a sudden, their flesh starts rising up when you try to pray. You take them to the Bible! They will say, "I don't care what that Bible says." For example, if you are a high strung person sexually, you have to talk about that. Now, let me say this, a man can't lust after his wife but you sure can get on her nerves. I am a preacher's preacher. You know these are things that you talk about because otherwise you are setting yourself up. You are setting yourself up for failure. The Bible says in all your getting, get an understanding. Be in agreement. And you can't have a headache all the time ladies. Nowadays men have headaches. We just have to deal with deceit out in the open. Now, you may be asking yourself, "What does any of that have to do with the devil?" *Everything*. The Bible says that the woman doesn't have control over her own body but it doesn't stop there. What else does it say? That the man is also subject to the wife. It is true? **The wife hath not power of her own body, but the husband: and likewise also the husband hath not power of his own body, but the wife** (I Corinthians 7:3).

103

KEEP YOUR MARRIAGE STRONG

You have got to set the scenery, husbands. Women, you have got to set the scenery. I am still talking about deceit. Because if you think you can keep your marriage strong any other way, you are sadly mistaken. Love makes the world go round. I am telling you. It is just something we have to talk about. These things are important. And if you figure there are some hiccups in there now, don't marry that person! Don't do that to yourself. They are going to fight you about coming to the church and about giving. You can't make people change. Don't do it to yourself! Don't lie and make people believe you are all sweet and know how to cook and all that stuff. You can't do that. Because time is going to tell. Making a man think that you wake up with rosy lips. Just cut it out! I mean you don't have to look like a barn in the morning either. You say, "I'm married now, I don't have to roll my hair." You get up in the morning looking like shockwaves have went through you. One person will always want to blame the other person. And when we have counseling with folks [speaking of her congregation], we will meet together with the people and then we meet separately. It always amazes me because the husband will say the same thing that the wife has said about him but they are supposed to be Christians. These are supposed to be people who sing, opening up the doors of the church, assist with tithes and offering but they don't even have peace at home. They are sleeping in separate quarters and they only connect when they get in the car; his seat and her seat. And then they come in, "Honey, honey." You are not loving each other. Some of you don't even sleep in the same house; let alone the same bed; let alone the same room. Love, faith, hope, forgiveness, they all start at home. It's just a collaboration effort. That all comes with you into the house of God, some of it good and some bad. You don't send folks to church; you bring them. You want a strong family then come with your wife! Come with your husband! Bring your children! It's the way God planned it. The Word says to teach your children and generations after them to honor God. The Lord commanded us to teach our children about Him. **Remember the days of old, consider the years of many generations: ask thy father, and he will shew thee; they elders, and they will tell thee** (Deuteronomy 32:7).

GOD WAS GRIEVED

Remember we are talking about Adam and Eve. The Lord had to trust them and did not look into their future to see what they would do on tomorrow. God was horribly grieved by Adam and Eve's failure. When soul's come to the Lord, the Lord never looks into their tomorrows before He washes away all their sins to see if they are going to back slide. What a gracious God and a merciful God we serve. 1 John 1:9-10 say, **If we confess our sins, he is faithful and just to forgive us our sins, and to cleanse us from all unrighteousness. If we say that we have not sinned, we make him a liar, and his word is not in us**. The Lord is not talking about keep on forgiving you every week. No! Jesus' blood did what the law could not do in that it was weak and could not remove the stain of sin. The law didn't have the power. The law could not take away the stain of guilt and the shame of sin. But the all power, all conquering blood of the lamb, Jesus Christ, it washed it all clean. Though your sins be as scarlet, I can make it white as snow. The Blood of Jesus! I love talking about the blood. I love reading about the blood. I love singing about the blood. What can wash away my sins? Nothing but the blood of Jesus. What's missing from so many churches today? The Blood! The hymns! The altars! Those hymns that talk about the blood; "Were you there, when they crucified my Lord? Were you there? Oh, sometimes causes me to tremble. Tremble! Tremble! Where you there when they crucified my Lord. They beat Him all night long. He never said a mumbling word."

THE SCENT OF SEX STILL...

So many churches have pulled up out their altars, altars that use to be filled on service morning with hungry seekers. People were flowing in to talk to God and make sure they were ready to receive His Holy Sacrament on Communion day. Now, people are putting gum in their mouth just before taking communion; some come right from the night club to take communion. They've been out all night long, dancing with the devil. Some even still wear the scent of sex all on their hands and yet they pop up ready to serve communion. **Wherefore whosoever shall eat this bread, and drink this cup of the Lord, unworthily, shall be guilty of the body and blood of the Lord. But let a man examine himself, and so let him eat of that bread, and drink of that cup. For he that eateth and drinketh unworthily, eateth and drinketh damnation to himself, not discerning the Lord's body. For this cause many are weak and sickly among you, and many sleep. For it we would judge ourselves, we should not be judged** (I Corinthians 11:27-31). *If you got sin in your body, you better leave that communion alone.* Don't touch it, it's deadly to the unholy soul.

CAST INTO HELL

And I say unto you my friends, Be not afraid of them that kill the body, and after that have no more that they can do. But I will forewarn you whom ye shall fear: Fear him, which after he hath killed hath power to cast into hell; yea, I say unto you, Fear him (Luke 12:4-5). You want people to think you're holy. Forget about what people think. It is what God knows that you are going to be judged by. Again, I John lets us know that you confess your sins, the Lord is faithful and just to forgive you your sins and to cleanse you from all unrighteousness. Now preachers and teachers who teach false doctrine, they cater to the flesh and that's the reason so many people accept it. They always cater to the flesh; cracking jokes, and having political conversations in the pulpits of God across America today. It's no service if you are not warned to flee the wrath to come. It's not a Jesus service if you haven't been reminded about the blood and how Jesus gave His whole life so you could and must live free from all sin. It's no service about the Lord, if warning about the need to separate from everything, to flee the very presence of evil, is not published. If the young girls are not taught to keep their virginity until their wedding night what good is it and our young men are not admonished to do the same, to be virgins as well. It's not a service of Jesus Christ if parents are not reminded of their awesome responsibility to train up a child in the way that he or she should go and when he is old, he won't depart from it. Not saying that he won't leave God but the way back has been instilled in him and if he ever decides to call on God. Parents, you have an awesome responsibility to raise children to fear the Almighty God but, if they talking back to you, how are you going to get them to fear God when they are not made to respect you?

MOMMA'S GOD IS OUR GOD

I use to think my momma and God were closely connected. I know I didn't want God to get me because I didn't want my momma to get me. You see how it is? We didn't have trouble respecting God because we respected our parents. We saw that example laid out before us. My mother would always fixed my father's plate first. We had responsibilities and we were held accountable for those responsibilities and that training helped us become who we are today. We had chores, we had allowances, we had responsibilities and we didn't watch TV during the week. We couldn't raise our voices at each other or anybody else. Just anything couldn't be discussed in our home. We never told our parents' business to anyone *outside of that house* - nobody. And you know what, for that much, they didn't talk grown-folks stuff in front of us. See, what I am saying? "Where is God?"

IN MY HOUSE

Then said he unto me, Son of Man, dig now in the wall: And when I had digged in the wall, behold a door. And he said unto me, Go in, And behold the wicked abominations that they [My People] do there (Ezekiel 8:8-9). The Lord said [in God's house], stealing the money, wounding and hindering souls. *In my church*, preaching false doctrine because they are worried about filling up chairs. *In my church*, people not even giving, not even paying their tithes. *In my church*, people are not even coming out, when they know it is their responsibility to be in the church to help spread the Gospel. *In my church*, people are watching football when they should be in church. They are washing and ironing clothes, when they should be hearing "Thus saith the Lord." *In my church*, at the casino during Sunday school time. *In my church*, He said both profit and preacher are profane. Where are the miracles? Where are healings? Where are the deliverances? Not in these so called houses of God, today because God is not even welcomed in His own house. They have the lock on the door. They let the rappers in but they won't let Jesus in. They will let false prophets in and people speaking in tongues at will, talking about they got a word from God. Don't know nobody got a word from God for me. If the Lord has something for me, He will tell me Himself. Don't you feel like that or you got itching ears. Don't you pray enough? Don't you fast enough? Aren't you in the Word enough that the Lord can speak to you? Isn't that what the Lord told us in Numbers? **And he said, Hear now my words: If there be a prophet among you, I the Lord will make myself known unto him in a vision, and will speak unto him in a**

dream (Numbers 12:6). I am fasting, crying out, talking to God and He is going to send *you* with a crooked finger? God's people love this! How in the world is the Lord going to help you in a situation when you were already cheating. You say, "I am going to go down there to the board. They owe me that money." How do they owe you unemployment when you were still working? That's hypocrisy, isn't it? Don't expect the Lord to help you if you are not doing right. Remember, the devil can tell you some truth but not *all* truth.

DIVINE BLOOD

Adam was created with divine blood in his veins. Many have never realized this. Divine blood was the reason Adam and Eve were to have lived forever. It had to have been divine blood to have preserved the flesh that God had made out of the dust of the earth. If Adam and Eve had not sinned, they would be just as young today, as they were when God created them. They did not have human blood like ours until the curse came. Losing divine blood was part of the curse. Not one person, since the fall of Adam, were born in the image of God. We had to get the blood of Jesus to make us humanistic. Adam and Eve were the only ones created in the image of God because they were created with divine blood. When we accepted Jesus Christ, if you are saved today neighbor, you have the blood of Jesus on your soul. Now, that blood has brought you into the image of God. But since the fall of Adam, no one was born in the image of God. How could you be in the image of God without the blood of Jesus? You can't.

CHAPTER 6

DO YOU RECOGNIZE SEDUCING SPIRITS
PART 1

Did you know you can't really study about something that is false until you know the truth about it? We are obedient to the will of the Lord. So many people who don't attend church on a regular basis, don't know that they are not saved. It is our responsibility to get the message out to them. We are going to be traveling today in that great book that I introduced to you some week's back, *The Deceit of Lucifer.*[14]" There are some books to read and there are some books to study. This is a book that you must study. Matthew 13:24-25 say, **The kingdom of heaven is likened unto a man which sowed good seed in his field: But while men slept, his enemy came and sowed tares among the wheat, and went his way.** The man servant wanted to know if they should pull up the tares along with the wheat. This is what the Master said, **"Nay; lest while ye gather up the tares, ye root up also the wheat with them. Let both grow together until the harvest: and in the time of harvest I will say to the reapers, Gather ye together first the tares, and bind them in bundles to burn them: but gather the wheat into my barn** (Matthew 13:29-30). So many people are wondering why the Lord has not taken action over so many things that are happening in the world today.

---

[14]   Angley, *The Deceit of Lucifer*

GREAT HAVOC

Neighbor, we had a major incident happen in our church many years back. We had just got on our feet. The television ministry was in full swing. We had large crowds each week. We had so many different groups in the church doing different things. It was flourishing everywhere or so it seemed. A few people were greatly deceived. No doubt some of them have blasphemed against the Holy Ghost having fought this work in such a way. It was horrible. I don't want to ever forget that time. I've studied it over and over again. I've learned so much from that experience. One of the most important lessons that I learned was how important it is to stay on top of things because people will take over your church if you let them. As I was reading this parable in preparation for today's lesson, it kind of reminded me of the will of the Lord for our ministry and the difficulties we experienced during that awful time. Can you recognize seducing spirits? Some of the people who were in our church at that time, seduced a few of the other members who were weak and gullible. Some of them have managed to survive and some of them are gone out – pushed out by God and I don't want those people ever to come back here.

WORKS OF SEDUCTION

People in this final hour, must recognize seducing spirits. It is imperative! The devil works through seduction. So many of the television programs are full of sex, violence and drugs. It's no wonder our children feel as if they must engage in sexual behavior as such young ages. Do you leave your children in front of the computer without parental controls? It's just something to think about. Even in our day, in our time, in our church, in our homes, in our lives, on our jobs and then in the government and the world. People wonder why God hasn't stepped in. When I was reading this parable, I thought about a time in our ministry when there were a lot of things going on. If you are a true pastor, if you are a true evangelist, you know all too well what I am talking about. When things happen and you are starting a ministry, when other souls are connected to that person's life, you are not so quick to take an action or make a move. I am soul conscious and that's why I tolerate so much for so long. Souls. Souls are connected to other souls, good and bad. You have to really get this today if you get nothing else. There are so many people who are connected to you. You hold souls in your hands. There are so many lives like tar, they are connected to your life. You have to be careful what you do and what you say. You must be careful with your persuasion. You have go to be careful with your influence. All of us have a sense of influence. You have to be careful with your influence because your influence can build up or destroy. Notice how precise the Lord is here. He is so perfect in giving us the scriptures and the things that we need. He is an on-time God! He knows what needs to be said and when it needs to be said. People are so hooked up on, "We are blood, we are blood!" What about the Blood of Jesus? What about the blood that was shed for the remission of sin?

WHO'S FIRST IN YOUR LIFE?

Don't be confused about your obligation to people. You owe all to your Lord, first and foremost. Your allegiance must be to the Lamb. The Bible is so magnificent. It will shed light on things taking place in your life, if you would just give God a chance. If you would just get quiet before Him in His presence. If you come before Him with a humble heart, He will direct, comfort and keep you. The Lord can only go so far. He will not compromise with sin and degradation. He does not compromise with any of the works of the flesh.

THE FIELD OF SOULS

Matthew 13:24 says, **The kingdom of heaven is likened unto a man which sowed good seed in his field.** Think about those of us who have studied about tending to a garden. This is bigger than a garden, it said a field – *field of souls*. When you have a garden, you have to put your seed in at an appropriate time. You just can't come out in December saying you are going to plant roses. As you know, roses are generally planted mid-April, depending on where you live. They will die because winter is still coming. Think about the timing of God. First, the ground [your soul] must be made ready. Your soul must be made ready for receiving of God's Word. So many people when they hear the truth of God, they cannot comprehend it because their minds are leeched. They have been seduced by false doctrine and by the things that they heard in the world, through friends, neighbors and kinfolks. Maybe it takes the anointed voices of the people who are singing or it might take the anointing of the people who open up the door and show so much love. Little by little, that person can begin to understand the Word of God. It's truly something how the mind words. Only God can truly understand it. Our Father, through the Holy Spirit, tries to work with each mind. Salvation starts in the mind. Did you know that? That's the reason the workers, no matter the capacity, must give their all toward each soul who comes looking for God. Everything we do in the house of God, we have to do it unto the glory of God. The singing might affect one soul but the skit might affect another soul. The hello may affect one soul and the ushering in and sitting with a single mother may affect another soul. We should do all things unto the edification of Christ.

WHILE MEN SLEPT

Unto a man which sowed good seed into his field: But while men slept, his enemy came and sowed tares among the wheat,

and went his way (Matthew 13:24-25). Somebody asked him, "What should we do?" It says, he that sow the good seed, is the Son of Man. The field is the world. The good seed are the children of the kingdom, but the tares are children of the seed of the wicked ones. The enemy that sowed them. The harvest is the end of the world. The reapers are angels. As therefore, the tares are gathered and burned into the fire. So, shall it be in the end of the world. The Son of Man shall send forth his angels and they shall gather out of his kingdom all things that offend and them that do iniquity. And shall cast them into a furnace of fire. They shall be wailing and gnashing of teeth. We just have to put all things in the hands of God. There's a lot going on in our lives, in our city, and in our government. We must trust God. If we don't trust God we will start leaning to our own understanding. Some may want to set other's house on fire because some bad person set their house on fire. The Lord will put everything in course. He'll set everything up in line. You may or may not be surprised that even in the churches people are speaking ill, having ill-will against the leader. They don't like the Gospel of Jesus Christ when it finds them in the corner. They don't want to do right when the Word comes forth. But, you must keep on pressing on. Even it is your momma, even if it is your daddy or your precious youngster. You must continue to look to the author and finisher of your faith, who is Jesus Christ. You have got to stand strong. There is a time in your life when you have got to separate and keep on separating. Only what you do for Christ will last in this final hour. Why spend your whole life doing something that will not benefit you in the end. Going to Heaven is the interest and dividends from pure and righteous living. Eternal life will prove a great profit in the end. Always "hello" and never "goodbye." Why would you want to enjoy the pleasures of sin and then die lost? Why? How can anything in this world compare to anything the Lord has to offer you?

LYING TONGUES

Can you recognize seducing spirits? Do you recognize when somebody is trying to draw you away from the truth? Do you recognize when somebody is trying to take you away from the church? You remember the story off Korah? People came in here with lying tongues. They were so deceived. I stood up and took authority. Some few people had been deceived. And now I see little microscopic effects of that same deceit trying to rise back up in different ones. I don't care if it is only five of us, we are going to be holy. I don't care if it's only three of us, we are going to praise God and be thankful because He has been good to us. And I just thought about this scripture, praying oh God. When you are dealing with people who are seduced, you have to be very careful because *that devil in them* will blame you. There was a young lady who was in our ministry, she's still in our ministry today. Some people from another church seduced her into thinking she should move and marry one of those fellows there but it was the deceit of Lucifer. She eventually married a nice young man in the ministry where she is a worker. Many times, I wanted to say something; I wanted to approach her but, when you are dealing with people who are seduced, you have got to be careful because the devil is *always* looking to have them blame you.

IT'S THE PASTOR'S FAULT

The enemy will *always* say, "You [pastor] are the one. You don't want the person to be married." Why wouldn't I want the person to be married to a good man? Why wouldn't I want couples to have a good home? But, when seduction is working, it takes the truth and turns it into a lie. And that which is wrong and that which is false, the enemy paints it all across the wall like it is something glorious. But to God be the glory for what He has done! He's our true king! He's our true leader. He's God! Praise you Lord! Yes, Lord! I was so concerned about the families that were connected to the person.

I was praying earnestly, "God, give me strength." I was crying out to God at night, "Lord, give me direction, Lord tell me what to do." And this person had so many family members in our church at that time. I just cried out to God, "They are not strong enough. They are not going stand, they are going to blame me." **The pastor gets blamed for everything when people make bad choices**. Slowly but surely, I would tell people something and they wouldn't believe me and they would turn around and write other people like I didn't know anything about it. When I wouldn't side with them, they would rise up. Finally, that person began to wake up. She was so seduced. Those with lying tongues had it all arranged. "You can come down here and you can live with me. You can come live with me." Nobody is going to take care of you. Stop being naïve and letting people seduce you. And what was the whole thing about, to point a finger at me and this ministry. Those people who God pushed out of here, I never want them back here and I can't believe some of you are still associating with them.

I'LL HOLD ON

Jesus say here, "Let the wheat and tares group up together." That is the reason I take as much as I do. That's the reason why your momma takes as she does off you. That's the reason why your husband takes as much as he does from you. That's the reason why your wife takes as much as she does from you. They have the reality, but yet you are sitting in darkness. Who else is going to deal with you? Who else is going to put up with you? Jesus loved you so much that He would lay down His life for you. But, you won't even give Him the tenth. That's God's holy money. This some good teaching. I try to deal with people as long as I can. I try to be long suffering with them. I try to hold on to them all that I can, with souls in mind. They may have a little sister; a little brother; a little daughter; their momma may go to my church. Isn't that right? As long as God holds on, I'll hold on. When He lets me know to stop praying and holding on, then stop I will. People think I am weak when *I don't act when and how they want me to*. I am not weak but soul conscious. Thank God for the mind of God! In Paul's writing, he said that we can have the mind of Christ. And I thank the Lord for that. If God pulled up the tares He might also uproot some of the good wheat too. If you act too quickly, you are going to injure an honest hearted person. You will injure an innocent person. People are not going to understand your actions because they won't know the entire story. You must have the mind of God. You can know the scriptures but, if you don't have the wisdom to apply it here and there, what good is it? You can be a loveable person but, if you don't know how to treat your wife because you don't understand her; what good is it? You can be a marvelous person but are you a godly wife? You may be a good student at school but are you obedient at home. You understand? You might have the knowledge of something, but do you have the wisdom to apply what you know? How? God is coming back for a holy people. I don't care what others may say; pure and righteous. Perhaps, you are hiding away and committing willful sin, thinking that no one knows about it but God knows. If unrepentant, you will become the tares that will be rooted up and thrown into the fire. Are you doing something wrong? Are you associating with those who are drawing you into sin – people full of deceit? People who fought this ministry and God pushed them out, how can they be your friends? They hate this Jesus ministry. They hate the light that is in the truth of the Word of God. Hate is one of the works of the flesh. Why are you listening to them? It's a mixed-up situation. The churches are in a mess.

DRAWN AWAY OF HIS OWN LUST

Do you recognize seducing spirits? You must check your life and find out if there are any influences taking you away from God and His work? God can give you deliverance from seducing spirits if you want to be free. But, when you love the power of Lucifer more than you love the truth of God, deliverance will ***never*** come. If you are devil possessed but fail to acknowledge that something is wrong, there is nothing that God can do. If you not living right, no one can make you. We can't make you get married. One person said, "Well, Reverend Thomas made us to get married!" Yes, because you were shacked up and living like animals. Let's be clear, I don't make people do anything. They were in total deceit and when things "started going south," that devil said, "See Reverend made you all get married. It's all her fault." Lies. Lies and more lies. You got married out of condemnation. When you came to church that Word was lighting into you and you thought, "I have to get this monkey off my back." Just as Lucifer is in control of a devil possessed person. The Holy Spirit has control of a person who is born again and filled with the Holy Ghost.

LUST IS

James 1:14 says, **But every man is tempted, when he is drawn away of his own lust, and enticed.** You were tempted when you were drawn away by your own lust. Have you ever stop to think what ***lust*** is? Webster's dictionary[15] tells us that ***lust*** is a pleasure of the senses, and sensual satisfaction; delight. Delight in that which God says is wrong -- off limits -- that which is forbidden. You have been drawn away by your own appetite for the wrong things. That's lust! You have your eyes fixed on something or someone, watching that porn. If my mother was here, she would say, "Who keeps on watching porn? Can they stop it?" If my dear, precious mom was here, she would say, "Who is still watching porn after nineteen years of preaching? Can they please stop it?" What do

---

[15]   Dictionary.com

you get out of watching porn? It must be something. Watching two men, two women. You must be getting something out of it; you're climaxing. Maybe you think you're safe because it's in the privacy of your own home. It's gross and that porn will send your soul straight to hell. Count on it. You are drawn away by your own appetite for the wrong thing; insisting on looking at that which is false. The enemy knows that if he can get you to look at it, you will begin to desire it. Have you ever noticed that when you are in the grocery store, you went in there for some black eye peas and you past the fruit stand? You don't care that much for fruit but today it's just shining and glistering. Suddenly, you wanted that apple, or anything else the devil might be shining up before you. And these high schools, they make you think something is wrong with you if you are virgin at 16. People make you think something is wrong with you because you are not messing around on your wife or husband because you are faithful. Our world is upside down; totally seduced and that which is right now is being looked upon as wrong, strict, impossible or fanatical. That which is wrong, lewd and indecent has become today's norm. **Lust** is what? To be eager; you are eager for that forbidden fruit – for that which God says "Thou shalt not." You weren't intending to do anything wrong.

I AM JUST JOKING

Webster says, **lust** is playful, sportive. Meaning it is done just for fun. Like some people crack jokes, and they say, "I am just joking," but, that was their sadistic way of poking fun at you. "You so stupid, ha, I didn't mean that. Your teeth are yellow, no girl, I am playing." Then they will go tell your friends, "I told them." You say you were playing but that was your evil way of telling them how you truly felt. "I don't see how anybody ever married you! Ha! Ha! You have big teeth, like a bunny rabbit," and then you laugh. You don't know when you are laughing with them, they are signifying and talking about you. Some say, "I don't understand, you go to church, Wednesday, Friday and Sunday. You are giving your life to that place." You reply, "I kind of do go a lot, don't I?" And then when you are by yourself, the enemy plants the thought, "Three days?" They call you on the phone on Friday. They ask, "What are you doing?" You say, "You know its Friday and I have church." They say, "Stay home tonight, you are giving your whole self to the church." You say, "What am I going to do then if I don't go to church?" "Well, I already know what we can do," the caller suggests. There you go. They already planted a seed when they were laughing at you. You thought they were laughing *with* you. They were laughing *at* you so they could get to you. We are studying deceit so we have got to get down to the nitty gritty.

EVERYBODY IS OFF LIMITS!

Lust is to be eager. You are eager for that forbidden fruit. You are not intending to do anything wrong, but you will. Lust of the flesh is inviting. It is deceiving. It encourages you to look at things you are not supposed to have. You may find yourself lusting for a woman or a man, who is off limits. When you are not married, *everybody* is off limits to you. Remember, you're supposed to be waiting for the one God *has just for you.* And whether you have sex *upstairs* [oral] or *downstairs* [penetration], it's all wrong. God is not into "testing" the good before marriage. There's no scripture for it. Deceit encourages you to look at things you are not supposed to have. And if you are married, and you are looking at somebody else then you are in trouble. James 1:15 says, **Then when lust hath conceived, it bringeth forth sin: and sin, when it is finished, bringeth forth death.** When sin is done with you then what? When will your eyes come open? When will you realize, you have been made a fool of? Maybe you lost your house. Maybe you lost your car. Maybe you go to the doctor and you have AIDS. Maybe you have HIV. Maybe you have three kids and you are raising them alone. Maybe none of your family want to be around you.

WHEN WE WERE KIDS

I was talking to a person who shared a very interesting story with me. He was living in fornication with this woman. They were living with this young lady and her immediate family. Suddenly the father took ill. The young lady that he was living with treated her father terribly. The mother and other siblings would keep him [the father] locked up in a room and they would slide his food under the door like a prisoner. And this person who told me, asked the young lady, "Why do you all treat your father like that?" She told him, "When we were kids and we were growing up he used to treat our momma badly." Isn't that something to think about? They kept him in a room. He wore diapers and his own children made no rush to clean up after him. This is a true story. This man's family would slide his food under the door. Please note, I am not saying that I agree with all this but I believe it needs to be shared with my readers and will bring more light to this chapter on deceit. The entire action was wrong on so many levels. Just think the father started out his youth, when he first got married, he never could have imagined that the "winter" of his life would be as such. It's funny how things turn out.

YOUR UNRECONCILED PAST

Today is not what's going to get you, ***it's your unreconciled past***. You have to live your life unto God each and every day that you have left. How many people [adults] are still in the fog of yesterday; something they did or said. It baffles the mind. Today, you might feel the necessity to tell somebody what is on your mind or to down your kids or to treat them bad; to cheat on your husband, or to cheat on your wife. Neighbor, please remember tomorrow is coming. Your tomorrows will one day become *"today."* They're coming. And I am not standing up for what the daughter did. She should have turned it over to the hands of God but none of them in the house was saved. And oh yeah, the momma was there and participating in all of this. Because when they were young, the dad treated the mom so bad. That poor father never thought about it. How many days did he dream of dying when he was in that room? How many days did this father wish for someone to come by and let him stay with them? I'm convinced the father was free of his deceit and knew why and how he arrived at this point in his life. He was very sick. He was the one who asked, "Can I come and live with you?" There's no way he could have ever surmised, they [his children and wife] would have even treated him in such a way. The Bible says in this life you are going to pay for what you do...and then there is the judgment. **And as it is appointed unto men once to die, but after this the judgment** (Hebrews 9:27).

STUDY OF SELF AND THE DEVIL

You must study deceit. To study deceit is to study and know yourself, God *and* the devil. That's what we are talking about today. You have got to *study* yourself. Often, we don't like what we see in other people because it is a hard, strong reflection of what we see in ourselves, most times. We hate it. A person is always talking about what they got and what they are going to do. Well, maybe it is because you haven't lived up to your potential. And you resent that person for being so motivated and getting stuff done. We are not talking about a person with conceit. They say, "Man, I got my Master's degree. Thank the Lord." And you don't want them to talk about that around you, why? Or when somebody fails God. They don't want you to talk about it around them. Why? Don't tell me not to talk about God because you go a whoring. You ever notice that.

Some may say, "Man, she is always talking about fornication." **When sin is finished, it bringeth for death** (James 1:15). This is the way sin works. You must study deceit. You have to study seducing spirits; deceiving, tempting, enticing until sin is birth; naked sin that leads to death and eternal existence in hell. Many do not know what lust is. They think it is merely a desire to be like the devil himself; a part of the devil. No, lust is a desire to *gratify the senses*. To be free from lust, you must be covered with the blood of Jesus, living holy and righteous in the presence of the Lord. Look honestly at yourself so that no deceit will enter. Now that is the key. Study yourself. What makes you happy? What makes you sad? If you get angry quick, why? What is it that sets you off? If you sleep all the time, why? If you are depressed, why? If you are unhappy, why? You have got to be in touch with yourself. You have to understand why you are the way you are to go on.

LESSONS LEARNED

I worked at a refinery. It was one of the biggest refinery in our area. We used to have these meetings called, *lessons learned*. In order for us to measure our progress, we had to go over the whole project to see where *we missed it*. You can't grow until you find out where you are missing it. You can't grow with Christ until you find out where you are missing it. You can't be a better person until you find out where you missing it. Some of you, you didn't get all the love you needed when you were a child. Any little thing sets you off. Some of you are jealous-hearted. For what? All you have to do is rise up. You have to have lessons learned with yourself this week. Why are you unhappy? Some hurt people have explosive anger and curse because they are trying to pacify a wound that is on the inside. When people act out outwardly, it is something tucked way inside the heart that needs to be healed; that needs to be made well.

LEGION

Mark 5:15 says, **And they come to Jesus, and see him that was possessed with the devil, and had the legion, sitting, and clothed, and in his right mind: and they were afraid**. The devil possessed man who had two thousand devils in him, when Christ healed him, the first thing he wanted to do was to cover himself up and look like he had some sense. Get in touch with yourself. Spend some time just reflecting. Take the Lord with you, take the Holy Spirit with you. Some of our young kids are growing up so traumatized. You don't think words can hurt your children. How you talk to them, and what you say to them will and does affect them as adults. Some days the sun is shining. And some days it rains. Some days you can go outside and don't need a jacket and some days you must bundle up. You must put on two pair of pants and you have got to put your boots on. You have got to have on your skirt, scarf and your thermals. You need your mask on. Don't worry about what people say, you live your life for God. Get your homes right! If you are a husband and you and your wife not right; get it right. Get it right! Get your home in order. You should be praying together. You should be having dinners with your family. You should be talking to your children. What a privilege you have to have a family. I wish I had my mom. I wish my son was still here. And I look at some of you. You have a great opportunity! Don't let stuff go on in your house and you got a miracle when you came here. Don't have conversations that will keep you from being set free when you come to this place; church. God is for truth and He's for justice.

CHAPTER 7

DO YOU RECOGNIZE SEDUCING SPIRITS – PART 2
MY BROTHER CAIN

I know you're going, "Oh man, he killed his brother right?" When you start studying about the devil, he comes after you and assigns his worst demons to you. Studying the truth about that ole boy will get that old hornet's nest aroused. This is not an hour for you to draw back. Hebrew 10:38-39 say, **Now the just shall live by faith: but if any man draw back, my soul shall have no pleasure in him. But we are not of them who draw back unto perdition; but of them that believe to the saving of the soul.** Luke says, **And Jesus said unto him, No man, having put his hand to the plough, and looking back, is fit for the kingdom of God** (Luke 9:62)**.**

WHERE DID IT START?

Where do you think seducing spirits started? Genesis bears record of the first success the devil had of using seducing spirits on a human being. Anytime you're studying the Word of the Lord, and you come across something that you don't understand, whether in the New Testament or the Old Testament, you should *go back to the very first time that it's mentioned in the Bible.* It will shed more light on the subject. In the book of Genesis there are a lot of *firsts* – a lot of events you will see happening for the first time. We see the formation of the first man with a soul. We see the downfall of man. In Genesis we also see murder, hatred to such a degree, and it follows from *generation* and *generation.* Going back to the first time will shed light and provide you with a great deal of understanding. We see the power of seduction right there in the book of Genesis. *That old devil* worked then in the same fashion that he works today. The same cunning way; why should he tamper with success? Ecclesiastes 1:9 says, **The thing that hath been, it is that which shall be; and that which is done is that which shall be done: and there is no new thing under the sun.** The enemy is still using the same tactics that he used down through the years and down through the ages. The tongue is the smallest member in your mouth but it can destroy a family, it can bring down nations, it can build up, and it can save lives. Angry – bitter -- and you want to get somebody back, and so you use your tongue. Some of you have talked the love right out of your marriage. Your siblings, some of them, don't want to be bothered with you because you're just so much trouble. The enemy started on the top of the mountain with deceit, beguiling a person who had once been perfect and holy which was Eve. She was perfect and holy until she went to the forbidden tree. Adam and Eve were created by God in perfection. Both were created in the image of and after the likeness of God. The Lord took the rib of a man and created Eve. *No one since Adam and Eve were born in the image of God.* When Adam failed that brought the curse on the known world. Many Bible scholars don't know that. They think and many teach that everyone is born in the image of God which is *false doctrine.* If we were born in the image of God, there would have been no need for God to send His Son, Jesus and for Jesus to give His life. Eve was perfect and holy but she failed God and so can you. The Lord gives us examples in the Bible so we can apply the Word to our lives. You will be able to take today's lesson and apply to your life, if you are truthful. As you read this, let this lesson help you with your mind, your attitude, something you said, something you did or maybe something you're contemplating. This lesson may save you from making a very bad decision. It will keep you from getting into trouble. See why you must study deceit?

TEACH ME THY WAY

In one of Paul's writings, he encouraged us to do more than just peruse the scriptures. He encouraged us to do more than take pen to parchment. We must study God's Word with the light of the Holy Spirit. **Study to shew thyself approved unto God, a workman that needeth not to be ashamed, rightly dividing the word of truth** (2 Timothy 2:15). **Teach me thy way, O Lord; I will walk in thy truth: unite my heart to fear thy name** (Psalm 86:11). **Jesus saith unto him, I am the way, the truth, and the life: no man cometh unto the Father, but by me** (John 14:6). When people are in court and to win, who do they call on? *An expert witness.* An expert is somebody who has studied extensively in a specific field; who is considered to be an expert by his peers. They have studied they have a lot of schooling, and that's the way you have to be about the things of the devil. You have to be able to recognize him [the enemy] first of all when he begins to rise up in you; not in other people but in you. You feel irritated. Why? You feel teary-eyed why? Why? When something is going on with me I want to know why? Why do I feel like this? Why do I feel like this? You can ignore and act like stuff is not affecting you but then it's just coming back again if you don't solve it. Why do you do the things you do? And if you're not acquainted with yourself [who you are], you will become a tool -- a ploy in the hands of the enemy. Understand why you feel like that. Why are you so angry all the time? Why is it so easy to get on your bad side? And then you have to turn around and give people a piece of your mind; you have to think about that. You have to study yourself. Why it is some people like black walnut and some people like butter pecan? It sounds funny but think about it. I like raw onions but I really don't like grilled onions but yet they're onions. I like strawberries on certain things but on other things I don't. I'm not really crazy about tomatoes but I love fried green tomatoes. See, so you have to peruse your life; you have to *learn* and *study* yourself. People want to go natural, I **can't** to do that. So what am I saying today? Just know yourself. Some people favor gray over black. Some people love bright red lipstick and we can't understand why. But that's their thing. You are catching on now. Everybody's different. Stay in touch with yourself. Some people can eat salads every day. Did you know a salad prepares you for the main course meal digestively? A salad prepares you for the rest of your meal digestively. That's why I encourage you to eat salad before your main course. It gets your system ready. Have you ever been watching a movie and you start crying? It's just a movie and you're just praying away. Do you ever find yourself praying like on *The Ten Commandments*? You're like Lord please just let them get across the Red Sea. They've been across for how many years? But in your heart you just carry that spirit of prayer. Lord please let them get away. The movie was out when you were a kid and you're still praying Lord just help them. Right it just shows your heart is soft. Your heart is soft, and when something comes up you tend to lean toward the Lord instead of taking matters into your own hands. So how do you react when you're watching the movies? Do you for the villain or the underdog?

TEMPTATION IS NOT A SIN

Don't ever think you are so close to God that you cannot be seduced by temptation that will lead to your fall. And this is the thing about temptation; being tempted is not a sin. You can't control all the thoughts, and everything that comes to your mind. But when you yield to that temptation and those thoughts, then *you assume ownership*. Keep that in mind. Being tempted is not a sin. You're a human being not a robot. "Well, I won't be bothered with that thought. When I go to the doctor the shot won't hurt. It's going to hurt," you might think. If you get the flu shot they are putting that needle right into your muscle. You can psych yourself out. There is no such thing as name it and claim it. Don't bother yourself with that mess. When the wrong thought comes in and you embrace it you will have to fight and battle to empty your spirit of that.

THE DEVIL, THE SERPENT, THE WOMAN AND ADAM

Let's examine more closely the role seducing spirits played in the downfall of Adam and Eve. Genesis 3:1 says, **Now the serpent was more subtil than any beast of the field which the Lord God had made.** The devil seduced the serpent first because he couldn't get to the woman directly. What does that mean? The enemy will work through others, often those close to you, but his whole point is to get you. He's going around sifting people trying to see who he can use – who has made themselves weak through a lack of prayer, fasting and living in the Word. Right now you're high on prayer, deep in knee bowing, and the enemy is very patient so he's going to use the ones that are close to your heart. They drop a word every now and then and you are not fazed, and that sly devil just keeps working – little by little. The devil is patient and he's very skillful. Many people don't realize how organize he and his army are. Again Genesis 3:1 says, **Now the serpent was more subtil than any beast of the field which the Lord God had made.** The devil seduced the serpent first! Had Eve taken one look at Lucifer she would have run off screaming. He had to cover up his plan and tactics. He didn't want it to be so obvious what his whole plan was so he camouflaged it.

WWB – WIGS, WEAVE AND BRAIDS

I want to share a funny story with you...about myself. Today I am able to purchase some really good weave. I'm in the *WWB* and everybody's invited. *WWB* stand for *wigs, weave,* and *braids.* I used to get a sew-in. Come on don't play with me you know what that is. When my kids were little, I couldn't afford really good weave; I was able to get a little bit here and there. I used to go to the hair salon and get a sew-in but I have hot flashes and my *"real hair,"* blink, blink use to rise up. I thought let me think about this. So what I'm going to do is buy me some really good hair, let my stylist tint some of it so she can blend it in mix it with the rest. My stylist is great too. My wigs that she makes for me matches my skin. I always get very nice compliments. Thanks Wendy. Then I said "What I'm going to do is have her make me a wig so I can wash my hair whenever I get ready. If I have a hot flash I will just flip off my cap [wig] and I'm cool right." Think about what I just told you. At first I use to get as sew-in but then when my new growth would come in -- when the new growth started coming in then those bangs started looking like a mountain didn't it [speaking to her congregation]? Don't your bangs start looking like a mountain when your new growth comes in? You can't even put your hair up in a ponytail; it's like woopty doo right. So I went around some other way but I got the same results; just like when I got a sew-in, *the real me is still underneath.* You are laughing but you understand much better what I am saying to you. Often we have a laugh at ourselves and it's nothing wrong with that. The good part about it is you don't tend to forget what made you laugh...about yourself. That's what the devil did. He's still trying to accomplish the same goal but he's just trying different ways. Get this today. The devil only has one goal and He's just trying different ways of accomplishing that goal. He wants to make you mad. He loves to make you cry. The wants you to curse because like Peter, you won't have salvation. These cursing Christians. Christians yes then are not. The enemy wants you to throw your hands up and give up, and he usually comes up the least way you expect. **Lest Satan should get an advantage of us: for we are not ignorant of his devices** (2 Corinthians 2:11).

LUCIFER'S TRUE FORM

I am convinced that if Eve taken one look at Lucifer's true form, she would have run off screaming. If he came straight at her, Eve would have recognized him. Young girls, you know what I am saying. If a *certain* [you know his name, don't you?] boy came to you when he first saw you and said, "My whole point is to get you to sleep with me because I like sleeping with virgins, and then I'm going to spread it all around the school, and tell everyone you're easy," you would be like, "Dude get out of my face!" But what he does instead, every now and then he drops a little word on you about how voluptuous you are; that you're packing. The devil plays on your personality, your insecurities. He plays on your fears, your personality, and your weaknesses. You don't think enough of yourself and the enemy know you more than you know yourself. You sit at the same lunch table around the same time. A certain young man just happens your way at the very time to remind you how thick you are, all the while his whole mission is to get you in bed and spread your dirty business around like business cards. You can holler back whenever you get ready. I don't have a problem with it. The enemy uses the same routine with making you cry and getting you to be frustrated. **There is no new things under the sun** (Ecclesiastes 1:9). It seems so simple as you read this but in life, it is just as simple when you go God's way. Face facts. I use to run around, chasing people and going to their homes, trying to work out their issues. I cut that out! People will wreck your nervous system. PFC [A Passion For Christ Ministries] is my university and I am close to getting my masters. You hear me? I have found out from the school of PFC, you'll do all of that and they'll still leave God! Some of the people I went the furthest for were the first ones to rise up and say, "She is no good." Well I'm really not going to be any good. I wrote my pastor about a particular incident and he told me "Good riddens." Hey! That was all I needed to hear. He said, "Beverly don't chase people. If they leave, 'Good riddens.'" I had heard from the man of God. I'm not going to chase people all night, be at the hospital and the morgue. I speaking to just a few right now. There are some very sincere people who have stood by this ministry and when they really need help I will be there. I am not talking about them. But I'm talking about *users* who want to use up your sleep, Bible study and time needed for sincere hearts.

FULL OF UNCERTAINTIES

Romans 8:28 says, **And we know that all things work together for good to them that love God, to them who are the called according to his purpose.** Now if you belong to God then you should be able to go to sleep and trust Him. You have to trust God. This life is full of uncertainties and you will ruin your nervous system unless you let the Lord build up your faith. You're not going to be ready for **the big one** that comes in your life; that comes in all of our lives. It might be death, it might be sickness, it might be a death notice, and the doctors might say that you're going to die. That doesn't mean you're going to die. God not man has the final say but your faith has to be able to match in the difficult times. How many times have you been to the doctor and they pull that little book out of their pocket? "Tell me you have bumps where, hold on. And then what happens do the bumps -- do they turn white on top? Ok let me go back to this way." You're at the doctor and he's going through his mobile Physician's Desk Reference right in front of your face! If he has a book in his pocket, that book looks like well-used Bible; certain pages are folded over and markings are throughout. Neighbor, you have to trust God. You may find yourself say, "Lord I praise your name. I have to take this pill but Lord I'm honoring you in the midst. Heal me God so I won't have to take any more medicines." If you are told that your cholesterol is too high but if you take this pill you might live ten more years then pray and swallow it down. If you have trouble with the pill, go back until they get it right. Thank

God for good doctors but they make mistakes too. If you don't agree with your physician, get a second opinion. That's your choice. But what I'm saying today is if you go to the doctor and you are prescribed a medicine that does not mean you're going to be on it forever! Do what they say. "I'm not taking any medicine," yup and then we'll see you in the doctor looking like a permanent stop sign; when all you had to do is take a little pink pill. And there you are in the hospital looking like a little stop sign. If God doesn't heal you then you're not going to be healed. The Lord put virtue in medicine to help you. He gives the doctors the wisdom and the knowledge to do whatever it is they need to do on your behalf. There are some people that the Lord reaches while they are on medicine and gives them a great miracle. Our God is great indeed. I thank the Lord for good doctors. Thank you Lord. You see how it all starts with God? If it had not been for God who was my side, where would I be today? Where would we be?

TRUST GOD

You have to trust God. You have to trust God. Trust Him with your future. Trust the Lord. Let Him know how you are feeling. "Lord my heart is broken today. I just need you to help me." Jesus Christ is your *personal* Savior. He died to be as close to as you will let Him. He wants to closer than a brother. Life is hard but you still have God. You have things happen in your life but you still have an anchor called God. A lot of people don't have that. You have God if He has you! See how it goes? You have God only if He has you. But if you don't you're just riding the storm-tossed seas alone. How sad. Can you weather the storm? Can you stay afloat in the midst of trials? That's what happened to Cain. The Lord through His word promised to bless you, promised to heal you; those are promises of God. But He also promised you trials, persecutions, and tribulations. The Bible told you to be a good solider. Jesus said you would go through trials [not trials of sickness] but He would bring you out of the depths of what; all of them. Jonah said from the belly of hell I cried. He said I looked toward God and God heard me. God will look out for you if you belong to him. Genesis 3:1 continues and says, **And he said unto the woman, Yea, hath God said, Ye shall not eat of every tree of the garden?** So there is the devil trying to get you to doubt what God says. The devil had picked the serpent because the serpent was more subtle than any other creature. No doubt the serpent walked upright at the time. He was charming uh-oh, he was magnificent, and he was able because of these things to seduce Eve. Maybe a charming guy is what she was looking for. Maybe that day Adam was busy naming the animals she felt smitten as if you know I'm here in all of my glory, and you go and name the fish. I'm the greatest catch you ever had! Come on girls you know how we act sometimes you know how we can be sometimes. Come on don't play with me! Right so it was something in what he was doing that got her attention. I t was something in what he was going that got her attention. So what does this go back to? Knowing yourself. What makes you happy? What makes you sad? What can get your attention immediately? What can get your attention like a slow cooker?

WE MAY EAT

Genesis 3:2 says, **And the woman said unto the serpent, we may eat of the fruit of the trees of the garden.** Looking at this lovely creature looking at this lovely creature she felt safe. He was fascinating. And after all she had no intention of doing anything But now she had developed an appetite and wanted to look just a little bit closer. She must have thought, "I know what's going to. I'm going home in just a minute," but she never made it back holy and pure. Just like some of you, you say to yourself, "I'm going to get my life right! I'm going to get my life right! I'm going to get my life right!" Yeah and hell is full of those same people. "Man I was going to church!" People want to say to me, "Why didn't you tell me he was no good?" You were not listening. I tried, through the Word of service days, but your ears were dull of hearing and that is why you didn't she was a witch dressed up in angels' clothes? You don't hear me! Eve wanted a closer look. Oh the devices the devil uses. He wraps himself in many disguises but he's still the devil when those wrappings are stripped off. Now Eve was engaged in a full-fledged conversation with the enemy. **And the woman said unto the serpent, We may eat of the fruit of the trees of the garden: But of the fruit of the tree which is in the midst of the garden, God hath said, Ye shall not eat of it, neither shall ye touch it, lest ye die.** Not only did he not want you to eat it, the Lord didn't even want you to touch it! Genesis 3:4, **And the serpent said unto the woman,** (Oh she's listening now; he has her attention). **Ye shall not surely die.** Verse 6, **And when the woman saw that the tree was good for food, and that it was pleasant to the eyes,** (It looks all right how can any harm be in this) **and a tree to be desired to make one wise, she took of the fruit thereof, and did eat,** (She didn't stop there what did she do after that) **and gave also unto her husband with her; and he did eat.** Going to the next chapter now talking about my brother Cain. Now you know where the foundation was laid for what happened to the rest of their family. Your family today what foundation are you laying for them? Neighbor, pastor, and evangelist those people who look up to you; the flock the great number of people who come to your church every Sunday, and sometimes during the week; what is the foundation that you are laying for them? Is it truth? Is it righteousness? Or is it that no one can live free from sin? You're setting them up to fail. In the fourth chapter of Genesis we read a terrible account describing one of the results of seduction, for which Adam and Eve had paved the way. Notice this. One child was killed and the other one was banished. But they laid out the foundation. Its ok you don't have to tell Reverend the truth. Don't tell her what's going on in my house. You're teaching your children them to lie and disrespect God. Keep that thought in mind.

GENERATIONAL CURSES

Seducing spirits had taken over Adam and Eve and now Cain was taken over too. His seduction exceeded that of Adam and Eve. Cain's parents did something so horrible but what their seed did was greater! It was greater! That's something to think about isn't it? Cain committed murder. So remember I told you that you see a lot of first things happening in the book of Genesis. Many down through the years have been seduced to commit murder. There is no way to number them. Most of the hideous crimes today, if not all are planned and plotted through *seducing spirits*. These seducing spirits will control a mind so completely that the person becomes like a demon from hell. Demons in the driver seat, thinking for that person. Sometimes a person plots to kill their mate, or a son, a daughter, or a parent. It's being done on a daily basis. Where did Cain get the idea to murder his brother? From seducing spirits.

CAIN TALKED WITH ABEL THEN KILLED HIM

Genesis 4:8 plainly tells us **And Cain talked with Abel his brother: and it came to pass, when they were in the field, that Cain rose up against Abel his brother, and slew him.** Where did that thought come from? There hadn't been a murder before. There hadn't been a murder before. Where did he get that thought from? Seducing spirits; it was a devilish thing man didn't have the knowledge even the thought to kill! Cain had never seen a dead human. But when seducing spirits took him over Cain gave his mind completely to them. How did they enter? Through envy. Cain was

Jealous of his brother. Paul stated there should be no schism in the body of Christ. There should be no fighting; no inward fighting, no jealousy, no backbiting, angry because another person is singing a solo. Jealousy, hatred, envy, grudges, hell has caused many to give over to seducing spirits. I can't stand that person and then when you really get down to it they don't have a reason. How many couples have I counseled and the husband said the same thing that the wife said about him. The wife said the same thing that the husband said. And I'm thinking to myself now the wife said the same thing about you. Your husband said the thing about you! Others seeking their own desires are captivated by those with seducing spirits. Cain was jealous of his brother and the Lord found out about it. And you know for people who say God knew that man was going to fail, why would God ask Cain where his brother was? He trusted Cain and he trusted Abel.

KING OF KINGS AND LORD OR LORDS!!

He's God of the universe and He can *choose* to know something just like He can *choose* not to know it. Come on we're talking about the Creator of *everything that's breathing*. He's the God of it; He said, "If it's another god bring him right here to Me I want to talk to him." **I am Alpha and Omega, the beginning and the end, the first and the last** (Revelation 22:13). **There is none other God but one. For though there be that are called gods, whether in heaven or in earth, (as there be gods many, and lords many,) But to us there is but one God, The Father, of whom are all things, we in him; and one Lord Jesus Christ, by whom are all things, we by him** (I Corinthians 8:4(b)-6). You'll never find it in the Word because it never happened and will never happen. No matter what you are going through I care because God cares. Always remember you are special to God. Man to study the devil that's some deep stuff and it challenges you to look inwardly at yourself. Keep the Word ever before you. **Thy word have I hid in mine heart, that I might not sin against thee** (Psalm 119:11). **Thy word is a lamp unto my feet, and a light unto my path** (Psalm 119:105). Didn't the Lord say draw night to Me and I'll draw night to you? That's what He's talking about. Keep the Word with you at all times. God wants us to be blessed. I want to challenge you this week to read the book of Genesis; it's so many things we can learn in the book of Genesis. Genesis is not an old book and it's not outdated, but we can all learn something from the book of Genesis. We want to be happy. We want to help people. We want to lift them up. We want to pray for them that the Lord will keep them strong. We want to pray for those who are sick, pray for those who are afflicted, pray for those who are sitting in the bereavement chair today because it might be us on tomorrow. It's not hard for somebody to come back and give you something that you gave them. But if you are not giving out anything it's hard. Give love this week and joy and happiness. You never know when you need a hand.

The Sinner's Prayer:

Oh God! Oh God! Oh God! Please help me! Please forgive me for sinning against you. But I have come home never to leave you again. Oh Lord I know there are many false Christ'. Oh Lord I know the Antichrist is in the world now, and if he's in the world now I know my only way out is to make it to Rapture ground; is to make it to Rapture ground. And by faith in the blood save my soul! Save my soul! Wash me in your blood! Cleanse me and make me whole! Save my soul! Save my soul! Come on in Jesus! And if you meant that neighbor He is there. Stay with God and He will stay with you. Are you ready? Let's go!

NOTES

DJG

NOTES

NOTES

DJG

NOTES

DJG

PART 3

GRADING PLAN

CHAPTER 8

A SCHEMING MOTHER

So many parents are not in the position they should be in. And you know when you begin to start a family, you are responsible for that family, and it's your responsibility to teach and train them properly. The Bible says to train up a child. **Train up a child in the way he should go: and when he is old, he will not depart from it** (Proverbs 22:6). You know when you start having children then your life is placed on hold, and those children become the number one priority. The family structure has been broken.

A TENDER BEGINNING

Isaac and Rebekah they had such a tender beginning. Abraham was old when the story starts about Rebekah and Isaac. He called for his senior servant, the manager of his entire household, and told him not take a wife for his son, Isaac from the daughters of the Canaanites among whom I live. But ye shall go to the country of his relatives, and take a wife for his son, Isaac. You can read the story in its entirety in Genesis 24 through 27 chapters. The Canaanites were a vile race. They were cursed by God and doomed to destruction. God would not have been pleased for Isaac to marry one of them. Although Abraham's relatives lived in Northern Mesopotamia, and they had idols they were at least a moral people who knew about God and respected Him, and they were decedents of Shem who were blessed of God. There's much knowledge to be gained here.

WHAT'S THE OBJECTION?

If you're engaged and are planning to marry a person who has an objection to your belief in the Lord, fasting, praying, living in the Word, and if they object to you paying tithes, woo ooh. You better think before you jump into that fire! You better not jump into that fire! And if you're not getting along now, don't ruin the rest of your life by marrying someone you can't get along with now. 1 Corinthians 7:39 says, **The wife is bound by the law as long as her husband liveth; but if her husband be dead, she is at liberty to be married to whom she will; only in the Lord.** 2 Corinthians 6:14 says, **Be ye not unequally yoked together with unbelievers: for what fellowship hath righteousness with unrighteousness? and what communion hath light with darkness?** Just think about how important it is for believers to marry believers; to marry the person God has planned for us. There are some who married before coming into the knowledge of the truth; when you both were unequally yoked. **My grace is sufficient for thee: for my strength is made perfect in weakness** (2 Corinthians 12:8).

BEFORE YOU GET MARRIED

<u>Before</u> *you get married,* you should be talking about very important issues such as finances and sex; the probability that you may or may not want to have children. You don't want to get married and then two years down the road decide that you don't want any children but your mate does. Your husband – your wife wanted children way before you both were married. If you are an active member in your church and you support them in a financial way, you have to get it all lined out. It is important that your soon-to-be spouse knows, "That I go to church, and I'm going to keep going to church when I say 'I do!' Do you understand that?" Ladies, there are some fellas out there that look pretty good, but they are wolves in sheep's clothing. They are going to tell you a whole bunch of tales. You're going to think they are *Supermen*; you're going to think they were underdog and now they have become *Wonder Dog*. But they're still a dog. Ya hear me? As soon as you say '*I do*' they do you right out the church, do you out of your money, do you out of being with your friends. There are some very critical things you must get an understanding about *before you get married*. You have to understand sexual matters. Some of you have high levels when it comes to intimacy. These are important matters that must be all worked out *before*. Some of you are just calm and quiet, you know you're a little slow, but you have power in your punch! You get what I'm saying? You have to discuss all these matters. Another example. You know you like your meal a certain way, some of you are very tedious. You have all your socks lined up a certain way and soon there will be *another person inhabiting your space*. Your soon-to-be wife, she might be a little miniature, diminutive packrat! So you have to get that all worked out. You're not marrying somebody to get them to come over to your ways, and you can't change a grown person. They, along with God's help, must want to change.

IT TAKES TIME

Genesis 2:24 says, **Therefore shall a man leave his father and his mother, and shall cleave unto his wife: and they shall be one flesh.** It takes time for that blending of the personalities even when the spouses are in God's divine will. There are growing pains. The key is both parties must be willing, with God as core, to stay and work hard at making a good Godly home. If you avoid talking about very important subjects such as sex, finances, and what you believe in, you will be setting yourself up for a fall. If you marry somebody without talking about having or not having children, you are setting yourself up for a horrible fall. Count on it. You want to associate yourself with good-thinking folks because you're going to mimic some of their traits and if you hang out with people that are up to no good you too will be up to no good! If you're hanging out with women who are talking about cheating on their husbands, you're going to *develop the same appetite*. Spirits are catching. We want to inspire and encourage our children to associate with people who are doing well and respect their parents. Every young person is not toting a gun; some of them are trying to make it to college and become independent, thriving adults. Some of our youth want to be an engineer of a great building. Some want to be architects. Some of them are thinking about what it's going to be like during the first year of residency and we want to inspire and encourage those young people. Hanging out with a street pharmacist [drug dealer] won't get you in medical school.

A TRIP TO HARAN

Abraham's faithful servant took the toilsome trip to the vicinity of Haran, where Abraham's brother had remained after Abraham had migrated to Canaan sixty-five years earlier. Abraham had assured the servant that the angel of the Lord would go before him. With that sense of divine direction he stopped at a well in the town of Nahor; which happened to be Abraham's brother's name. He prayed that God would bring *the right girl* to the well and lead her to offer water for his camels. It was a very specific request for exactly the proper mate for Isaac. Take notice that through all this time since the servant left Abraham's house and searched for a wife for Isaac, he [the servant] always put God first. Abraham always prayed to the Lord every step that he made; seeking direction. "Now Lord you have blessed me with a good job what's the next thing? Lord I know I can't pay you back but is it something I can do for the ministry? Can I offer my car to be of assistance to help somebody else?" Are these your thoughts when the Lord blesses you? Do you think like this?

GOD IS METICULOUS

All the things that the Lord has done for you to be in the right spot in your life; these things didn't just happen. God is meticulous. He has specific plans for you. He wants to bless you. He wants to direct *all* your steps. **The steps of a good man are ordered by the Lord: and he delighteth in his way** (Psalm 37:23). But just like the servant who was in Abraham's life, we can't lean to our own understanding, but ask the Lord to direct our paths – every step -- in everything that we do and everything will work out for our good. "Lord is this your will for me," must be our cry all the time. **For he flattereth himself in his own eyes, until his iniquity be found to be hateful** (Psalm 36:2). **Be not wise in thine own eyes: fear the Lord, and depart from evil. It shall be health to thy navel, and marrow to thy bones** (Proverbs 3:7-8). We're traveling along we're studying about Rebekah, and then as you get the background and history about her then you will see where she messed up her life and the life of her children. All the things God went through for her. What a plan the Lord had for her life. Sometime, when people get out of God's will, He is not able to fix it. Getting ahead of God is just as dangerous as lagging behind. We must stay in step in this last and final hour.

SHE WAS A VIRGIN

Rebekah, the granddaughter of Abraham's brother, came out with her jar on her shoulder and the scriptures say that she was very beautiful, and was a virgin. **And it came to pass, before he had done speaking, that, behold, Rebekah came out, who was born to Bethuel, son of Milcah, the wife of Nahor, Abraham's brother, with her pitcher upon her shoulder. And the damsel was very fair to look upon, a virgin, neither had any man known her: and she went down to the well, and filled her pitcher, and came up. And the servant ran to meet her, and said, Let me, I pray** thee, drink a little water of thy pitcher. And she said, Drink, my lord: and she hasted, and let down her pitcher upon her hand, and gave him drink. And when she had done giving him drink, she said, I will draw water for thy camels also, until they have done drinking. And she hasted, and emptied her pitcher into the trough, and ran again unto the well to draw water, and drew for all his camels (Genesis 24:15-20). These folks were busy. Abraham's eldest servant ran to meet Rebekah as she ran to get some water for him and the camels. Come on I'm getting on your porch but that's all right I'm going to ring the bell in a minute. It says she emptied her jar into the drinking trough and ran back to the well for some more, and she drew enough water for all ten of his camels. That confirmation of the fleece was exactly what Abraham's servant had prayed for. It's good to always put a fleece out two ways. Now some men say, "If I find a wife I find a mighty good thing," but then they go out searching and publicizing their search on all the local billboards. "If it doesn't work out then I will know it's not God's will," many conclude.

BLESSED BE THE LORD

What a girl she was! Rebekah was beautiful, vivacious and voluptuous. I added that. She had to be friendly and outgoing. Rebekah showed that she was unselfish and energetic. When the servant found out that she was the granddaughter of Abraham's brother, he bowed his head and worshiped the Lord. Genesis 24:27 says, **And he said, Blessed be the Lord God of my master Abraham, who hath not left destitute my master of his mercy and his truth: I being in the way, the Lord led me to the house of my master's brethren.** Abraham's servant was so thankful that the Lord had fulfilled His promise. He was so thankful because the servant felt responsible for what Abraham had asked him to do. Do we feel responsible for the direction our children take? Do we feel responsible for our companion's happiness? We should. Do we feel responsible for meeting his or her needs? When you said 'I do' some didn't read that fine print. The servant was so glad. Look at the greatness of God. Look at the power of God. Look at the obedience of the servant. Look at the willingness in Rebekah's heart, and how the Lord preserved her. No man touched her. The Bible says that she was a virgin. She was not selfish! Then it blows your mind to see the way her ended! To study deceit a scheming mother. This is important and you need to understand the history of all of this.

THE BELLY OF HELL

How could they have failed God after such rich teaching? How could they have failed God after all the things God had done for them? Bringing them up out of a horrible pit; Jonah said I was in the belly of hell but from that belly of hell, I lifted my eyes and called on God! I will now look towards the heavens and call on God. I will lift up my eyes to the hills from whence cometh my help. When a problem is stronger than me, I will look to the rock that's higher than I am; higher than my thoughts; higher than my flesh and carnality. I will look to God. *Flesh talk is weak talk*. It was obvious from the onset of this story that God is the real matchmaker in a marriage. When the servant recited to Rebekah's family the indication of God's guidance both brother and father agreed. They followed God's lead. Do you follow God's lead? Mama and daddy must be in agreement about the rearing of the children. That husband *might not* be in support of what the wife does in the church, but he better not let those kids see it because she's honoring God. Momma's prayers may be what keeps you from may be having cancer. Her prayers at midnight may be what's keeping you from something awful. You should thank God if you have a holy wife. You should thank God that you have a

God-fearing husband. No matter what kind of problems a marriage may encounter they will be easier to solve, if both the husband and the wife have a settled assurance that God has brought them together. Difficulties will not be conquered without a firm assurance and faith in God. He must be glorified in the home.

WILT THOU GO WITH THIS MAN?

Rebekah faced an immense decision in her life; leaving her home and the family she would never see again and traveling nearly five hundred miles on camel back with a total stranger to marry a man that she had never met before. Genesis 24:58 says, **And they called Rebekah, and said unto her, Wilt thou go with this man? And she said, I will go.** It was her assurance of God's sovereign direction that motivated her decision, and revealed her courage and trust. Certainly the hours of travel were filled with talk of Isaac. No doubt Rebekah must have thought about what a good husband he was going to be to her. How could she have doubted? Look how everything flowed so smoothly. The family agreed. He sought God for direction and no doubt the old man all his talk was regarding the will of God. How could Rebekah not have been excited? "To think the daddy of my future husband has so much faith in what I am going to be, and what I shall do, and what I'm able to do, that he sent somebody to get me! Hey!" She said, "I'm going to go with this man." Think about the long hours of travel. Genesis 24:63-67 say, **And Isaac went out to meditate in the field at eventide.** Here we go. Here we go. I'm giving you a little history now. Isaac was in the field meditating at evening time when the caravan -- the camel caravan -- approached carrying his precious cargo. Rebekah dismounted from the camel when she saw Isaac. She covered herself with a veil as was the custom. After he heard all the exciting details of the eventful trip, and a providential guidance that had found him a bride we then read in Genesis 24:67 say, **And Isaac brought her into his mother Sarah's tent, and took Rebekah, and she became his wife; and he loved her: and Isaac was comforted after his mother's death.** It was a tender, tender beginning. Further on in Genesis we find great deceit. Lying devils, seducing spirits where, in a mother. Rebekah, Isaac's wife was given a promise by God concerning her twins.

TWO NATIONS

Genesis 25:23 say, **And the Lord said unto her, Two nations are in thy womb, and two manner of people shall be separated from thy bowels; and the one people shall be stronger than the other people; and the elder shall serve the younger.** Ahead of time, remember, God had given truth; the elder shall serve the younger. But Rebekah allowed lying deceiving spirits to take her over. That was the same Rebekah that Abraham had sent his precious, trusted servant to find her for his dear son. And I've seen it neighbor. Our ministry is almost 20 years old and I've seen it too many times. People will come to the church and they'll lie and deceive and plot against me and this ministry, and take seduced people right out of the church; people that God has worked and worked to get on a path of truth. Seducing spirits eventually filled Rebekah with great sorrow. She lost both of her sons and was separated from her favorite son for the rest of her life. The elder serving the younger was against everything Rebekah had been taught but God had told her that Esau would be the servant of Jacob. The years passed. It came time for the sons to receive their father's blessing and Rebekah grew overly anxious. Isaac was about to pronounce the blessing of heritage, of power, of authority, and he was going to give it to Esau. *Rebekah put herself in God's place.* She took God's place. How terrible. Just like so many today who claim, "I'm going to help God out. God said

He was going to give me a wife you're the one! I'm going to help God out." It's something when you put yourself in God's place. "I never put myself in God's place." When you give your opinion about something, you put yourself in God's place. It's tight but right. You might have to have a spiritual skin graft. *A skin graft is a type of graft surgery involving the transplantation of skin. The transplanted tissue is called a skin graft. Skin grafting is often used to treat: extensive wounding or trauma. Burns.*[16] This Word is finding you out!

IN GOD'S PLACE

Rebekah put herself in God's place. Seducing lying spirits controlled her and through them she in turn took over Jacob. I want you to get this. Those kids' downfall was her fault. How many children are in jail today because of something that mama told them to do *but it was wrong*? I have seen people in these stores around my neighborhood. They [the parents] will be in the store and outside the store begging with their little kids. What are they teaching their kids to do? Beg and steal. I have seen them all over town. I'm not talking about people that are sho-nuff in need; that's not what I'm talking about because it's some sho-nuff homeless families in great need. I'm talking about the gimmicks and the schemes that people partake of and include their children. They have their kids in the store and they have them steal for them; they are *training them* to be thieves when they grow up. A carton of eggs under their jacket; you don't think little Johnny is going to remember that when he gets a little older, and he's going to keep on stealing. Whatever is in you grows up in you, grows up with you, grows up through you, and eventually becomes you! You are a product of what happened to you in childhood.

---

[16] Wikipedia – skin grafting.

I WILL APPEAR AS A DECEIVER

Rebekah in turn took over Jacob through seducing spirits. She must have thought or even told her son, "Jacob you're going to pretend," but isn't that a lie? Isn't that deceit? Isn't that a scam? She was scheming against not only her son, and husband, but the will of God? God already laid out the plan and was generous enough to let her know some of that plan! "Now Jacob this is what you're going to do, you're going to pretend that you're Esau," his mother said to him. Jacob was trying to get out of it. Jacob was trying to understand -- trying to rationalize with her! "But I'm not hairy like he is mom! My skin is smooth! Even though dad is blind when he touches me, he'll know that I'm not Esau! I will appear as a deceiver" "We'll take care of that," Rebekah schemed. "Don't worry about that. Let me tell you what we're going to do. Bring me back a kid, we'll kill it and we'll use the animal's coat to cover your arm and neck. When your father feels the hide he'll think that you're Esau." With great deceit a mother and a son worked, guided by cunning arts of seducing spirits. Rebekah, she knew the truth. Had she just waited on God, her son would have not been forced to flee for his life. So many times people are taken over by seducing spirits because they *get ahead of God* and fall into doctrines of devils. Rebekah acted in a way that said God was not able to perform that which He said. She acted in a way as if to say, "God forgot about His promises to me!" The Bible says that the Lord does not slumber and that He does not sleep. The Bible says that the Lord proclaimed that His word shall NOT come back to Him void! But it MUST accomplish what He has said! I'm talking about the God of the universe not some statue you have on your centerpiece in your home. I'm talking about a God with a capital G not a low g with an S on the end. Rebekah knew the truth. **Had she only waited on God**. Again so many people are taken over by seducing spirits because they get ahead of God, and fall into doctrines of devils. She didn't know at that time her deceit would cost her a son. *The devil hides the outcome of deceit.* Father Isaac, he, was also deceived. Now see how this all affected a whole family? A whole family would be destroyed. A whole family neighbor -- your actions affect everybody around you. Not until Esau came to receive his blessing was Jacob found out. Dad knew he had blessed the wrong person but it couldn't be undone. Genesis 27:41 says, **And Esau hated Jacob because of the blessing wherewith his father blessed him: and Esau said in his heart, The days of mourning for my father are at hand; then will I slay my brother Jacob.** "As soon as I get finish mourning my dad, I'm coming after you!" And Jacob had to live almost his entire life in fear of the possible anticipated meeting with Esau knowing he wanted him dead.

I BLESSED THE WRONG SON!

Rebekah's husband was up in age and nearly completely blind, and he had to die with that thought in his heart and in his mind. "I blessed the wrong son. It was the wrong son." Just think as he lay there getting so close to death, Isaac must have thought, "My wife, my wife conspired against me." The Lord didn't bring the message to Isaac for Isaac to tell Rebekah. He wanted Rebekah to know that He was sho-nuff God and was going to do this! She did something different. Neighbor you have to stand for truth. No matter who it affects, no matter who it hurts, you have to stand for truth because the days are long, but the years are short, meaning only what you do for Christ will last.

CHANGE THE COURSE

You're a product of your parent's decisions. But guess what, you can change that course. You don't have to stay on that deceitful path. Maybe you didn't get enough love when you were coming up, but see you can change that now. When I was growing up my parents did the best for us they could. If you don't like what's going on in your life change it. Stop blaming folks; playing the blame game; just blame everybody. "It's my mama's fault." We all get despondent and discouraged but don't let that take control of your life. Somebody's [some soul] watching you. What are you teaching them? Where are you taking them? Don't be a part of anybody's downfall. Don't be a part of any person getting in trouble in your school. Don't be a part of any child's downfall in your family. Don't talk derogatorily in front of your children about their mama. Don't talk negatively in front of children about their daddy!

CHAPTER 9

ON THE RUN, TWO BROTHERS

When you have children, you have an awesome responsibility to train up a child in the way that he or she should go, and when he is old he won't depart from it. That doesn't mean that the child won't leave God but that seed will be planted in him; that if his back is ever against the wall, and he feels the need to call on Jehovah God, that seed that was planted in him will start churning inside him, and those scriptures will start coming back to his mind, and he'll start remembering about the love of God, and that will, if he yields, it'll draw him back to Calvary.

I WILL KILL MY BROTHER

Genesis 27:41says, **The days of mourning for my father are at hand.** Esau said, "Just as soon as I'm finished mourning for my father, I'm going to find you and I am going to kill you. I don't care if you are my brother. I don't care if you are my twin. I don't care if we held hand hands in the womb; just as soon as I am finished mourning the death of my daddy, I'm going to kill you!" Sounds like the heart of so many today, doesn't it? Siblings fighting one another, stabbing each other over nothing. Genesis 27:41 says, **The days of mourning for my father are at hand; then will I slay my brother, Jacob.** Both Jacob and Esau they had to with that for the rest of their lives. Every step that Jacob took, he wonder how far behind was Esau. That all started with deceit from mom. Jacob simply followed his mother's instructions. God had already assured Rebekah but that wasn't enough. I want you to hear God telling you today, "Let Me work." Don't try and put things into your own hands but let God be God. Let Him work. Don't get ahead of God or you might not be able to get it straightened out in this lifetime. What a waste. And just think Rebekah never saw her sons again.

RUNNING FOR MY LIFE

Jacob was on the run. The threat of Esau being on his trail was resonating in his mind, and continued resounding in his ear. "Esau is going to kill me," Jacob must have thought many nights. Jacob is running out in the desert night; somewhere he finds a stone for a pillow. He's frightened and alone. In the desert, Jacob made a covenant with God. God knows how to get our attention when we run out of options. Sometimes God has to wait until you are down to your last piece of bread to acknowledge Him because people so quickly forget who gives us them strength to get the wealth we have. *People forget that without God they are nothing.* Sometimes it takes being on the run for your life to really sit down and think about, "How did I get here? My kids are not talking to me. I can't get along with anybody." So many people wake up in jail. Jail stops them and allows them to slow down and think about life. Until a person finds themselves in *that* spot in life it's everybody else's fault. Neighbor you hear me? It's everybody else's fault. You're running, running, all the while you in the bed sleep; your sleep has left you. You're running but you just got on the platform to catch the Metra train but you're running in your heart; you're running in your mind, you're running in your spirit. You're on the run but you're getting your hair done; but you're still on the run. You're on the run but you're going right back to punch into that job; that job that you have been at for thirty years; but you don't know if today is going to be your last day. You are running in your mind and heart. How many people in America thought they would get up and serve God but slipped on into eternity without a Savior on their side? Some of you might be sitting down, you might be behind a prison cell, but you're running. You're on the run from something, from someone, something in your past, something you've done, and you've got to get it figured out!

IF YOU WILL BE WITH ME

Genesis 28:20-22 says **And Jacob vowed a vow, saying, If God will be with me,** (Now notice what he's asking God to do) **and will keep me in this way that I go, and will give me bread to eat, and raiment to put on.** (He wasn't asking for a Lincoln for a 2015 Impala, he wasn't asking for Fubu and boo-boo, and all these named brand clothes. Jacob said if you just feed me and put some clothes on my back. Isn't that something? When you didn't have any money, you didn't even care just, "Give me something to eat man." The Lord moves for you and now you have to have name brand stuff. **And Jacob vowed a vow, saying, If God will be with me, and will keep me in this way that I go, and will give me bread to eat, and raiment to put on, So that I come again to my father's house in peace;** (Underline that if your Bible is a workbook. How did he want to come back home? In peace) **then shall the Lord be my God: And this stone, which I have set for a pillar, shall be God's house: and of all that thou shalt give me I will surely give the tenth unto thee.** Don't tell me he didn't know about tithing. People won't volunteer in the house of the Lord; many of clock watchers and want to be paid enormous amounts of money. Even when people owe you money, they try to pay you back in piece mill. Come on somebody! You have loaned them one hundred and they want to give you twenty a week, and want you to forget about the last ten. Jacob had been sent by his mother to her brother, Laban's house. A brother who was also possessed by what? Seducing, deceiving spirits. You have to keep in mind Jacob was seduced. Where did his mother send him? To somebody else that was seduced. Rebekah repented in bitterness for the wrong counsel which she gave to Jacob for it was the means of separating him from her forever. What Rebekah told Jacob was her opinion and her advice was the reason should would never see Jacob again in her life. Jacob was compelled to flee for his life from the wrath of Esau, and his mother never saw his face again. Isaac live many years after he gave the blessing to Jacob. Rebekah should have stayed in *her* place. Let God do the things the way He wants. As a matter of fact, if you're going to go His way that's the only way you will prosper. It must be His way.

A DECEITFUL WEDDING NIGHT

Jacob was not happy in his marriage relations so notice this just notice this. Go with me to Genesis about his wedding deceit just begat deceit; Just deceit, deceit. So if you start reading in Genesis chapter 30 you'll start reading the story about (you can read it at your leisure) when Jacob came to Laban's house. He saw Laban's daughter, Laban promised him Rachel but he deceived him and he gave him the older weaker sister Leah. Jacob was not happy in his marriage relation although his wives were sisters. He formed the marriage contract with Laban for his daughter Rachel whom he really loved. After he served seven years for Rachel Laban deceived Jacob and gave him Leah. So this is what I want you to see today; just because the mom died; that deceit kept going on. This is important for us as parents. This is important for us as workers in the church. This is important for us who have influence in the lives of other people, and that's all of us. You don't want to have anything to do with someone doing wrong! You don't want to have anything to do with a lady leaving her husband nothing! You don't want to have anything to do with a man cheating on his wife, leaving his wife;

keep your mouth off people! Because even though you might move on in your life that influence is still turning and churning in their life, and the result of it, you're going to have to pay for some of it.

STILL PAYING

Even though Jacob's mother died, he was still running for his life years later. He made a contract with Laban where he would work seven years for the woman that moved his heart but Jacob didn't even get Rachel. He was still paying for listening to his mother. Did she not say earlier in Genesis, "Listen to me?" Even after her death, Jacob was still paying. Some of you can clearly identify with that. Bad decisions that you are still paying for. Have you ever been in a situation where you're just asking yourself, "When will I complete the payment for this thing that I've done?" Have you ever done something in your life and you're just constantly asking yourself, "When is my debt going to be paid? When am I going to be finished paying for what I have done?" What the devil does not tell you while you are immersed in self, flesh gratification, is how big the price will be; the magnitude of it so great -- so massive! It seems like you're married to it!

MARRIED TO YOUR PAST

I remember when one of children got in trouble. He said mama, "It seems like I'm married to this thing." When he was participating in it, listening to his friends, allowing his friends to deceive him, he never gave the outcome any thought. Fast money, quick money, easy money, man this is easy money Gee; but in the end he paid dearly. It is very important that you stand up for what's right no matter who it's against. You stand up for what's right if not, you're the one who will be paying for it later on. Young people, don't worry about being accepted in school. Do you know how fast high school is? It's quick. ***But you can make the wrong mistake and spend the rest of your life trying to unwind.*** Make good choices. Preserve your body, preserve your youth. Don't let men all of over you, and handle you any kind of way. Don't let women all over you, and handle you any kind of way. Take pride in yourself. Think highly of yourself or else nobody will. Yes! It's something for you to think about today.

SEVEN MORE YEARS

Jacob worked for seven years for Rachel but Laban had deceived him and gave him the weaker wife. When Jacob realized the deception that had practiced upon him, and that Leah had participated in part to deceive him he hated here. The deception just kept on multiplying. Jacob ran down to Laban's house. So you see how deceit goes? It just passed on like a bad cold. You have to cover your mouth and be sure to wash your hands often. You don't want to give someone else your germs which will make them sick also. Well the Bible says who could lift up holy hands? Only those with a pure heart. You have to keep washing your hands with truth. You have to wash your hands with righteousness. When Jacob realized the deception that had been practiced upon him, and that Leah had acted in part with her dad to deceive him; he could not love Leah. Laban deceives Jacob but Jacob came to Laban's house already deceived.

BE CAREFUL WHEN HANDLING DECEIT

It's hard to work with a person who's deceived because they think you don't know what you're talking about. You have to be careful when you work with a person who is lost, not only lost in salvation; but lost in reality; lost in that which is true because the enemy will point the finger at you and make that person focus on you, like you're trying to keep them from something great. Deceit is so slimy, it's so slick. It's worse than black ice. It's so slimy, it's so slippery, and it's so slick that if you're not in the truth you will be deceived. You have to live real close to God because the devil he seeks to deceive you, every day, every way, all day long. He wants to deceive you and he's going to deceive you by using your personality and your weakness.

THE WEAKER VESSEL

Leah was the weaker sister. She knew the history; she knew the customs and traditions of marriage. Leah knew that what Rachel shouldn't have gotten married to him first. She knew that and so what did she think? Jacob was looking good. Laban was talking constant deceit to her, trying to make her feel worthy and justified; just like some parents do today. "You don't have to tell your wife everything son. Have yourself a separate bank account, keep your old cellphone." Leah knew the rules. Jacob, not doubt, was walking around there winking his eye at Rachel all day. Leah, however, would be the one to dress up and pretend, for one night of passion, that she was Rachel. When Jacob woke and realized the deceit and trickery, he no doubt, hated Leah for the rest of her life. Come on somebody look how this deception went down. Leah went to death's door having baby after baby. She had baby after baby and every time she had a child, search the scriptures, she said maybe my husband will love me now. Every time she had a baby she said, maybe my husband will love me now. But he never did. I want to share something with you.

WILL YOU MARRY ME?

There were these two people I knew, husband and wife. This happened nearly twenty years ago. The husband was in a previous relationship but he wasn't treating his wife right. And I can't say that the way she went about everything was right but stay with me, you will get what I am trying to show you a minute. The husband would antagonize the wife; he would verbally abuse her. He would talk down to her, saying such things as, "You aren't any good. Nobody likes you. Nobody loves you. Nobody cares about you." This was his daily conversation to his wife. He refused to help her with the children on certain day; wouldn't help her out around the house. However, when he came out around his friends, he acted like he was the most holiest and loving man anybody knew. People who didn't know the inside story of abuse, had the upmost respect for him. Again, they didn't know the truth! After a long period of time and many years of abuse and disrespect, the wife decides she will simply get rid of him! Finally they get a divorce. Please take notice. I'm not saying everything she did was right. This is important and that is why I have included it in our lesson. So they get a divorce. The husband is so bitter an and angry. His wife wasn't as weak as he thought she was. She wasn't as timid as he thought she was. He used to say very derogatory things to her. I knew these people very well. This is the person you married and all you hear all day is negativity. "You mean I can't even make a bologna sandwich right. What does it take but two pieces of bologna and put mayonnaise and or mustard? How can I mess that up," this lady must of thought many times over. When you hear it all day from a person who is supposed to care for you; don't tell me it does not shape your opinion of yourself. I said it shapes your opinion about how you think of yourself. Someone you have once held close to your bosom, somebody you said was going to be with you for all time, and then things start turning around. You have to come out to work, you have to go up to the school where the kids are and just put on a happy face, knowing the hell that you are experiencing at home.

DOUBLE TAKE

She divorced the man. The husband was so bitter he would come up to his former wife's house and bang on the door, and cause all kind of trouble. Sometimes she would have to call the police and have him removed from the property. The husband would pass out lies and rumors saying that she was all kind of stuff. But what he did was he found him a prostitute who happened to favor the wife a little bit. Watch it! When they were married they tried to have children but the wife couldn't conceive and it was good she couldn't. It would have been terrible for the child. Deceit is deep. It's slimy. It has killed millions. Not only did he find this prostitute that kind of favored his previous wife, but he asked her to have a baby for him. All of a sudden here he comes with his pregnant wife and they started showing up at places where the ex-wife was. He was still tormenting her, still taunting her, still pointing his finger at her; still talking down to her.

LET NO MAN DECEIVE YOU

The new wife found out what his plan was and what he was up to; that he marriage her to get revenge. She realized that she, all this time, was just a tool in his scheme to make the ex-wife feel bad. She has been treating him like a dog ever since. He is sick now and can't do anything but look; can't raise his fist, can't fight anyone. This is the God's heaven truth I'm not making this up. He can't raise a fist. He almost died a couple of times. His wife comes and goes as she pleases. She has her boyfriends; doesn't try to sneak or hide. She doesn't even give her husband a thought. See how it goes? See how it goes? He thought he was in control just like some of you. You think you're in control thinking you can use people and talk down to people and treat people bad. But as sure as you're breathing today God will not mocked; that whatever you sew is coming right back to your door. It's something to be old and sickly and your kids treat you like a dog. They won't even change your diaper. Your food is slid under the door like you're in prison because you made a difference between them and treated their mother badly.

ESAU WILL KILL ME

These two brothers had the same mother, they had the same father, had the presence of God in their lives, had the hope of God in their lives, had the favor of God in their lives, now they're on the run! Everywhere Jacob went, how many times did he think about Esau and his vendetta. "I'm going to kill you!" See how deceit separates you?

ANOTHER SEVEN YEARS

Jacob works another seven years and finally marries Rachel; that was the one he really wanted. Can you imagine how that household must have been? Finally he married Rachel the love of his life. But isn't it something she doesn't even live long. She dies during child birth to his youngest son. Then there was Esau. He wasn't any better. Esau took two idolatrous wives. He married somebody that worshiped idols; which was a great grief to Isaac and Rebekah. Notwithstanding this, Isaac loved Esau better than Jacob. And you don't think the other kids knew that? So Jacob was Rebekah's favorite and Esau was Isaac's favorite. The other kids knew that? Your actions matter and the way you treat people matters. Esau had two idolatrous wives for the time came Jacob married Rachel, and it was time for him to move out of Laban's house. That's something to think about.

Jacob confronts Laban about the deceit and Laban says, "Well, I just couldn't give you the younger daughter before the elder married." Like duh duh. Don't you know the families rules? Duh. Laban did give him Rachel but Jacob had to serve another seven years. Some guys don't have to wait seven days.

WHAT DID YOU GET FROM A ONE-NIGHT STAND

They just give it up on a one-night stand the young lady often never sees him again and they leave you with a present that keeps on giving. Do you know how many one night stands people have? They don't know anything about that person [man or woman]. You don't even know anything about dude or the woman! You know how conscience people are about their feet? They don't want you to see their feet, and you have to think about the mental capacity of somebody who has a one night stand. People pay more attention to their feet than who they give themselves too. You will never see the person again then you're left wondering why your body isn't right; why you are always at the doctor. You find out you have HIV, Chlamydia, Trichomonas, Gonorrhea, or even Syphilis. In a night stand and you sleep with all the people that that person slept with. But you're cool, you're doing it. It's your thing you're doing it anyway you want to do it. Right some of you all are too young in here but some of you all know that record right. And now you're left alone with HIV, with a STD. So many of these STD'S make you sterile. Five or ten years down the line when you finally meet a half decent person, your body is giving you trouble; can't have a baby.

LIES

Laban would just lie to Jacob over and over again. Finally Jacob gathered up his herds, his servants, his wives and his children, and set his face towards mount Gilead. **Then Laban overtook Jacob. Now Jacob had pitched his tent in the mount: and Laban with his brethren pitched in the mount of Gilead. And Laban said to Jacob, What hast thou done, that thou hast stolen away unawares to me, and carried away my daughters, as captives taken with the sword** (Genesis 31:25)**?** So Jacob married to Laban's daughters but Laban accused Jacob of taking his daughters. Some parents still try to hold on to their daughter when they are married. Let them go. Tell your daughters, "Go home with your husband and work things out. Go home to your wife, son and work it out." Keep everyone out of your marriage. You married one another not your spouse's parents. There are some very godly parents who can be an asset and provide direction but for the most part keep others out. The Bible says when a man leaves his mother and his father, it didn't say the carriage and the horses, and goes to his wife; it didn't say the wife and the mother-in-law. The Bible didn't say the husband and the dad, and all his trophies from high school. Find your own life together; you and your new companion, with God as your compass. If you both stay before God the Lord will give you answers.

HE COMETH TO MEET THEE

Laban starts after Jacob but the Lord visited him in a dream and told him not to mess with Jacob. So Jacob has it set in his mind I have to go back to Canaan, and remember that promise that the Lord had made him? He asked the Lord to bless him and, if he would keep him safe, keep a roof over his head, and clothes on his back, and just let him return to his daddy's house in peace; only would he serve God but he would give the Lord the tenth. Jacob gathers up the courage to travel home. Genesis 32:3,6 say, **And Jacob sent messengers before him to Esau his brother unto the land of Seir, the country of Edom. And the messengers returned to**

Jacob, saying, We came to thy brother Esau, and also he cometh to meet thee, and four hundred men with him. Let's go back to verse one. **And Jacob went on his way, and the angels of God met him. And when Jacob saw them, he said, This is God's host: and he called the name of that place Mahanaim. And Jacob sent messengers before him to Esau his brother unto the land of Seir, the country of Edom.** Notice Jacob is trying to get things all setup. "I'm going back home and I have this is the time that I will see my brother, Esau. I wonder if he still hates me. Does he still hate me?" His whole life for twenty something years he lived wondering about this day; twenty something years he lived like this and it's all started with momma. This is what I am trying to get you to see; Mamma's dead, in the ground, but the sons are still living with the residue of her deceit. You see what I'm trying to tell you? You must be careful how you lead people. You must be careful what you tell people – giving your opinion. If you don't want to be involved with somebody don't play games because people are crazy. Don't make false promises.

MY LORD ESAU

Genesis 32:4 says, **And he commanded them, saying, Thus shall ye speak unto my Lord Esau.** Jacob is just so humble now. He said that he is a servant to Esau; my Lord. He has calmed down; note the humility working in his voice. Jacob said this is what I want you to say to him. Notice his whole persona is different now. He just doesn't want his brother to come with all his folks and kill his family. But when Jacob started out it was just him and his ego. But now see he has a family. He does not want his family to pay the price for his deceit! That's what he is saying. I don't want any of my kids to pay for anything I did because they have experiences sho-nuff they have to pay for just living this life. I don't want them to pay for my past failures! I don't want my grandkids to pay for something because I didn't stand up for what's right; because they have to live their own lives and they have to face challenges already laid before them from the time they came into the world, and was slapped on their bottom and cried for the very first time. Life is a setup. There will be heartaches, disappointments, it's already setup. We all came in the world on the block -- the green mile -- everyone who has been born, since the fall of Adam, came in the world *a wanted man*. They were born wanted men, women, boys and girls and the only way to freedom is that they obtain redemption through the blood of our Lord and Savior Jesus Christ. Yes we were all born on the block. Verse number 4, **Thus shall ye speak unto my Lord Esau; Thy servant Jacob saith thus, I have sojourned with Laban, and stayed there until now: And I have oxen. And asses, flocks, and menservants, and womenservants: and I have sent to tell my lord, that I may find grace in thy sight.** Now Jacob is accountable for so many more people he does not want them to be slain for his mistakes. You don't want your kids suffering for what you did. So do what's right. You married couples, cut it out! And you know what I'm saying whatever you're doing cut it out.

400 MEN

And the messengers returned to Jacob, saying, We came to thy brother Esau, and also he cometh to meet thee, and four hundred men with him (Genesis 32:6). Esau was not coming by himself. Notice this in verse six, he's coming with four hundred men. Jacob must have thought, "Somebody is dying today. Somebody is going down today." Can you see Jacob's eyes almost popping out of his head when the messengers said, "Your brother Esau, we saw him and we counted about four hundred men with him, somebody is going to die today. Somebody is going to die today! I think it is going to be you Jacob because I'm going to fall back when they start coming man I'm going to fall back so deep I'm going to disappear."

TODAY WE DIE

Then Jacob was greatly afraid and distressed: and he divided the people that was with him, and the flocks, and herds, and the camels, into two bands. And said, If Esau come to the one company, and smite it, then the other company which is left shall escape (verse 7)**.** Who do you think Jacob put in that first company that they could possibly get killed by Esau? Leah and all the kids he had with her. All has come full circle for Jacob and Esau. Dooms Day. Even still, Jacob thought he could run away from it but its back at his door. ***Finally***, Jacob has to face himself. Whatever you did you have to face it! You have to face it! You have to face it! You hooked on pornography you have to face that! You don't know how to show love you have to face it! You needy, hypersensitive you have to face it! Always blaming other people you have to face that! You have that! There is not putting it under the rug and putting it out of your mind. Where do you think split personalities came from? Trying to act like it does not exist, that problem, that burden, that suffering, that molestation, that insect, that abuse, trying to act like it does not exist; that's where split personalities come from the brain is so powerful, and it's so strong, some traumatic event that has happened in your life that you have not been able to cope with, that you have not been able to process causes your mind to develop another character. Face life. Learn to face life.

DEAL WELL WITH ME

Genesis 32:9 says, **And Jacob said, O God of my father Abraham, and God of my father Isaac, the Lord which sadist unto me,**

Return unto thy country, and to thy kindred, and I will deal well with thee. Jacob was trying to reason with the Lord. He was just trying to hold on to the promise of God. Verse 11, **Deliver me, I pray thee, from the hand of my brother.** What Jacob did not know was that God had gotten a hold of the heart of his brother Esau. Esau wasn't coming for war. He no longer had a vengeful spirit, and Esau had changed. When he saw his brother the Bible lets us know that they came and embraced, and they wept on each other's shoulders so nobody died that day. The Lord changed the heart of Esau. He had forgiven Jacob and Esau greeted Jacob with arms open wide. The mother was not there to see her kids in embrace; she wasn't there to see the reconciliation, she wasn't. What a wonderful reunion. It took twenty something years; twenty something years of each son wondering how the other was going to react when they saw one another. Twenty years of wondering does he still hate me today? Twenty years of wondering Lord this weight is so much I can't bear it alone; what I've done, What I've said, how I have mistreated people. Twenty years twenty years does he still hate me? Does he still hate me? God is a God of love.

A GOOD ENDING

Jacob and Esau's final encounter was one of peace. God had granted them much in that one meeting. God can turn things around for your too neighbor. Study the life of Jacob and Esau.They both paid tremendously for what they did. Rest assured, your sins will find your out, no matter how long it takes. You may be very old but God will remember. He doesn't forget. He doesn't sleep. Find please now. Find peace today. Like Esau and Jacob, some of you have been traveling uncertain paths.

I STILL LOVE YOU

How in the world can you sweep incest under the rug? Molestation, being hated by a parent, being hated by a sibling, you can't sweep it under the rug. But I heard the word of God say, that when your mother and father forsake you that I'm going to take you up. Come unto me All ye that are laden. All ye that have such a heavy burden, and I will give you rest. Though your sins be as scarlet I can make you whiter than snow. This is the Father's love for His children. Are you a child of God? You can be. How many siblings leave this earth abandoned by and alienated from family and friends. There are married couples who live in the same house but they don't sleep in the same room; they treat each other like a dog, but when they get out in public they are just lovie lovie. Who wants to live like that? Fighting devils on the job, people looking down on you in the church; you have to deal with so much stuff at school, and sex sex sex everywhere. Not to mention when you get home you're just another low down dirty dog. Can't do anything right; can't make anybody happy.

YOU NEED PEACE

You need peace today. You need peace today. Come on let's say the sinner's prayer lift those hands up asking God into your heart. This is a very important time, not a time to place. This is a very important time. Be wide awake to this hour. It is very critically hour. Come on lift those hands up and everybody saying the sinner's prayer. Everybody saying **Oh God! Oh God! Please forgive me for sinning against you. But I have come home never to leave you again! God help me today! I need you help! I don't want to hold anything in my heart against anyone because I need a miracle! I need a healing! I need my mind healed! I need my heart regulated! I don't have any time to not forgive! I don't have time for grudges! I don't**

have time for backbiting! I'm going to turn my enemies over to you and I'm going to love everybody because I know that's the only way you're going to hear my prayers. You're going to hear my prayers you're going to come and see about me. You mean more to me than any hurt or harm, than any disappointment, to anything that has happened in my life. You mean more to me today than you did on yesterday. You mean more to me today than you did on yesterday. Come into my heart Lord! Heal me of all this hurt all the pain Lord that I can love like you did. Come into my heart Lord. Come into my heart Lord. Set me free! If you meant that today the Lord is with you, don't go down the same path. Do some fasting and stay in the Word and that will help you. God bless you!

Call out to the Lord. He's waiting.

CHAPTER 10

THERE'S NO PLACE LIKE HOME
D. THOMAS

I want you to write down the word "**study**," because you have to understand what *study* means. Those of you have been in school and those of you that have had time to study, and those of you that have been in a place where you had to study a lot, you understand what I mean. It means *a well- defined organized branch of learning or knowledge. Something produced as an educational.*[17] Did you know studying is an exercise for the mind? You have to learn how he [the devil] operates. Some of you may think you know a little bit about the devil, but boy when you start studying him, that devil will start acting up in people. He will manifest himself through people. Count on it. Don't let your guard down. *You have to study.* 2 Timothy 2:15 says, **Study to shew thyself approved unto God, a workman that needeth not to be ashamed, rightly dividing** (what) **the word of truth.**

KNOW THE TRUTH

You have to study the truth so that you can recognize deceit. You have to know the truth about matter before you can tell if something is false. How can you tell if something is false without first knowing the truth? When you are full of deceit you will misinterpret God's Word. That's what has fooled so many people down through the years. Deceit was in their hearts and they were blinded by it. **And he spake a parable unto them, Can the blind lead the blind? Shall**

---

[17] Dictionary.com

they not both fall into the ditch (Luke 6:39)**?** When you study with a deceitful heart and you open up the Bible, you interpretation will be distorted and you will believe a lie and be damned. **And with all deceivableness of unrighteousness in them that perish; because they received not the love of the truth, that they might be saved. And for this cause God shall send them strong delusion, that they should believe a lie: That they all might be damned who believed not the truth, but had pleasure in unrighteousness** (2 Thessalonians 2:10-12)**.** Without truth, you'll get deceit out of the Word – a misrepresentation. If you're always looking to find something wrong then you will. Haven't you been in a situation like that? I believe you have. Every time you say something positive to somebody, they want kick it down with something negative. "You're going to find something wrong with everything I say," is often how you are left feeling. They just don't want to hear anything positive about what you're saying. Some few have done that and that's why they exist in deceit. Don't get angry or bitter. Just recognize **self** and make the necessary changes.

I HAVE ALL THE ANSWERS

I [Pastor David] remember when I first started coming this great ministry. I was deceived about a whole lot of things. I thought everything was going the way I wanted, and I thought to myself, "Man I have all the answers," but all I had was what the devil was feeding me. The pastor began to preach those wonderful messages back then in the *apartment days.*[18] I allowed God to finally open my eyes. I realized "I'm in deceit! I'm deceived about many things," and because I cried out to the Lord, like Peter, I was able to get saved and come to the Lord! I had to accept the truths of God. **Even**

---

[18] When we were the *prayer group.*

the Spirit of truth; whom the world cannot receive, because it seeth him not, neither knoweth him: but ye know him; for he dwelleth with you, and shall be in you. I will not leave you comfortless: will come to you (John 14:17-18). **But when the Comforter is come, whom I will send unto you from the Father, even the spirit of truth, which proceedeth from the Father, he shall testify of me** (John 15:26). **Howbeit when he, the Spirit of truth, is come, he will guide you into all truth: for he shall not speak of himself; but whatsoever he shall hear, that shall he speak: and he will shew you things to come** (John 16:13).

THE WIZARD OF OZ

I want to read a familiar childhood story. A lot of you may know this story. *The Wizard of Oz*[19]. According to *Wikipedia*[20] the story takes place in Kansas in the early 1900s. Dorothy Gale lives with her dog, Toto, on the farm of her Aunt Em and Uncle Henry. Dorothy and Toto gets in trouble with a ruthless neighbor, Ms. Almira Gulch, when Dorothy's dog bites her. However, Dorothy's family and the farmhands are all too busy to pay attention to what's going on. That does not mean there wasn't any love there. It says that they were just too busy at the time. It's a lot of things to do on a farm. Sometimes you know you have to bring things home. Sometimes you can feel misunderstood about certain things in your life because you feel like unloved or you feel because someone didn't speak to you at that time that they don't love you, but it's just your insecurities manifesting themselves once again. It's *self*. You must be careful when going through hard times or you will find yourself *pointing-the-finger* at

---

[19] *The Wizard of Oz (1939 film). Wikipedia, the free encyclopedia. 18 October 2016. Wikimedia Foundation, Inc.*

[20] Ibid.

other people, instead of looking inside where the problem is. Again, the article that I am reading from states that the farmhands were too busy doing their own thing to notice Dorothy and Toto. Ms. Gulch arrives with permission from the sheriff to have Toto euthanized; which means to have him put to sleep. The dog is taken away but manages to escape and returns to Dorothy's arms. She then decides to run away from home with Toto to escape Ms. Gulch. If you saw the movie, you will know that she was a pretty mean woman. Ms. Gulch was famous for say, "I'm going to get you." While on the run, Dorothy meets professor Marvel, a phony kind of fortune teller. He really wasn't. He realizes Dorothy has run away, and tricks her via his *crystal ball* into believing her aunt was ill, and Dorothy must return home. So there she is and phony fortune teller urges, "Ooh you must return home." He knew that's where she belonged.

BUCKLE DOWN

Loved ones this message is so important for you. The devil is deceiving a lot of you into leaving home; and it's not just the kids, it's not just the young people, it's parents because they're going through a lot with their children, and just want to take off and start running. I can understand because I've been where you are. I had five different personalities and different people who wanted to do things their individual way. You have to buckle down, and say, "Let's trying this again." It takes great courage to be a parent in this final hour; the world is so wicked. Our pastor often says people should be bring children in the world who they cannot take care of in a physical and spiritual way. It's craziness to do otherwise. We're going to find out where the deceit is coming in at so that you and I both can become a better vessel for the Lord. Professor Marvel tells Dorothy to go back home and she starts for home. Suddenly a powerful tornado develops. Unable to get into her family's store cellar, Dorothy seeks safety in her bedroom. A wind- blown window sash hits Dorothy on the head and she falls unconscious on her bed. She begins dreaming, seeing the house spinning into mid-air, and held aloft by the twister. The twister had the house suspended in the air just spinning around. You all who have seen this, isn't your mind going back to the story? While I was reviewing this for today's lesson, I thought of the movie and decided to incorporate it into today's sermon. Still dreaming, Dorothy watches the storm outside the window and sees an elderly lady in a chair; several farm animals, two men rowing a boat, Ms. Gulch, she's still there, still peddling her bike. Remember when Ms. Gulch use to visit on the farm, she used to come on the farm riding her bike. Suddenly Ms. Gulch is transformed (Ms. Gulch) into a cackling witch flying on an ugly broomstick. The farmhouse crashes down in Munchkin Land in the Land of Oz where Glenda, the good witch of the North, and the munchkins welcome Dorothy as their hero.

FOLLOW THE YELLOW BRICK ROAD

The house lands on and kills the wicked witch of the east, leaving only her feet exposed. Her sister, the wicked witch of the west, arrives to claim the magic ruby slippers worn on her sister's feet but Glenda the good witch, transferred them to Dorothy's feet instead. Do you all remember that? And the wicked witch of the west swears revenge on Dorothy and Toto for her sister's death. Glenda tells Dorothy to follow the *yellow brick road* to the Emerald City where the Wizard of Oz may be able to help her get back home. I'm trying to get you to understand there is no place like home – that's strictly my reason for sharing this article with you today. No place at all. You know about the tin man and the cowardly lion, and the scare crow. You know all about them but we're going to skip all that for now. At the Emerald city, the Wizard delays their request. They're standing in front of the Wizard but he delays their request for some obviously well-deserved rewards. The Wizard was attempting to teach them what they were looking for was within. They simply needed to look within themselves for what was needed. However, they were outraged and the group argues with the Wizard. As they are going back and forth with the Wizard, Toto runs in the back and pulls back the curtain and exposes the Wizard as a normal old aged man. He wasn't a true wizard; he was just pretending. You all remember the story don't you? The Wizard then had to admit that he was just operating and controlling *the image* of the Wizard. He admits to being a *humbug*. The Wizard gives each of them tangible items but all they really needed was locked within. He gave the scare crow a diploma, the lion a metal and the tin man a watch which was shaped like a ticking heart. He granted their wishes and convinced them that they received what they had come for. He then prepares to launch his hot air balloon to take Dorothy home but Toto chases a cat; Toto runs out of the balloon and tries to chase a cat. They miss the balloon. Glenda, the good witch, comes and tells her there's a way, "Just click your heels three times and say, 'there's no place like home.'" Finally, Dorothy does as instructed and wakes from her dream. When she woke up who was standing around her, Dorothy's much loved family. I wanted to read that to you all to bring something to you to study deceit and there's no place like home.

THE HILLIARD HOMES

I want to share with you a little bit about my life growing up. While some of you may have heard this before, it merits repeated here. We lived in the projects and we had these long, long porches. Those of you who have lived in the projects, you know exactly where I'm coming from. Those porches were so long that by the time you would get to the end of them you wanted to stay outside. One day it was snowing really bad and man my older brother wanted to ride his new bike with training wheels on the sidewalk. My mother and father were totally against it because the weather was extremely bad. At his insistence, my parents gave in and allowed him to ride his bike in the snow. At the time he was wearing glasses. When he would go outside to ride the bike in the snow, his glasses would fog up. My brother would come back in the house, let the glasses clear up and he would go back out there. But I was thinking about the love that my mom and dad showed at that time. Even though it was snowing they wanted my brother to do what he wanted to do. That was a lot of love. There was another time I remember my father allowing me to cut something; I would watch my dad cut. I was standing behind him one time, and he looked over his shoulder, and he saw me standing back there and said, "Do you want to cut it?" "Yes," was my instant reply. He was trying to show me how to carefully use a knife. I was so gung-ho [hasty]. I grabbed the knife and started cutting something and I almost cut my thumb of. My dad then said "See you're too anxious. You just thought you were ready, didn't you? You were not ready." Just like Dorothy said, "There is no place like home." Think about Dorothy for a minute and think about this story. Dorothy had an unusual dream but yet her request was still what? "I want to go back home." I almost cut myself and my father was trying to show me the right way but I thought just by looking, I had it all figured out.

PICK OUT WHAT YOU NEED

On another occasion, my dad use to always carry change in his pocket. He would reach in his pocket, with all of that change and pull it out. He would then stand before me and my older brother. He would hold out the change and say, "Take out what you need."

To me, I am just a kid, it looked like a lot of money but it wasn't. He would say, "Pick out what you need," and I would pick out quarters. "Are you sure that's all you want?" Again my dad was trying to teach me not to be greedy. You see that's love. There's no place like home. He would say "pick out what you need." I would pick out a quarter, and pick out different coins. And one time my father put a dollar or two in his hand, so I moved the two dollars out the way and took the change. He looked at me and said, "You don't want the dollar?" I said, "No," but he gave it to me anyway. Again, my father was trying to show me something. So many parents are not teaching their children as they should be. They have left that to the computer and the television shows. They're not showing their children how to be responsible in this hour, and that's where the deceit comes in at. Some buy their children so many different things; name-brand items and so much of it is completely worldly. They are following people that are *supposed to be* their friends. Children have been allow to pierce their ears, and they are given name-brand jeans, boots, etc., but that is not teaching them responsibility at all. When they get out in the world the children will believe that so much is owed to them. You will have to live with the results of your actions. Can you keep up with their desires, wants, and demands? You have to teach your children how to be responsible for the things that they get or else you're going to raise a monster. They will have learned to expect something without responsible or working for it. When the truth is being told like this, people can't take it; people don't like the truth. Who wouldn't want to be free? Well acceptance of truth is the road to freedom. In freedom is love. In freedom there's purity and a strong thinking mind. You might have to battle but you will have a peace of mind when you're free. When the truth is on your side you don't owe allegiance to anyone but truth. Jesus said to know Me is to be free.

I AM THE LIGHT

I am the light of the world: he that followeth me shall not walk in darkness, but shall have the light of life. If the Son therefore shall make you free, ye shall be free indeed (John 8:12, 36). **If ye continue in my word, then are ye my disciples indeed; And ye shall know the truth, and the truth shall make you free** (John 8:31-32). Jesus is all that we need. **I am the living bread which came down from heaven: if any man eat of this bread, he shall live for ever: and the bread that I will give is my flesh, which I will give for the life of the world** (John 6:51). However, when you're false, ***you will*** teach your children to lie, and manipulate others; to steal and tell them it's alright, nothing will happen to them. You're actually telling them lies because something will happen to them if they go on in that way. Just think so many parents are paying for the things that they have done or *not done* regarding raising their children but they will have to admit the reason for their suffering was a lack of honoring God in the home. Remember when you are parent, you are that child's primary teacher, leader, guide and corrector; you lay the foundation – good or bad. When you decide to become a parent, you are responsible to ensure that your child has everything they need to grow into a mature adult and that includes teaching them about God. Some parents resent how their children have turned out but they are the cause because they failed to give their children much-needed direction. Grant it, parenting does not come with a manual but that's why we all need God in every area of our lives. We need His wisdom and knowledge. We must acknowledge Him in all our way. **Trust in the Lord will all thine heart; and lean not unto thine own understanding. In all thy ways acknowledge him, and he shall direct thy paths. Be not wise in thine own eyes: fear the Lord, and depart from evil** (Proverbs 3:5-7). And that's where the deceit comes in at. Our house use to be immaculate.

IS THIS THE PROJECTS?

While we may have lived in the projects [*The Hilliard Homes*] our apartment was immaculate. Let me tell you. People use to come in our house and say, "Is this the projects?" My dad was just that type of person which made us different people growing up. What I mean by "different people," we were a different family. We stood out like a sore thumb because my mom and dad took us to counseling sessions so we would learn how to speak proper English. They wanted to see a difference come out of our lives. My parents didn't serve God at that time but they tried to do the best that they needed to do for us at that time. We would talk to people our peers and they thought we talked strange. They thought that we talked different from them and some would say "Why do you guys talk so proper?" To me, we talked normal but to them it was a difference, and then they hated us and fought us. Many would say, "You mean to tell me you 5 kids have the same mom and dad?" See, there were many who lived around us who had different moms and dads. You had two that had the same mom and different dad. You know what I mean? That's just how it was. We stood out like a sore thumb. But it was so much love and unity in our home until arrived. Proverbs 14:12 says, **There is a way which seemeth right unto a man, but the end thereof are the ways of death.** Ezekiel 28:15 says, **Thou was perfect in thy ways from the day that thou was created, till iniquity was found in thee.**

MY FATHER'S ABSENCE

My father ended up leaving the home, which resulted a broken family. Ultimately, all the things that I told you about now started to crumble. No more counseling sessions because now my mom had to raise all five of us right. That's where the deceit came in you know. Don't get me wrong my dad is not like that anymore. My mom is here in the ministry serving God with us now. These things that I grew up with in my childhood -- I am sharing with you today. Our family was broken. I use to cherish the times when my dad would come and pick us up after he had left the home but my concern was why he wasn't there in the home any more. What happened? Every child needs a father; look at our society. So many missing dads. Many children have found themselves asking the same question over and over again. My father's absence impacted me in a great way. When he would tell my mamma that he wasn't coming to get us, *which would make me so sad*. I remember one rainy day, I was folded over as I was waited for him to come and get us and it was just raining, and my mom came and told me "He's not coming today." Oh I cried and cried. The rain didn't shed as many tears as I did that day. Those words made me feel horrible because *I depended on my dad*. He was just my rock; he was everything to me. You see how it is *everything* when your parents are in the home? You see how we can be as parents when we get selfish and we start thinking of our own selfish ways; because your life actually stops when those children come. Those kids become your life until they are grown. You say, "Oh I've done wrong," well that's not their problem. That's your problem and you've have to get your life right. That's deceit to think you can have a life outside the children you brought into the world. You have to study and get an understanding up under your umbrella of life.

WHO IS THIS STRANGER?

I watched my dad in the home and I noticed how he was changing and it terrified me. I didn't know what was going on, and I saw him changing how he treated us and from that point on I hated him. He had lead me to believe that he was one person but then I had saw a different person. "Who was this stranger?" Until I received salvation and all the hate, resentment and bitterness was washed out of my veins like a person on dialysis, God flowed the blood of His son into me and made my soul righteous. Oh Hallelujah! This is for some of you today. Dads are you showing your sons and daughters one thing and then you're doing another? And you think he's not being affected; are you showing your son that you're this strong person, and yet you're really weak. What are you showing your son? What are you showing your children? Are you showing your son how to wear his hat cocked when so many young men are getting killed and shot for that purpose? Are you making him grow up to be just like you and your life is 'toe up from the flow up?'" Consider these things. You're always looking over your shoulder and you're not teaching your son or daughter the correct way. Moms, dads are you cursing in the home, in front of the children and then asking where they got it from. That's deceit! Where do you think they got it from? **They got it from you**. What are you teaching your children? How are you guiding them? Why are you blaming everyone else for your situation and not blaming yourself about what is going on? There are so many people in this world; a great percentage of the people that are in the world wish they could go back home. Others have had bad experiences in the home and *they never want to go back home*. But Jesus is the healer; He is the revealer of secrets. He'll keep every secret. Jesus will never take your secret and put it on display. You can come and talk to Him about anything and He will rescue you. We sing a song called *God is able* to deliver from the fire. He can rescue any soul that wants to be rescued all you have to do is trust the Lord and give your heart to Him and He'll let you know He's there. The Lord has a special way of talking to His children; He has a way of drawing you out and showing you great love. I've been there and I know what I'm talking about.

FALSE PROMISES

John 3:16 says, **For God so loved the world, that he gave his only begotten son, that whosoever believeth in him should not perish, but have everlasting life.** One day I discovered that my dad wasn't the man I thought he was. My dad changed and what did that do to me? It brought so much anger, bitterness, division, lies, and no trust; and that's what the churches are doing to people today. They're drawing people out with false promises and telling them that they have answers to their problems. But they're taking the world and bringing it inside the churches, and teaching the people they can live any way they want – that God understands – and they will still prosper. It is good when you have a good church to go to. It's good to have a church where you can go and learn about the Word of God; it's a wonderful thing. But it's not a good place when you can go to a church and have something that *looks good* but behind the scenes it's rotten to the core. There are some homes like that. People only let you see what *they want you to see* but they don't tell you the whole story. I watched this family on T.V. they were prospering and had money. It looked like they were doing very well, like they had it all. Kids were clean, clothes were nice and fresh, mommy would kiss daddy in front of the kids. Behind the scenes, however, there were some terrible things happening. And they got exposed on T.V. some of you know exactly who I'm talking about. They claimed to be Christian, claimed that they were doing so many different things in the name of God, but then the truth came out. The truth came out, and the Lord said that which is done in the dark will come to light. He said your sins will find you out. Galatians 6:7 says, **Be not deceived; God is not mocked: for whatsoever a man soweth, that shall he also reap.** You have to understand how God operates.

...SUPPOSED TO BE THERE

Let's talk a little bit about the prodigal son. *To study deceit, there's no place like home.* Have you discovered yet why there's no place like home? Protection is *supposed to be there.* Why is there no place like home? There is *supposed to be love there.* Why is there no place like home? The home *is supposed to be* a place where you can be yourself. If somebody broke into your home how would that make you feel? That's the place that you have established for your family, your kids but if you're destroying your home on the inside, people don't have to break in. You've already broken it up. Follow me now if you're doing things in your home that is ungodly, if you're doing things that you think your children are not listening to, and watching you; if you're doing things in your home and you claim up and down to yourself that it's all right, you're in great deceit. If you're not doing right by God, and not raising those children the right way, you're breaking hearts and you're going to have to deal with the outcome of it. You have to take it serious when you are raising a child, and therefore, if you take raising a child seriously. Sometimes when you are raising a child you don't have all the answers right away, but you know that love you have in your heart, you'll reach for the right answers. You ask God and you know He'll direct you in the right way.

GIVE ME MY STUFF

Luke 15:11 says, **And he said, A certain man had two sons: And the younger of them said to his father, Father, give me the portion of goods that falleth to me. And he divided unto them his living.** Think about the love the father must have had. He knew his son wasn't ready but yet he still granted his request. Now think about the deceit the son in. Didn't he say, **give me the portion of goods that falleth to me**, which meant give me all. And the devil deceives young people into believing that they can have everything they need *outside of the home*. Everything you need is inside of the home! I'm talking a God-fearing family where God is honored; that has love in the family. I'm not talking about a broken home because I know all too well why young children run out and escape from home. People must get themselves together when it comes to family. This nation must return to the ways of the God. We need answers that come from Him and His Word. Stop blaming others and forking over the responsibility to somebody else. It's always somebody else's fault. Young girls have children and they don't know what to do once the baby gets here; then they get angry, bitter, and mad when something is being told to them about what they are doing wrong.

A WASTED LIFE

Luke 15:13 says, **And not many days;** that means not many days from when he left the home! **And not many days after the younger son gathered all together, and took his journey into a far country, and there wasted his substance with riotous living.** He hadn't even got out of the door good before he lost everything. Why? Because that's the way he was thinking; but just like I told you in the beginning about my father, when he tried to talk to me about how to properly cut something, the prodigal son thought to himself that he was ready. The father knew he wasn't ready but he had so much love for his son that *he let him go*. When mama is trying to teach you something young people, humble yourself and shut your mouth! You don't have all the answers. As a matter of fact no one has all the answers, especially without God's direction. Our total dependence must be on Him. You're too young to have all the answers. I don't have all the answers and I'm much older than you and I'm still learning! The man of God, our home pastor, has been in the ministry for sixty-two years and he said he is still learning. So why do you think that you have all of the answers? Dad when your son comes to you and tells you about his problems, don't shun him to the side but listen. Get rid of the marijuana! How in the world are you going to understand him and you're high all of the time? And you say that you can't be free but you can be free if you want to be free! How bad do you want to be free? That's deceitful thinking and the devil is doing your thinking. This young person told me a long time ago when I was coming up "Man I drive better when I'm high." Deceit! He was deceived and he really believed that he did. How many people believe that when they get drunk and high, they can do things better? That's devil-possession to the fullest.

DEMON POSSESSION

Did you know that any person addicted to drugs or alcohol is devil possessed? Well it's true. When that person's turns their mind over to those influences, the devils come right on in. That person wakes up to find himself different but unable to determine who the difference is. You had given your mind and our body so completely over to that alcohol that you were rendered helpless and lying on the ground. You put yourself in that senseless condition; and by doing so, you opened yourself up to demon possession. Demons have taken over many people while they were under the influence of alcohol or drugs. Those demons won't settle until you keep on feeding them. The effects of demon possession when a devil possesses a soul that person becomes whatever that demon is. For example, there are murdering devils that desire to kill. If it sounds disgusting, that's because it is. People don't know what they subject themselves to when they turn their minds over to drugs and alcohol. Demon possession occurs in different ways but being under the influence of drugs and alcohol is one. You have to be delivered and you have to be set free! That's what it's all about. I use to drink, get high, smoke and I use to have this really bad thing in my heart about what I did. I believe I influenced my younger brother to start embracing the drug scene. I was so deceived and seduced by lying devils, causing me believe that I was doing the right thing by, showing him the path that I was on. I was so deceived about myself I thought I was really prospering but I wasn't really prospering; I was dying. I could have been a better light for them. I could have been a better strength for them if I would have known better. My older brother left home and he went and did his own thing. I started to get high and drink and I brought my younger brother with me. It was just a bunch of mess! Now I have come into the knowledge of the blood, and the blood has set me and my brother free. Now, I will teach other young people the right way. I was spending my money and trying to stay alive but I wasn't living -- just merely existing. I was not living the way that I wanted to live but I had now power to change. I thought to myself, "How can I keep going on this way without something terrible happening to me?" I saw destruction all around me! I didn't have the strength but I didn't want to die! I had to get to a point where I had to humble myself and allow the Lord to introduce Himself to me. I ask God to help me, and He did!

THE LOVE OF MONEY

Look at this. Luke 15:14 says, **And when he had spent all, there arose a mighty famine in that land; and he began to be in want.** Many people are trying to get rich. They *love* money. The love of money is the root of all evil, and most people love money. Of course a ministry needs money too; a true, blood bought ministry will take that money and put it back in the ministry, and use it for the ministry, and won't live high and mighty. It's nothing wrong with having riches but it's what you do with it; it's where your heart is. For the Word clearly tells us that you cannot serve two masters. We care about souls and more souls. The young prodigal son spent all of his money, not thinking to himself, that something would ever happen in his life. The Bible says as soon as he spent his money a feminine? The prodigal son didn't anticipate this time in his life; it was so far from his mind. He just thought, "Let me spend it; let me get it all now!" He didn't think, "Wait a minute let me put some of this money up; maybe something might happen in my life and I will need it." And sure enough a famine arose; but the son had nothing to help him; nothing to rely on. He left home where all the help was. The prodigal son spent it all and now he was in want. Luke 15:15 says, **And he went and joined himself to a citizen of that country; and he sent him into the fields to feed swine.** Now the son went and joined himself to somebody of that country. But the person that he joined himself to did not care anything about him. "Go feed the swine," was all he had for the son. Isn't that what it says in the Word? He was treated just the world treats you when it's done with you. Listen to what I'm saying to you. Nobody is going to love you like mama. You're married and your wife has put up with your mess. She took care of the home while you tried to move up in your career. She put her life on hold for you to gain! Now your wife finds herself going through in her life. She's battling depression and maybe has gained a little weight. You thinks she's no longer attractive to you but what about her attraction of sacrificing her life for you; so that you could have something and vice versa. This goes both ways; maybe it was the husband who sacrificed for the wife. You understand. Now you have got a little weight off and you're looking in the mirror at yourself and now nobody can tell you anything. Oh, you're doing well now but you forgot about the sacrifice that was made for you. That's deceit! Home is where the heart is. Things happen in life and you have to be ready for those sudden changes. When you are a leader of your family -- when you are a parent – it's your responsibility to get your children ready for life. You're getting them ready to be an outstanding citizen. You do the best you can, not the least you can. You search for ways to raise those children! You search for good ways to bring them up! You search for ways to make sure that they have a coat and a hat! That's your responsibility. You cannot raise a child trying to go to school and do these fifty different things; somebody is going to get lost in the mess, Your like is put on hold. You have to take care of that baby. It's so easy lying down when that man tells you on the phone (because his voice sounds like *Barry White* [famous deep-voiced singer from back in the day]) that he loves you. His voice is so heavy yeah but what about the future? What about things that matter? His voice does not matter! That's deceit working in you! The devil is doing your thinking.

AM I SAVING THE LOST?

Freedom is what we are looking for. Freedom is what we are looking for. And you can do all the things in the churches, you can open up so many avenues, you can give people so many different opportunities as far as different things you have in the church. They can have worship service, they can have the praise team, and you can have groups of individuals do different things in the church. You may have different ideas that you want to come up within your church. But you have to ask yourself as a leader and as pastor, "Am I saving the lost? Are they being set free and delivered?" Have you allowed the world to come into your church? If they are doing things of the world then your church is a *world church;* it caters to the world. Did you know that the church is supposed to be hated of the world? So if everything is going on in the church and the world loves the church there's a problem! There's a problem! The church is supposed to be a second home. Why is that? Because there is supposed to be strength and power there; just like in the home. So many people and churches have left the old way. That was the accusation that

Jeremiah brought against the people of his day. **Thus saith the Lord, Stand ye in the ways, and see, and ask for the old paths, where is the good way, and walk therein, and ye shall find rest for your souls. But they said, We will not walk therein. Also I set watchmen over you, saying, Hearken to the sound of the trumpet. But they said, We will not hearken** (Jeremiah 6:16-17). They have left the old time way. The prodigal son eventually ended up going back home. He was a better young man and more humble. A mom is not always a person that gives birth. A mom is a person that takes care of that baby and sacrifices her life for that child. You can have a child but if you abandon that child you're truly not the mom, you're just the birth mom that's all. But if someone comes along and takes that child and shows him love like Jesus did me; overshadowed me with His wings of love; He saw me drowning in my own blood, and He said this is a time of love. If a mom can do that then that's the mom! Don't be angry with the truth. Let the truth set you free! Let the truth set you free.

The Sinner's Prayer:

Oh God! Oh God! Oh God! Please help me! Please forgive me for sinning against you. But I have come home never to leave you again. Oh Lord I know there are many false Christ'. Oh Lord I know the Antichrist is in the world now, and if he's in the world now I know my only way out is to make it to Rapture ground; is to make it to Rapture ground. And by faith in the blood save my soul! Save my soul! Wash me in your blood! Cleanse me and make me whole! Save my soul! Save my soul! Come on in Jesus! And if you meant that neighbor He is there. Stay with God and He will stay with you. Are you ready? Let's go!

NOTES

NOTES

NOTES

NOTES

DJG

PART 4

CLASS PARTICIPATION

CHAPTER 11

I WILL, BUT I DON'T KNOW HOW
[D. JOHNSON]

I looked up the word *"will."* **Will** means capable of. Keep that definition in mind as we go along in the lesson. *Will* also means capable of; can, determined; or sure to. You go to church. You go on Sundays even when you have to work. You pay your tithes. People know. You attend counseling when required. People think that's strange. They think the things of God are *strange*. People who are of the world believe the things of the world are normal. They think cursing somebody out is normal; slashing people's tires is normal. But, what we do is not normal? It is just a sign of the times. Again the definition of **will** is; capable of; can; determined; or sure to. I know that makes you want to say, "Hmmm." This word is awesome. Especially, when your mind is open and you can discern understand. I am not talking about what you want to understand. Even when you are being corrected. If your heart is right, "Man Lord, wow." It is amazing to find out something for yourself about yourself through the Word. It is something that your heart and understanding are open; that you want His correction. You want His reprove. Like the book of Proverbs says. Another word I want you to notice is **yield**. The Lord is always searching for willing and yielded vessels to fulfil His plan in this hour. He is always searching. The Lord is searching even now. He's searching hearts. Our Lord does not worry about the outward appearance. Are you willing? Are you a fit vessel to fulfill His plan in this final hour? We may not know how or understand what the Lord has called us to do or what is totally required of us. We may not understand right now but we will trust the Lord as He leads and guides us. This is not the time to run off and lag behind or get ahead of God. Many have failed by taking such steps. This is simply the time to stay yielded and obedient.

HE IS THE SUPERVISOR NOW

On my job I had a situation where the supervisor wanted me to do something. He is the supervisor right? Here is the thing, it does not matter that we started together as train men. He or she is a supervisor now. I know a couple of people, we all started working on the trains together but now they have been elevated to a supervisor. That means that I have to listen to them; they are supervisors now. Keep that in mind. So, the supervisor told me to do something and I just did not feel, in my mind, was right. Other people heard about it. You know people, they were saying, "Well, you don't have to do that." Well, that's not the way we do things. If I don't feel like something is right, I have the option of going to another individual to verify protocol. So, I went to the manager. I called the manager by name. I was a train man with him which this manager was promoted from train man to a supervisor. Now he is a manager. He is above the supervisor. I said, "Chris, about this situation." He said, "Don't worry about it, you don't even have to do that." See that was the right way handle my uncertainty about what I had been asked to do. When the Lord tells you to do something, just because you don't know how to do it, or you don't feel comfortable doesn't mean that you don't follow through. Hear me. Just because you don't feel comfortable doing it or you don't know how to do it, doesn't mean you don't do it. That's the time to be yielded and obedient.

BE STRONG AND OF A GOOD COURAGE

We will review a couple examples. The Lord would not ask you to do something and not equipped you. He won't ask you to do something -- The Lord won't call you to do something and not equipped you. You might not have the understanding at first. You may not have the understanding of preaching the Gospel at first. You may not have the understanding of all the songs that you have been given at first. That doesn't mean to run off. Deuteronomy 31:6 says, **Be strong and of a good courage, fear not, nor be afraid of them: for the Lord thy God, he it is that doth go with thee; he will not fail thee, nor forsake thee.** If the Lord calls you, He is going to be with you all the way as long as you remain obedient. Why would the Lord call you and leave you in the night? That is not the type of God we serve. Some of you might have an inkling of what the Lord is asking you to do. That is not enough; wait on God. He will confirm and manifest His will for our life. This is also not the time for to run off. Maybe you think you should be doing something else. Or maybe you just don't understand. That's the time to yield and be obedient. That's the time to yield! Say that you don't understand. Okay, you may not understand but deliverance will be at hand for you, if you obey and yield. Deliverance comes through yielding. That's how you got saved. Whosoever calls on the name of the Lord shall be saved. You yielded to that if you have real salvation. You said, "That's right Lord, I need you Lord. Save my soul. I am wretched and undone." He saved you because you believed He had the power to not only save you but keep you as well. You believed that God's Son, Jesus Christ, was raised from the dead. Thou shalt be saved. You yielded and you were obedient. So, you were delivered. I am delivered. I have been set free. Right? Those of us who have that testimony. The Lord came to deliver you. **He will not fail thee, nor forsake thee** (Deuteronomy 31:6).

BACKSIDE OF THE DESERT

Now Moses kept the flock of Jethro his father in law, the priest of Midian: and he led the flock to the backside of the desert,

and came to the mountain of God, *even* **to Horeb. And the angel of the Lord appeared unto him in a flame of fire out of the midst of a bush: and he looked, and, behold, the bush burned with fire, and the bush was not consumed. And Moses said, I will now turn aside, and see this great sight, why the bush is not burnt. And when the Lord saw that he turned aside** (he yielded) **to see, God called unto him out of the midst of the bush, and said, Moses, Moses. And he said, Here am I** (Exodus 3:1-4). Did he run off? No, not like some of us might. Some of us have the nerve to say we want to see an angel. They say, "When I rise Lord, I want a big angel hoovering right over me, in Jesus name." Of course, the Lord does not allow that to happen because He knows you are not ready for that. You want to see an angel or a devil? Exodus 3:5-6 say, **And he said, Draw not nigh hither: put off thy shoes from off thy feet, for the place whereon thou standest is holy ground. Moreover he said, I am the God of thy father, the God of Abraham, the God of Isaac, and the God of Jacob. And Moses hid his face; for he was afraid to look upon God** (Exodus 3: 5-6). Sometimes we have to be shaken. Sometimes, we have got to go back. Sometimes, *we have to go back to really move forward.* I am not talking about slipping back in sin. That is not what I am talking about. Sometimes, we have to go back to see where we came from – count our blessings one by one and see what the Lord has done. Go back in our memory and reminder just how far the Lord has brought us. We have to remember and tell our children what God did for us, so those praises can go up. So, those praises can be louder. So, that we can give more. So, that we can fast and pray more. So, that we can be more grateful. So, that we can be more ready to go forward. When the enemy tries us, we can say, "No! No" because what the Lord has done for us. We can't afford to go back. *I can't afford to come clean again. I can't afford that.* There may not be another chance for me. There may not be another *come clean* message for me! I can't afford to do that and neither can you.

I KNOW THEIR SORROWS

Exodus 3:7-10 say, **And the Lord said, I have surely seen the affliction of my people which are in Egypt, and have heard their cry by reason of their taskmasters; for I know their sorrows; And I am come down to deliver them out of the hand of the Egyptians, and to bring them up out of that land unto a good land and a large, unto a land flowing with milk and honey; unto the place of the Canaanites, and the Hittites and the Amorites, and the Perizzites, and the Hivites, and the Jebusites. Now therefore, behold, the cry of the children of Israel is come unto me: and I have also seen the oppression wherewith the Egyptians oppress them. Come now therefore, and I will send thee unto Pharaoh, *that thou mayest bring* forth my people the children of Israel out of Egypt** (Exodus 3:7-10). What did Moses say? **And Moses said unto God, *Who am I*** (Exodus 3:11)**?** Moses complained, *I am just a baby who got rescued out of a creek, Lord.* Who am I?" Moses continued, "You want me to do what? To lead people? To lead a stiff neck, hard headed people?" **Who am I, that I should go unto Pharaoh, and that I should bring forth the children of Israel out of Egypt?** "Lord, you have got to be mistaken. You have got to be talking about somebody else. You cannot be talking about little old me. Did you forget, I slew somebody? I killed somebody. I am not fit. Not me? Lord, I don't know how. I am afraid." There is nothing wrong with telling the Lord that but, are you willing? He wants to hear that "I will" even from the beginning. Yes, you are afraid. Yes, you don't know how. But, our Lords wants to hear "I will" in the beginning. "I will Lord but I don't know how." Yes! If you will then the Lord will! Exodus 3:12 says, **And he said, *Certainly I will be with thee.*** Our Father didn't say I might, or it's a chance. We have got that mixed up. The Lord said, "*I will* be with thee. I will supply your needs. I will provide you a job. I will, I will, according to My riches and glory. **But my God shall supply all your need**

according to his riches in glory by Christ Jesus (Philippians 4:19)**.** You can check that out. It is in there. Shall. Will. Action! **And he said, Certainly I will be with thee; and this shall be a token unto thee, that I have sent thee: When thou hast brought forth the people out of Egypt, ye shall serve God upon this mountain** (Exodus 3:12)**.**

THEY WILL NOT BELIEVE ME

Exodus 4:1 says, **And Moses answered and said, But, behold, *they will not believe me*, nor hearken unto my voice.** Now you know how our leaders at times. Can you see them crying to the Lord and say, "Lord, it doesn't matter what I do. It doesn't matter what I say, Sunday after Sunday; Friday after Friday. They call me on the phone. They disturb me at work. They send me emails. You know, I tell them what to do. They say, 'Okay.'" But, if you are going to do what you want to do, why waste time? I just feel like the Lord does not like that. **Now the just shall live by faith: but if any man draw back, my soul shall have no pleasure in him** (Hebrews 10:38)**. But without faith it is impossible to please him: for he that cometh to God must believe that he is, and that he is a rewarder of them that diligently seek him** (Hebrews 11:6)**.** Seriously, our leaders, their time is so precious. You talk about *borrowed time*. That is it. True leaders will crying out to the Lord for their flock. If you are going to do what you want to do, don't call them. Don't seek counsel. Don't go to counseling, if you are going to do what you want to do. If you have it made up in your mind that you are going to be stubborn and rebellious, don't go to counseling, it will be no use and you will be wasting your time. The frown of the Lord will be upon you. He knows you. The Bible says, the Lord has made them watchmen [that includes women] over us. **Son of man, I have made thee a watchman unto the house of Israel: therefore hear the word at my mouth, and give them warning from me** (Ezekiel 3:17)**.** "You better warn them. Whatever, I tell you to say. Even if you have to lay your coat right there and preach and leave, or preach and run out. Speak My words." Now, you know how Steven and Paul felt. But, that's what you better do. You better deliver your soul. Moses cried, "They won't hearken unto me, **for they will say, The Lord hath not appeared unto thee** (Exodus 4:1). Just like we feel. The Lord was really looking at Moses heart. So, what Moses was really saying was, "Lord, I'm willing and I am trying. I will, but I just don't know how. The Lord challenged him. I love this.

A ROD

And the Lord said unto him, What is that in thine hand? And he said, A rod. And he said, Cast it on the ground. And he cast it on the ground, and it became a serpent; and Moses fled from before it. And the Lord said unto Moses, Put forth thine hand, and take it by the tail. And he put forth his hand, and caught it, and it became a rod in his hand: That they may believe that the Lord God of their fathers, the God of Abraham, the God of Isaac, and the God of Jacob, heath appeared unto thee. And the Lord said furthermore unto him, Put now thine hand into thy bosom. And he put his hand into his bosom: and when he took it out, behold, his hand was leprous as snow. And he said, Put thine hand into thy bosom again (Exodus 4:2-7). See what happens? Just like some of you. You say you are using your faith. **And he put his hand into his bosom again; and plucked it out of his bosom and behold, it was turned again as his other flesh. And it shall come to pass, if they will not believe thee, neither hearken to the voice of the first sign, that they will believe the voice of the latter sign** (Verses 7-8). What else do you need? My hand is normal. I put it in my pocket and it comes out white as leprous. The proof is in the pudding. If we were not being taught right, there would be no miracles. There would be no healings.

WHEN THE TRUTH IS PREACHED

When the truth is preached, God will confirm His Word. **And they went forth, and preached every where, the Lord working with them, and confirming the word with signs following.** (Mark 16:20)**.** The anointing that flows here [speaking to his congregation] is working in your life. The Lord would not be moving if the truth was not preached here. **Then Philip went down to the city of Samaria, and preached Christ unto them. And the people with one accord gave heed unto those things which Philip spake, hearing and seeing the miracles which he did** (Acts 8:5-6).

THESE TWO SIGNS

Exodus 4:9 says, **And it shall come to pass, if they will not believe also these two signs neither hearken unto thy voice, that thou shalt take of the water of the river, and pour it upon the dry land: and the water which thou takest out of the river shall become blood upon the dry land. And Moses said unto the Lord, O my Lord, I am not eloquent neither heretofore, or since thou hast spoken unto thy servant: but I am slow of speech, and of a slow tongue** (Exodus 4:9-10). You say, "Lord, I am trying. Lord, I have this deformity. I got things going on with me. I just don't understand. I am just in a fog." The Lord understands that. He wants to let you know, He understands that. But, that does not mean not to go forth. The Lord reasoned with Moses. He could have said, "Get out! I will pick somebody else." But, you can attest tonight, as you sit here, He did not do that. He gives you chance after chance because He has invested so much in each and every one of us. The Lord is a hopeful God. He believes in us as long as we are moving toward Him.

CHANGED MY APPEARANCE

I remember when I first came to this ministry and I was finding out about the truth and what this ministry was all about. I was wearing jeans. I was wearing boots. But, a little while, the Reverend let me do some small things. As I continued in the knowledge of the truth, I decided I was going to keep doing it. I wondered why I was not collecting tithes and offering and why I was not doing other things but that Wednesday when I changed. I came into the knowledge of the truth and wore a shirt, tie, slacks and some dress shoes, like I was supposed to be doing. But, see no one got on me. I listened to the Word, found myself and changed my appearance. It made me feel good that I discovered this with the help of the Lord. I remembered that. They did not say, "You need to be wearing a shirt and tie. Or go on down to J.C. Penny." They did not do that like some places would have done. You let people self-correct. That is why you have to be led by the Spirit. You must have **tact** and **contact**. Those two elements are very key is not only winning souls but keeping souls.

WHO MADE MAN'S MOUTH?

Exodus 4:11-12 say, **And the Lord said unto him, Who hath made man's mouth? Or who maketh the dumb, or death, or the seeing or the bling? Have not I the Lord? Now therefore go, and I will be with thy mouth, and teach thee what thou shalt say.** So, there is your alibi. You say, "I don't know. I know that I am called to do this. Or I know I am supposed to do this. I don't know if the Lord is with me." Here are your alibi breakers; along with the scriptures and Deuteronomy 31:6. You can match it up together. **Be strong and of a good courage, fear not, nor be afraid of them: for the Lord thy God, he it is that doth go with thee; he will not fail thee, nor forsake thee** (Deuteronomy 31:6). **Now therefore go, and I will be with thy mouth, and teach thee what thou shalt say** (Exodus

4:12)**.** You know you need to be taught. You are not going to have things figured out right away. Just like some of our jobs. Lord knows, mine! I didn't figure it out right way. It took me sometime. I operate a train. When I was driving a train on a station called the "Red Line." It is fine driving south. But as I went up north, past streets called Wilson, Sheridan and Addison, the train track became real raggedy. In the beginning, I would have to ease up on the signal and make sure it was a clear signal. But, now I can tell. Not to say that I am relaxed. I can tell if the signal is clear. I am not as timid now. I am still a little timid – careful -- in certain areas. But, I am being taught. There are different things but I am being taught as I go along. When I got assigned to that area I could not just sit at home and say, "No! I am just not going to work." Or one may say, "I am not going to preach until I figure out what it is all about." "I am not going to tarry." "I am not going to give the Holy Spirit any liberty until I figure out what it is all about. Then, I will give Him liberty. Then, I will tarry!" No! That is not how it works. You will taught as you go along and stay in truth. You are taught how to give yourself to the Holy Spirit. You are being taught. You are willing. I am willing every Monday, Tuesday, Wednesday, and Thursdays etc. Sometimes seven days a week. I am willing. "But, I really don't know how." The Lord has been teaching me and He is with me. I do what He wants because I need Him and I want Him to stay with me. That's how it works. I have been successful so far with the help of the Lord.

THE ANGER OF THE LORD

And he said, O my Lord, send, I pray thee, by the hand of him who thou wilt send. And the anger of the Lord was kindled against Moses, and he said, is not Aaron the Levite thy brother? I know that he can speak well. And also, behold, he come forth to meet thee: and when he seeth thee, he will be glad in his heart. And thou shalt speak unto him, and put words in his

mouth: and I will be with thy mouth, and with his mouth, and will teach you what ye shall do. And he shall be thy spokesman unto the people: and he shall be, even he shall be to thee instead of a mouth, and thou shalt be to him instead of God (Exodus 4:13-17). All Moses had to do was trust God. He really didn't need Aaron; he just thought he did. Moses was so into himself. He was so timid. Moses had some issues but he was willing. He had some doubts. As you see, he got over that and was able to help deliver his people. He was able to be a great leader for the Lord. The Lord was really able to use him when he got over those fears. When he got over those insecurities. What was he really saying? He was saying, "I will Lord, I just don't know how. I just don't know what to say." Instead, we should trust in the Lord. That is what we have to do. When you don't understand, lean on Jesus. Roman 8:28 says, **And we know that all things work together for good to them that love God, to them who are called according to his purpose**. That scripture tells you that you will be alright no matter what happens if you are living in the divine will of God. The great voice of the Lord is crying out, "You will be alright because I have called you to take my gospel to the whole world." He has given you talents. The Lord has called you to work for Him; it may be different areas and different things. He has called you to work for him. But some of you will not believe that scripture. You may believe it only with human faith but you won't use divine faith then you talk doubt to yourself and to others. Moses was talking doubt and he suffered greatly for not using divine faith. If he would have used divine faith at first, he would not have needed Aaron and Miriam. He regretted it later. Definitely! Moses probably thought to himself, "If I would have just listened. The Lord told me He was with me. If I would have just listened, I would not have had this problem." "You are just dealing with Moses!" That was Miriam and Aarons' attitude. Well, why would He deal with you? Are you in a position that the Lord can use you? Something to consider. Miriam, as a result of her speaking against God's plan, she was turned into a leper. Who had to pray for her? Moses was instructed to tell Pharaoh. "Pharaoh! Pharaoh! Let my people go!" In the beginning, Moses didn't really know how to go forth; he didn't know how to handle a people who were so disobedient and stiff-necked. Moses had to develop the attitude of "He will." As he accepted that will, God helped Moses to go on and lead His people.

WAIT ON THE LORD

Wait on the Lord; be of good courage, and he shall strengthen thine heart: wait, I say, on the Lord (Psalms 27:14). Maybe you don't understand. Maybe you haven't figured it out just yet. But, that is the time to wait. While you are waiting, you are being obedient and you are yielding. Check and be sure that you are waiting in the right waiting room. Be of good courage while you wait. He says to do what I tell you to do until the understanding comes. Right? **And he shall strengthen thine heart: wait, I say, on the Lord** (Psalms 27:14). Proverbs 3:5-6 say, **Trust in the Lord with all thine heart; and lean not unto thine own understanding**. Don't lean to your own understanding because your understanding is no good. It's the Lord who gives you understanding, right? Yes, your understanding is no good, unless the Lord gives it. First Sam 16:7 says, **But the Lord said unto Samuel, Look not on his countenance, or on the height of his stature; because I have refused him: for the Lord seeth not as man seeth; for man looketh on the outward appearance, but the Lord looketh on the heart.** Remember earlier I stated that the Lord is *always* looking and *always* searching. He is looking for willing vessels to fulfill His great plan. Even though, you may cry at times, there is nothing wrong with telling the Lord, "I will, but I don't know how." Is your heart in the right place? Are you sincere and you just don't know? If you need the Lord to help you more or you need Him to guide you more, there is nothing wrong with telling Him that; that's why we have the Comforter. Those are the things you need to be telling the Lord in your prayer time. **But the Comforter, which is the Holy Ghost, whom the Father will send in my name, he shall teach you all things, and bring all things to your remembrance, whatsoever I have said unto you** (John 14:26). **Nevertheless I tell you the truth; It is expedient for you that I go away: for it I go not way, the Comforter will not come unto you; but if I depart, I will send him unto you. And when he is come, he will reprove the world of sin, and of righteousness, and of judgment** (John 16:7-8)**.** You need to be talking with the Lord. What do you do in your prayer time? Is it just always, "Give me, give me, and ask, ask, ask?" Or is it, "I need this, and I need that, and that sure would be nice?" Is that your prayer time? Are you talking with the Lord? I like to talk with the Lord. I like to tell Him, "This is going on with me. You know, I felt this way. I said this. I said that." Moses was willing. He had some bumps and bruises. He cried and I am sure he wept at times. Moses did a great work for the Lord, just like you can.

TO OBEY IS BETTER

First Samuel 15:22 says, **And Samuel said, Hath the Lord as great delight in burnt offerings and sacrifices, as in obeying the voice of the Lord? Behold, to obey is better than sacrifice, and to hearken than the fat of rams.** Go on and read the rest of that great chapter. Our answer should just be, "Yes, Yes, Yes! I'll just say, yes. I'll just say yes to your will and your way!" Isaiah 1:19 says, **If ye be willing and obedient, ye shall eat the good of the land.** You can underline that statement if your Bible is a workbook. Romans 6: 16 says, **Know ye not, that to whom ye yield yourselves servant to obey, his servants ye are to whom ye obey; whether of sin unto death, or of obedience unto righteousness?** You can get ready for your miracle and healing. You can get ready to tell God,

"I will but I just don't know how." You can tell God, "I really don't know how to release my faith, Lord but I have faith according to your Word. Lord, you gave me a measure of faith and I going to use it." You have to reason with Him. "I will Lord, but teach me how to use me faith. Teach me how to exercise my faith." Mark 11:22 says, **And Jesus answering saith unto them, Have faith in God.** Just four words. You have got to trust Him. "Lord, you called me to this ministry. Lord, you brought me here. You word says your spirit drew me. I could not come here by myself, unless your spirit drew me; unless Your Holy Spirit draw me. I know you wouldn't call me Lord if you didn't believe that I could do it." The Lord has faith in you. Your leaders have faith in you and that should mean so much. As the young people say, "If they are down with you, then." If they are for you, then who can be against you. Why can't you do it? Well, if you just don't know how; just be willing. The Lord said He would be with you and you will eat the fruit of the land. You will eat that fruit which is understand, peace, knowing how and coming into knowledge as the Holy Spirit teaches you.

HURRY FRIDAY

In *"Hurry Friday*[21]*"* The author says, *In the midst of all that heavenly joy, something weighed on my heart: When the Lord had taken my burden of sin, it was as though He traded burdens, taken the one and giving the burden for the lost. He was calling me to carry the wonderful, precious message of His salvation to a lost world. From the very beginning of my new life in Him, I felt His call to preach His Gospel, but I wanted to be sure.* He must have thought, "Lord, I just wanted to be sure! I don't understand why you are choosing a little

---

[21]   Angley, Ernest (2004) *Hurry Friday, Autobiography of Ernest Angley.* Akron, Ohio: Winston Press.

farm boy like me. You are choosing me." The author continued, *I knew if God meant for me to preach, I would be a success. Now I was down by my bed crying and praying: "Lord, I will preach, but I don't know how! I will preach but I don't know how!"* Neighbor, you may find yourself saying today, "Lord, I will but I don't know how. I understand you are calling me to preach but, I just don't understand why you are choosing me to preach? Lord, you are choosing me to sing the songs of Zion? Lord, you are choosing me to 'present the Gospel live?' Lord, you are choosing me to be a watchman; just to watch the door? Lord, you chose me to be in a ministry like this? You chose me! The curse stopped with me, with AIDS and drugs and alcohol. I don't understand." Today, so many have called themselves. The Bible is clear about this. Jeremiah 23:21, 25-26 say, **I have not sent these prophets, yet they rain: I have not spoken to them, yet they prophesies. I have heard what the prophets said, that prophesy lies in my name, saying, I have dreamed. I have dreamed. How long shall this be in the heart of the prophets that prophesy lies? Yea, they are prophets of the deceit of their own heart.** Today, the drunk is a prophet; the prostitute is a prophet. Everybody is a prophet.

I COULDN'T THINK OF ONE SERMON

The testimony continued. I will preach but I don't know how!" *After all the times I had been in church, all the sermons I had heard, now I couldn't think of one sermon. But the Lord didn't want me to preach someone else's sermon; He wanted me to preach His message. With tears of submission rolling down my cheeks, I said a big Yes to my Lord. The Holy Spirit sang through me in English: I'm going through, yes, I am going through, I'll pay the price whatever others do. I'll take the way with the Lord's despised few. I've started for heaven and I'm going through. I stood up. It was all settled. I had my call from God: I was to carry His Word.* Notice this. The author said, *with tears of submission.* What did I say? Yielding and obedience. Did he run? No! He said, *I don't know how Lord, but I am willing.* He said, *with tears of submission rolling down my cheeks, I said a big YES to my Lord.*

Neighbor it has to be settled with you as well. Whatever the Lord wants you to do. Some of you have an inkling. Some of you do not know. Some of you do not understand. Settle it today that you will obey and the understanding will come later. I will assure you. It must be that way with each and every one of us. Don't be afraid to tell the Lord in your prayer time just how you feel. If you are sincere, the Lord is there each and every time you come before Him. Oh how wonderful. Isaiah 1:19 says, **if ye be willing and obedient, ye shall eat the good of the land.** Don't be afraid to tell the Lord, "I will Lord." Tell the Lord you will. Don't just say the first part, "I just don't know how." No! Say, "I will," Be willing and obedient. Even if tears run down your cheeks and your face is towards the floor, or whatever you have to do cry out child of God. He is waiting for you there at the altar. He will help you. Just like he did Jeremiah. Just like He did Moses. Just like He did Reverend Angley. Remember, they were just men...with God on their side. There is no other way we will be able to make it in this hour if we are not totally obedient and willing. But, the Lord will help us. He promised He would help us. Joshua 1:5 says, **There shall not any man be able to stand before thee all the days of thy life: As I was with Moses, so I will be with thee: I will not fail thee, nor forsake thee.** Now go on and reason with God. Let's go on and do this great work. Let's be willing and obedient.

CHAPTER 12

THE DEVIL'S MAN
THE ANTICHRIST, THE FALSE CHRIST

The spirit of the Antichrist has covered the whole world. And so many leaders and teachers won't talk about the devil, let alone the Antichrist. Many of them won't teach from the book of Revelation. You have to teach the whole Word of God. Some preachers teach about salvation but you must teach about hell also. We talk about heaven, angels and Jesus watching over us. As preachers and leaders, we are also called to warn God's people. The Lord told Ezekiel, **Son of man, I have made thee a watchman unto the house of Israel: therefore hear the word at my mouth, and give them warning from me. When I say unto the wicked, Thou shalt surely die; and thou givest him not warning, nor speakest to warn the wicked from his wicked way, to save his life; the same wicked man shall die in his iniquity; but his blood will I require at thine hand. Yet if thou warn the wicked, and he turn not from his wickedness, nor from his wicked way, he shall die in his iniquity; but thou hast delivered thy soul.** *Again,* **When a righteous man doth turn from his righteousness, and commit iniquity, and I lay a stumblingblock before him, he shall die: because thou hast not given him warning, he shall die in his sin, and his righteousness which he hath done shall not be remembered; but his blood will I require at thine hand** (Ezekiel 3:17-20).

THE ANTICHRIST AND 1968

The Antichrist is in the world today. I believe he was born in the latter part of 1968. The spirit of the Antichrist covers the earth.

That's something to give great thought to. That is why we have an eruption of violence and it's going to get worse but don't let it affect you. You will see more and more suffering. You will see the powers of darkness settling upon the earth more and more, as people yield to the power of darkness. But you must yield to the power of the God's light; His light of love and grace and it will light up all of your paths. Do not be afraid. The Lord doesn't want us to be afraid. He has promised to walk with us all the way, as we walk with Him. Here in Chicago it's the wild, wild West. Chicago was on the international news because of the spike in violence. At this writing, there have been 729 homicides; whereas at the end of 2015 there were 492[22]. This is an hour of great deceit, and an hour of so much destruction. So many young people are dying at a pandemic rate but we have to hold on to God and remember His Word. **This know also, that in the last days perilous times shall come. For men shall be lovers of their own selves, covetous, boasters, proud, blasphemers, disobedient to parents, unthankful, unholy, Without natural affection, truce breakers, false accusers, incontinent, fierce, despisers of those that are good, traitors, heady, highminded, lovers of pleasures more than lovers of God; Having a form of godliness, but denying the power thereof: from such turn away** (2 Timothy 3:1-5). No matter what happens we have to make sure that our anchor and what we believe in really rests in the almighty God. We have to make sure that what we are receiving is coming from the mouth of God.

---

[22] Chicago Tribune. *Crime in Chicagoland.* http://crime.chicagotribune.com/chicago/homicides

WHO SHALL SEPARATE YOU?

Who shall separate us from the love of Christ? Shall Tribulation, or distress, or persecution, or famine, or nakedness, or peril, or sword? As it is written, For thy sake we are killed all the day long; we are accounted as sheep for the slaughter. Nay, in all these things we are more than conquerors through him that loved us. For I am persuaded, that neither death, nor life, nor angels, nor principalities, nor powers, nor things present, nor things to come, Nor height, or depth, nor any other creature, shall be able to separate us from the love of god, which is in Christ Jesus our Lord (Romans 8:35-39)**.** The hour is too late to go or depend somebody's opinion or theories. Stay with the Word. Stay with God. Some folks need to be shaken *up* so they can wake up before it's too late. We must walk in the steps of Jesus and do the work that the Lord has ordained for us to do. We are being offered everything that we need for this your last hour. The Lord is offering it to us now. Do not doubt God's. Do He loves us with an unending love. But some of you, you cannot believe that He love you. You can't really believe that He loves you but He does love you. Feel His love and be secure in His love and you will have strength, grace, and help. All the help you need for yourself and for others in this final hour. And that's really something to think about that we're going through so much in our lives now and you know some people; the greatest weapon that the enemy [the devil] has against them, is that most of the Christian world don't really believe that the devil is alive. They don't really believe that he's in the world today he is in great fashion. So when we really begin to talk about the Antichrist it's so far above them. They don't really understand what's going on. But the spirit of the Antichrist is in the world right now. And so you may ask why would you bring a message like this at this time? It's the right time. It's the right time for the world. It's the right time for people who are sitting in false doctrine and it's the right time for God's children if they are planning on making the Rapture.

WIDE AWAKE

We must be wide awake. It's the right time to clear up boggled minds, and people who are sitting in a stupor; people who are slumbering, and sleeping. It's the right time to wake people up. People need to be alarmed about what's going on; alarmed at the destruction. They need to be able to recognize the things that are happening in the world and take them right to the Bible. Matthew the 24th chapter is on center stage right now. People are sitting in darkness but the Lord promised us through His Word that the light we need is in His Word. If people look to that light they'll receive salvation and they'll receive redemption. What is that light? *It's the truth that's in God's Word!* The devil's man, the Antichrist, the false Christ. In the Old Testament, the Jews were promised by the God of Heaven that He would gather them back to the Holy Land. History tells us that since 1921, the greatest gathering in the history of the Jews has taken place. In 1948, the Jews, at last, became a nation. Today the Jews are stirred like never about going back to their homeland. Since 1948 when the Jewish state officially became a nation, we have been on our way to Rapture ground. You can study in Matthew the 24th chapter. It teaches us the parable of the fig tree and we know that fig tree in prophecy represents the children of Israel. The Bible teaches us that Jesus is coming back and it will be sudden. **For yourselves know perfectly that the day of the Lord so cometh as a thief in the night** (1 Thessalonians 5:2)**.** It's not going to be anytime to pray, and if you really understand the magnitude of the power that the Antichrist will have and are not getting ready, something is wrong. You want to be a part of what is going to take place for seven years – the hell that will be unleeched -- seven years of damnation. I want you to think, when you are left, you could have made it! You could have been with us. You could have made the one flight out! When you miss the Rapture you're going to realize what a fool you were! If you have been a part of this ministry you're going to know from event to event what's going to happen next, because you have been taught it in truth right here at this church. You're going to realize the bickering in the home, the pornography, not paying God His tenth, not raising your children right, not submitting yourselves, not walking humbly before the Lord, not standing up for righteousness, not standing up for the blood-stained banner, and making people believe you were something that you were not. You're going to realize it was all a waste! It was just a wasted life!

WAITING IN THE WINGS

The devil's man, the Antichrist, the false Christ is on the earth right now. But he's waiting in the wings to come out. The United States of America, the way our economy is, the way people are without jobs, the health care system, all the fighting that's going on in the government, and the wars and rumors of wars – America would welcome the Antichrist right now with no problem! Do you know why they would welcome him? You need to study and find out. The Antichrist cannot be revealed until the church [the Bride of Christ] is gone. In other words, think of the church as a dam. As the dam holds the water back, the church keeps the Antichrist from making his appearance. When the church is removed, then the Antichrist will rush in and make a covenant with the Jews for seven years. Everything that must be fulfilled before the Rapture can take place has been fulfilled with regard to the gathering back of the Jewish people unto their promised land. Anyone who knows anything about Bible prophecy and is teaching in truth, they know that all of the prophecies concerning the second coming of Jesus Christ have been fulfilled with the exception of gathering in of the final harvest [souls]. That's the only thing that we need to do. But <u>all</u> of the other prophecies about the second coming of Jesus Christ have been fulfilled. You don't think you need to get yourself together? You don't think you need to wake up? You don't think you need to come out of your stupor? You don't think you need to wake up out of the coma you've been in? Maybe you're a scoffer today and you might be saying within yourself, "Yeah they have been talking about that for a long time. They've been talking about Jesus' return for a long, long time." Yeah but if they've been talking about it for a long time, doesn't that mean that you're closer to it today than when you first heard about it? That's what that means!

THE GODHEAD

In the Trinity of the Godhead, we have the Father, the Son, and the Holy Ghost. Well in the Anti-God head there is the devil, which is the Anti-God, The Antichrist which is the Beast, and the Anti-Spirit which is the False Prophet or false doctrine. Pastors and leaders controlled by the devil are teaching the devil's doctrine right from the pulpit of God! Teaching people in the name of the Lord to blaspheme His name; it's the Anti-Spirit. I heard Paul say in Philippians 3:18-19, **(For many walk, of whom I have told you often, and now tell you even weeping, that they are the enemies of the cross of Christ: Whose end is destruction, whose God is their belly, and whose glory is in their shame, who mind earthly things)** (Philippians 3:18-19)**.** Galatians 1:8-9 say, **But though we, or an angel from heaven, preach any other gospel unto you than that which we have preached unto you, let him be accursed. As we said before, so say I now again, If any man preach any other gospel unto you than that ye have received, let him be accursed** (Galatians 1:8-9)**.** The devil's man is the Antichrist and you better wake up and realize it! You better throw your theories and opinions out and get with *Thus Saith the Lord*! Some people are so stubborn, they are so rebellious, and they won't accept this message. But this message will either be used for you or it will be used against you. It's up to you. You cannot be of God and speak something that is false. **For he whom God hath sent speaketh the words of god: for God giveth not the Spirit by measure unto him** (John 3:34).

WE KNOW THAT THOU ART A TEACHER FROM GOD

Listen to Nicodemus' testimony. **There was a man of the Pharisees, named Nicodemus, a ruler of the Jews: The same came to Jesus by night, and said unto him, Rabbi, we know that thou art a teacher come from God: for no man can do these miracles that thou doest, except God be with him** (John 3:1-2). Jesus is of truth. He can't speak false because He is truth! **Jesus said unto him, I am the way, the truth, and the life: no man cometh unto the Father, but by me. If ye had known me, ye should have known my Father also: and from henceforth ye know him, and have seen him** (John 14:6-7). **I am the true vine, and my Father is the husbandman. Every branch in me that beareth not fruit he taketh away: and every branch that beareth fruit, he purgeth it, that it may bring forth more fruit. Now ye are clean through the word which I have spoken unto you** (John 15:1-3). Christ can't speak doubt because He is of faith. He can't speak weakness because the Lord paid the price for all of us to be strong! Many of you know what I am teaching you is right, but you just don't want to hear it because you want to stay in the lust of the flesh. But go ahead it is, after all, up to you. Free will - that's the one thing that we did not lose when Adam failed. We did not lose our free will and it's up to you. You can go the way that seemeth right or you can go the way that you know is right. Now many people are not getting this kind of teaching that you're receiving and you need to do something with it! You need to do something about your life! Right? As this is a Holy Ghost dispensation, the Holy Ghost works in the interest of Christ. He is not working to glorify Himself but the Father and the Son. In that day the Anti-Spirit will be working to glorify the Antichrist and the Devil. He will deceive men with the great miracle he is able to perform, and he will tell those who dwell on the earth to make an image of the Beast. **And he had power to give life unto the image of the beast, that the image of the beast should both speak, and cause that as many as would not worship the image of the beast should be killed.** Now he caused <u>all</u>; listen to it -- all.

666

The devil's man. **And he causeth <u>all,</u> both small and great, rich and poor, free and bond, to receive a mark in their right hand, or in their foreheads** (Revelation 13:15-16)**.** In the middle of the Tribulation period, that's three and a half years into the Tribulation period, they are going to start holding up stations all around the world demanding that you take the mark. And see the spirit of the Antichrist is convincing people to do things such as you can start your computer with your fingertip. You can go to the store and instead of flashing your credit card you can do it with your fingertip. A lot of places are doing away with cash; they only want you to use a credit card. It's slowly but surely migrating into *world order.* **And that no man might buy or sell, save he that had the mark, or the name of the beast, or the number of his name. Here is wisdom. Let him that hath understanding count the number of the beast: for it is the number of a man; and his number is six hundred threescore and six** (Revelation 13:17-18). The number of a man is stressed so we know he is a devil man – 666. People ought to wake up. How wide awake are you today? Are you really Biblically awake? Are you awake to the fact that we don't have long? That's the reason the Spirit is being poured out and all of it being poured out. But some of you are not even running for the Holy Ghost; not even for old time salvation. Some claimed to be saved but you're never really been born new; you've never really left the world. No, you can't do the things that you do, the place you go and watch the things you watch. The devil is bringing it right into your homes. It's just as sinful as if you went to a saloon or whole house and watched but the devil will make you think it's no harm. He will whisper, "You are going to those places. You are not harming anybody." You need to become somebody in Jesus and you would realize that you are harming yourself and will never make it to Heaven doing those things. Sin makes you a no body. Porn makes you a no body. And some will say that they can't keep away from it [porn] then you can't keep away from hell. You can't keep away from the Tribulation period. You can't keep away from the lake of fire and once you are in hell, it is forever. There's no changing your mind. The choice is yours now but some of you, you don't even count it worth a few dollars; selling your soul to the devil for a handful of ashes, like Adam and Eve. You may think how they were, they already had their mansion in heaven. This earth would have been paradise thousands of years ago and the devil would have been in the lake of fire for at least 6000 years.

FREE CHOICE

The Lord gave Adam and Eve free choice, just as He gave the angels free choice. They no longer have free choice; they made their final decision. Some went with Lucifer and some stayed with God and that decision is final and forever. We have no record of Adam and Eve ever getting right with God. I believe God would have put it in His Holy book so we would have known that they got things right. We don't know but it is something to think about because we know that God didn't walk with them any more in Eden. Heaven was swept away from them. Good health was swept away from them. They began to cry; they began to weep sorrow after sorrow. They had a funeral for the first time, buried a dead body, a son that had been murdered by another son. Did their offspring learn? Most of them did not.[23]

YOU WILL WAKE UP...IN THE TRIBULATION PERIOD

Tragically, many Christians are asleep. Some of you are asleep too! You will wake up in the Tribulation period! I will assure you. You know all that the Lord has given us, all that the Lord has done for us; some people are not going to wake up because they are smarter than God. Isn't that what the Lord said about Adam and Eve? He had to move the tree of knowledge of good and evil away from them. He said because what? **And the Lord God said, Behold, the man is become as one of us, to know good and evil: and now, lest he put forth his hand, take also of the tree of life, and eat, and live for ever: Therefore the Lord god sent him forth from the garden of Eden, to till the ground from whence he was taken. So he drove out the man; and he placed at the east of the garden of Eden Cherubims, and a flaming sword which turned every way, to keep the way of the tree of life** (Genesis 3:22-24)**.** Right now in America the stage is set for the Antichrist. It's set right now; all the unemployed, the bad economy, the government, people in the government, they're supposed to be looking out for us and they're fighting against one another, and the way they treat

---

23   Angley, Ernest. *The Love Language, Part 579, The Mount of His Glory, Part 46*. Akron, Ohio.

Angley, Ernest. *The Love Language, Part 582, The Mount of His Glory, Part 49*. Akron, Ohio.

the senior citizens regarding healthcare and other matters is really something else. You can hardly get a raise but all of your taxes still continue to increase.

THE DAY OF CHRIST IS AT HAND

Second Thessalonians 2:2-4 tells us what the Bible says about the hour we're now living in. **That ye be not soon shaken in mind, or be troubled, neither by spirit, nor by word, nor by letter as from us, as that the day of Christ is at hand. Let no man deceive you by any means: for that day shall not come, except there come a falling away first, and that man of sin be revealed, the son of perdition; Who opposeth and exalteth himself above all that is called God, or that is worshipped; so that he as God sitteth in the temple of God, shewing himself that he is God.** Thessalonians is not talking about a falling away from the churches. The churches are getting jammed pack. They're building bigger and bigger churches and cathedrals. It's *a falling away from the truth and the standards of God!* It's a falling away *from holiness and righteousness.* That's where the falling away is. It's not a falling away from the churches because the churches are jammed packed. Some of these churches they are so big until they have to bus people to the main service area. You park your car and they actually have a shuttle bus to bring you to the main building. I'm not against big churches. We come from a big church. Our home church is massive. But it's a falling away from the standards of God, it's a falling away from true holiness and righteousness, it's a falling away from separation, it's a falling away from consecration, and honoring the things of the Lord! That's where the falling away is! It's a falling away of morals, standards, and teaching our children right. It's a falling away from father's being in the home, and moms being the moms that God called them to be. That's the falling away we're talking about and that is being brought out in 2 Thessalonians. The Bible says that without holiness no man shall see God. I don't care how rich you are, you can't buy a born-again experience. If Christ was for sale, none of us would be saved. None could afford Him. His price is far beyond rubies. His home, the streets are paved with gold. Come on somebody! You can't buy a seat in Heaven, thank God. **Blessed are the poor in spirit: for there is the kingdom of heaven. Blessed are they that mourn: for they shall be comforted. Blessed are the meek: for they shall inherit the earth. Blessed are they which do hunger and thirst after righteousness: for they shall be filled. Blessed are the merciful: for they shall obtain mercy. Blessed are the pure in heart: for they shall see God** (Matthew 5:3-8).

LET NO MAN DECEIVE YOU

2 Thessalonians 2ND chapter says, **The day of Christ is at hand. Let no man deceive you**. What? **By any means.** Don't let them fool you. Don't let them play down that everything is going to get better! That's it America has had her chance. She will not be great again. Our outgoing president of the United Stated of America has declared that we are no longer a Christian nation. Things are not getting better! At one time we were sending missionaries to places and now they're sending missionaries to America, of all places. This is the nation that people came to because they could enjoy religious freedom they wanted to serve the true and the living God. Not anymore! You can teach witchcraft openly in school but you can't pray over your food. You can teach astrology but you can't pray over your food. It's something to think about; we are messed up and the only remedy is to get yourself ready to get out of here. Get ready to go up. America had her chance and things will not be getting any better. **For that day shall not come, except there come a falling away first, and that man of sin be revealed, the son of perdition.**

Here it is. Who what? **Who opposeth and exalteth himself above all that is called God, or that is worshipped; so that as God sitteth in the temple of God, shewing himself that he is God** (verses 3-4). Now this is what is going to happen in the middle of the week [middle of the Tribulation period] with the Jewish nation. They thought that Christ was an impostor but when the Antichrist goes up and proclaims himself *Messiah,* they're going to realize he's the Antichrist and they killed their true Messiah, the Christ. They're yearning for him now. Their long awaited Messiah they're going to realize he's really the Antichrist when he goes up into the temple, not to proclaim himself the Son of God but Lord God almighty! Then they're going to realize that Jesus was really their master. They're going to realize Jesus is the one He is really their Messiah. They're going to realize as a nation, for the very first time, they really did kill their redeemer. There has never been a people on the earth like the Jewish people who have rejected Jesus Christ. But you know who's running second? The Gentiles that He grafted in. **Thou wilt say then, The branches were broken off, that I might be graffed in** (Romans 11:19). The Antichrist one day will do the very thing; he will sit in the temple and declare himself not to be the Son of God but God. The world stage is being set for the appearance of the Antichrist right after the coming of the Lord. And the coming of the Lord is nigh and it's at hand that's thus saith the Lord from what I'm reading here. It has been foretold in the Word of God, a prophecy one hundred percent accurate, that when the Antichrist appears he will make a covenant with the Jews. The Antichrist's covenant with the Jews will last for seven years. But in the middle of the seven years [middle of the week]; the prophet Daniel lets us know the covenant will be broken. The eyes of the Jewish people will be opened at last to the truth that the man that they thought to be their long awaited Messiah is really the Antichrist. Just think about that it's going to be something else. What's going to alert them that he's not their Messiah? The Antichrist acts of setting himself up in the temple of

God in Jerusalem proclaiming himself to be God; even now the spirit of the Antichrist is at work throughout the earth. It's something to think about isn't it? Laying the groundwork for his cruel takeover in the Tribulation period; Jesus let us know in John 5:43 **I am come in my Father's name, and ye** (what)? **receive me not: if another shall come in his own name, him ye will receive.** Now when the Rapture takes place and the Antichrist comes on the scene oh my Lord everybody's going to love him. They're going to think he's just a man of great wonders. But he's the devil's man. You better here me today! Some of you need to be shaken out of your sins! You're playing around with fire, eternal damnation and you'll never get out! You will never get out! Second Thessalonians 2:6-7 say, **And now ye know what withholdeth that he might be revealed in his time. For the mystery of iniquity doth already work: only he who now letteth will let, until he be taken out of the way.** This refers to the Holy Spirit who is holding back the Antichrist's all out takeover; who at the Rapture of the Bride of Christ, will leave with the Bride from the earth.

MANIFESTATIONS EVERYWHERE!

Although the Holy Spirit is now keeping the Antichrist from making his appearance, we see the manifestations of him, and his works everywhere. We see the manifestations of the Antichrist everywhere. We have black on black crime here in Chicago; we have *black on black* crime all around the world. We sit through our history lessons and we hear about being enslaved. Well what's our excuse? We're supposed to be lifting each other up. We're supposed to be supporting one another and it's *black on black* crime. We need to stop talking about slavery and emancipation. We need to rise up! We need to lift up a standard! A whole generation is being annihilated right in front of our eyes! It's the spirit of the Antichrist. Those murdering devils, they're going all around the world; they're going through families, fathers killing their daughters, and husbands killing their wives. It's the spirit of the Antichrist! Lust, sexual devils just have to rape and rape. They won't even be relaxed until they make the person they've possessed rape. That porn devil -- that's that pornography devil, you're not satisfied until you're in with the computer! You can't even get any sleep! You need that devil cast out! You need to be free! Pornography will send you straight go to hell! You can't have an addiction and say you are of God because that's saying the blood is not working. The blood will never lose its power. You can't be of God and of the devil at the same time.

IN LOVE, ADDICTIONS

A child of God can't be possessed. A child of God won't have any addictions. Addicted to nicotine; you're not a child of God. If you're addicted to porn, you're not a child of God. The blood of Jesus cures of addictions. If you're addicted to alcohol or drugs you're not a child of God! Demons latched onto the soul of those who are addicted to drugs, alcohol, porn, etc. Jesus said who are you? Remember, he said, "We are Legion for we are many." **But when he saw Jesus afar off, he ran and worshipped him, And cried with a loud voice, and said, What have I to do with thee, Jesus, thou son of the most high God? I adjure thee by God, that thou torment me not. For he said unto him, Come out of the man, thou unclean spirit. And he asked him, What is thy name? And he answered, saying, My name is Legion: for we are many. And he besought him much that he would not send them away out of the country. And all the devils besought him, saying, Send us into the swine, that we may enter into them. And forthwith Jesus gave them leave. And the unclean spirits went out, and entered into the swine: and the herd ran violently down a steep**

place into the sea, (they were about two thousand;) and were choked in the sea (Mark 5:6-10, 12-13)**.** Notice the swine drowned, *not the devils* that bound the man. The Bible says that when the demons were cast out, the man came to his right mind. He didn't light a cigarette, didn't take a drink, didn't go watch porn, and didn't put any drugs in his system. But what did he say when the man was [delivered] in a sober mind? "Lord I want to follow you." That's the devil's man, it's the Antichrist and he's in the world right now.

ALL OUT TAKEOVER

The verse that I just read from Thessalonians refers to the Holy Spirit who is holding back the Antichrist's all out takeover; who at the Rapture of the Bride of Christ will leave with the Bride from the earth. (Speaking of the Holy Spirit). Although the Holy Spirit is keeping the Antichrist from making his appearance, we see the manifestations of the Anti-Spirit everywhere. Second Thessalonians 2:8-10 say, **And then shall that Wicked be revealed, whom the Lord shall consume with the spirt of his mouth, and shall destroy with the brightness of his coming: Even him, whose coming is after the working of Satan with all power and signs and lying wonders, And with all deceivableness of unrighteousness in them that perish; because they received not the love of the truth, that they might be saved.** The Lord, as we have discovered, has great signs and mighty wonders. The devil uses false signs and lying wonders. Lying wonders are common in the occult today. And many are being. We believe that the Antichrist was born in the latter part of 1968; maybe in October.

YOUR HOMEWORK ASSIGNMENT

You need to do some homework with this message. You need to go and go on the internet and find out all you can. Ask the Holy Spirit to help you. The 1960's turned the world upside down. Did you ever watch that movie maybe some of you did; called *Rosemary's Baby*? That was when this lady became impregnated by the devil. She didn't really know how she was penetrated. Do you know how close that was to the birth of the Antichrist? The Antichrist was not born of a virgin; his mother was not a virgin. The Bible says that the Holy Spirit overshadowed Mary and told her that the thing that was in her was conceived by the Holy Ghost. So if Jesus was conceived by a woman, don't you think a woman birthed the Antichrist into the world? *Rosemary's Baby* what was that all about? A lady getting pregnant by the devil; if that wasn't close to the Antichrist's conception I don't know what was. *The Exorcist was* devil-possession right in your very eyes; and if you go on to study it, if you Google *The Exorcist* movie, so many strange things really happened when they were making that movie because the devil was in it one hundred percent! You can't play around with the devil and not be affected because he leaves his mark on you. You can't watch porn and then don't want it. When you are a liar, you think everybody lies. When you cheat, you think everybody's a cheat. When you're living a lie, you think everybody's living in a lie. The devil's man, the Antichrist, the false Christ. I want to challenge you today to read Revelation chapter 6 where the Antichrist bursts on the scene as the rider of peace on a white horse. Now while white is a symbol of peace the devil is going to come with false peace deceiving people. He's going to deceive the Jewish nation.

ONE WEEK – SEVEN YEARS

The Antichrist is going to make a covenant with them for seven years, or for the last week for the seventy weeks of years. Daniel 9:27 says, **And he shall confirm the covenant with many for one week.** So to really understand what I'm talking about as far as the Antichrist, you have to also study the book of Daniel. Don't get frustrated with prophesy, just as for God's direction through the Holy Spirit. Nothing is covered up in this final hour. The Bible is no longer a secret. That's how close we are to the Rapture. God gave Daniel prophecies about our day, gave him prophecies about his day, he gave him prophecies about the Rapture and the Tribulation period. Daniel 9:27 again says, **And he shall confirm the covenant with many for one week.** This is talking about the Antichrist. The Antichrist. The United States of America, they will accept him; and by that I mean they're going to reach out to him. They're going to recognize him to be someone great. The Antichrist will come in splendor. He's going to *have all the answers*. He will appear as a crowned king, not humble like Jesus Christ. Now you have to think about that's one of the major reasons why the Jews didn't accept Jesus Christ; because he didn't come born in a palace but yet He's a king. He is King of Kings and Lord of Lords! Yes, Hallelujah! See, this is going to be one of the reasons why most people are going to accept the Antichrist. Listen to it he's going to be crowned not with the humility of Jesus, but he will show worldly power. The Antichrist will offer everything to Israel she could ever possibly want. They're going to say oh yeah he's the one! Oh yeah he's *our* superman! Oh yeah he's the man we need! He's our man for this hour! But he's going to be the Antichrist. Daniel 11:24 **He shall enter peaceably.** He's going to come on the scene with so much peace. He's going to be sharing everything with everybody. And he's going to be making a way for everybody. There is probably not going to be any unemployment, everybody is going to have jobs, it might be free healthcare, he's going to look out in the kitchen lines making sure everybody is fed. But right in the middle of the Tribulation period he's going to take it all away. He's not any different from any other drug dealer. No he isn't. Doesn't the drug dealer give you some for free? Then when you're hooked he knows you have to come back and pay. You better wake up. Just think when the Antichrist appears on T.V. for the very first time to *tell people who he really is*. He's going to have so much power. If you don't have any God in you or don't have enough God in you, you will bow because his presence will compel you to bow! This is the hour that you've come into. Accept it or reject it. You can be happy about it or you can be mad about it. This is the hour that you were born into and you were not born by mistake.

MISSED OPPORTUNITIES

You came into the kingdom for such an hour as this. You came into this world with an opportunity to serve the true and the living God. You came into this world with an opportunity to serve Jesus the Christ. You came into the world and you can make a difference. It's up to you what you do with your opportunities. But what a great opportunity you have in this final hour to be receiving such truths. If you are a young person, you can keep your virginity until you get married. It doesn't matter what these people say. And people who talk against you, it's because they're spoiled. They're angry and they realize that all the hype about having sex wasn't what they thought. And then they had it all they had left was a venereal disease and a baby on the way. Daddy is gone! Junior is gone making more Junior's! That's what they are mad about. They're mad that every time they see your virtuous self; here you come you're happy, haven't been spoiled, and maybe all they have is their second venereal disease, and all they have is baby daddy drama, baby mama drama. Now keep yourself have something to take on your wedding night. Have something to take on your wedding night, don't be I and out of bed like a dog. Keep yourself together you haven't went crazy yet! And if some of these married people were honest they'll tell you they're crazier now. Right; everything that everybody else is doing is not for you. Find your own way. Find out your own way in life. Find out the plan of God for your life. Find out what he has for you. Stop being a follower and rise up and take the lead! The Bible says in Acts 2:14 there is Peter he use to follow along all the time. But the Bible says he lifted up his voice above the eleven and said hold up my memory is back now. I'm out of the slumber and the sleep I've been in. Yes! These men are not drunk but its prophecy fulfilled prophecy fulfilled! Wake up! Jesus is coming back in your day. You are the Rapture generation. Jesus is going to come back in your day. What are you doing about it? What are you doing about it? What are you doing about? Jesus is going to come back in your day. What are you going to do about it?

DO SOMETHING ABOUT IT...YOUR LIFE

How are you going to change your life? If you don't like the life you have now do something about it! Do something about it while you have a chance. The Bible says again in Daniel 11:24 **He shall enter peaceably even upon the fattest places of the province; and he shall do that which his fathers have not done, nor his fathers' fathers; he shall scatter among them the prey, and spoil and riches.** The Antichrist shall divide the spoil among the people. No other dictator has ever done that. Believing his promises Israel will enter into a covenant with him and be betrayed. Now many people have speculated that maybe Hitler could have been the Antichrist. But he couldn't be the Antichrist because the Antichrist is going to make peace with the children of Israel. The Antichrist is going to share with Israel. Hitler hated them he killed the Jews and a lot of Christians too. Right? The devil's man you need to know who you're fighting against. This spirit has covered the whole world, and you have to decide what you're going to do about your life. What are you going to do with the opportunities given to you? What are you going to do about yourself? You have to get you self together. Jesus went there to raise Lazarus. Do you think he did everything? No! He told Mary and Martha to do what they could. He said move the stone I have the power to give life.

TURN ME LOOSE! THE MASTER IS CALLIN

Free yourself from the bondage of sin. Jesus died so that you could enjoy life more abundantly. You run from that fornicating relationship! No you bust that computer if you can't get rid of the porn! In an adulterous relationship? Get some self-control and God will lift you up! He will raise you up! But you have to let the world know that you mean business! "I'm coming out of this! I'm coming out of this!" You have to let the Lord know that "I'm tired of living like this! I'm tired of snorting cocaine! I'm tired of being a liar! I'm tired of being one way at home and being another way at church! Lord I'm bound but set me free! Loose my shackles and set me free!" You have to tell cocaine dealer, The Master has need of me. Let me go!" You have to tell whoring, fornicating, shaking up, committing adultery, lying, stealing, not paying your tithes, "Loose me! Jesus is calling! Loose me. Jesus is calling! Loose me. Jesus is calling! Let me go! Let me go! The Master is calling me!" Did you not know that's why Jesus had to say "Lazarus?" Everybody who died in Christ would have busted their graves open and said did you call me? They would have been trampling over each other in the street. Jesus called me! Jesus called me! He had to say Lazarus! Because the graves would have burst open and all of the righteous would have come forth and said, he called me and I have to answer! Give the Lord praise in this place. Yes! Yes! You are living beneath your privilege I tell you. God has power I tell you! God is great I tell you! They had John on the island of Patmos and they tried to boil him in oil but the Lord said not so! God has power I'm telling you! Korah and those boys came up against Moses and Aaron, and he opened up the ground, and they went to hell immediately. God has power I'm telling you! He has power to cast your sins into the sea of forgetfulness. He has power to tell the raven to find you something to eat! He has power to be with you when the whole world is against you! He has power to blow air out of his nostrils and make the rain to come, and hoist up an ark and send it in the water! He has power! God has power I'm telling you! Don't underestimate him!

THE YEAR "1968"

The devil's man, the Antichrist; The Antichrist, he's on the earth right now. He was born in the latter part of 1968 as I said before. The world has never been the same since the sixties. We are living in the days like those of Sodom and Gomorrah. Martin Luther King Jr. tried to help the black people and he was shot down in 1968. So many things happened in 1968. The U.S. announced the worst toll of the Vietnam War. In 1968 Robert Kennedy was shot. The Democratic National Convention; ten thousand demonstrators gathered, they had twenty- three thousand police and national guardsman. The *Time* magazine talks about the year of 1968. One of the restaurants where they had just open orgy's was Alice's' restaurant. One good thing that happened in 1968 was that Apollo 7 was launched from Florida for an eleven day journey in Orbit. The flower children came on the scene then. All kind of things started happening in 1968. You can just type the word the word 1968 on the internet and its so many so many things about 1968. But the Antichrist he was born in 1968. And do you remember when Jesus was conceived? And Mary and her cousin Elisabeth she was carrying John the Baptist which was Jesus' cousin; and the Bible let us know that John the Baptist was the forerunner of Jesus the Christ. And John proclaimed to everybody that I must decrease so he must increase. John told the people that I'm baptizing you one way, but when Jesus comes he's going to baptize you with fire and with power. And just like John the Baptist was the forerunner of Jesus Christ, there is a forerunner of the Antichrist, and he is in a high place in the government. And you think that you can face this world alone. If you know anything about Bible prophecy you know Russia is going to kick off the Battle of Armageddon. But our current sitting president turned over our space program to Russia. An act of all out devilment; the devils man the Antichrist the false Christ. And look at you. Where are you going to be? You won't be able to buy one thing; you won't be able to sell. Think about if you take high blood pressure medicine, or think if you have diabetes, and you have to give yourself a shot. In the beginning of the Tribulation Period just think about it for seven years, we're going to be having the marriage supper of the Lamb in heaven. And for seven year's it's going to be the worst time of your life because you yielded to the spirit of the Antichrist it's the devils man. The Bible says in 1st John the 4th chapter verse number 1, **Beloved, believe not every spirit, but try the spirits whether they are of God.** The gospels tell us that many walk, many walk, they walk in the way of Christ but they are not of him. We have to have the Holy Spirit to discern who's really of God and who's not. The devils man the Antichrist the false Christ; the Bible tells us in the gospels it's many Christ'; its people out here actually saying they are Christ. But the Bible tells us don't let them deceive you. Jesus told us in the book of John; Let not your heart be troubled neither let it be afraid. He said I'm going away to prepare a place for you, and if I go away; which we know he did. He said I'm going to come back and receive you unto myself.

Beverly Thomas

THE BIBLE IS RIGHT

Let your heart take joy today as you listen to this great message from heaven itself; the devils man the Antichrist the false Christ. Neighbor I hope you were blessed today. Don't let anybody deceive you; not companion, or children, don't let man, or woman, don't let the devil himself deceive you. The Bible is right and everybody else is wrong. The Bible says let God be true and every man a liar. Jesus will come back in your day. The world is in such a horrible shape. Do not think that these calamities and these tragedies that are happening, neighbor they are al not coincidental. But the Lord is allowing some of these things to happen to wake his people up. The Lord knows what a state it's going to be for people who are left. Neighbor get yourself together and I want to pray with you now.

The Sinner's Prayer:

Oh God! Oh God! Oh God! Please help me! Please forgive me for sinning against you. But I have come home never to leave you again. Oh Lord I know there are many false Christ'. Oh Lord I know the Antichrist is in the world now, and if he's in the world now I know my only way out is to make it to Rapture ground; is to make it to Rapture ground. And by faith in the blood save my soul! Save my soul! Wash me in your blood! Cleanse me and make me whole! Save my soul! Save my soul! Come on in Jesus! And if you meant that neighbor He is there. Stay with God and He will stay with you. Are you ready? Let's go!

NOTES

DJG

NOTES

NOTES

DJG

NOTES

DJG

PART 5

EXTRA CREDIT

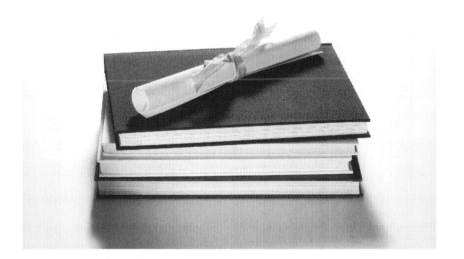

CHAPTER 13

FROM HARLOT TO BRIDE

From Harlot to Bride. I have a couple of definitions for you. **Adulterer**[24] *is a man or woman who has voluntary intercourse between a married person with other than his or her lawful spouse.* Write down the word, "**idolatry.**[25]" *It is the religious worship of idols. Excessive or blind adoration, reverence or devotion.* Write down the word, "**proposition.**[26]" *It is a plan or scheme proposed. The act of offering or suggesting something to be considered, accepted, adopted, or ordained.* This lesson is going to cover all of our lives. Isn't it so marvelous that we can go to the Word of God and find all we need, including the wonderful stories of redemption? Maybe you have made so many mistakes in your life. Now, the Lord doesn't heal you and fix you and do all these great things for you to *continue in sin.* When the Lord saves you, He empowers you to live free from sin. Why? Because you have to in order to make it to Heaven. Ezekiel 18:4 says, **the soul that sinneth, it shall die.**

SON OF MAN

Ezekiel 16:1-7say **Again the word of the Lord came unto me, saying, Son of man, cause Jerusalem to know her abominations.** The Lord wanted Jerusalem to know just how wicked she had been. Have you ever heard someone tell you a story and the story was about you all the time? Maybe the person telling the story did not

---

[24] Dictionary.com

[25] ibid

[26] ibid

know your past, your situation, or where you had been in your life but as they are telling the story, you thought, "That sounds just like some stupid stuff I did." You would never admit it to them. You simply nodded your head and played along and agreed, "Yes, that sure was stupid what they did." All the time, you are thinking, "I did that same thing." Sometimes things are brought to your attention and because people are so easily seduced and deceived; some do not realize until it is brought right to their face, "That's me."

YOU ARE THE MAN

Do you remember the story of David and the prophet of his day, Nathan? Do you remember David? You know the story. King David, in order to cover up deceit, had a person's righteous husband killed. He then took that lady to be his wife. Deceit, after deceit until the man of God, Nathan, came and confronted David. Nathan came to David with the Word of God. Nathan was God's mouthpiece [prophet] and had influence in David's life. All of these things played a part in David giving an ear to what was being said. Why would Nathan tell him something wrong? The Lord had used Nathan previously to help David to win battles. I am trying to get you to see something. There was the man of God, Nathan, telling David a parable. It was not until Nathan pointed it out to him that David realized the person Nathan had been speaking about was himself. From a different perspective, it always looks like what somebody else's does is bad? You might think, "Why would they do that?" Come on, you have been in that situation. You think, "Why would he do something like that? Or why would he stay with her?" I say, "Why are they staying with you, since you asked the question?" I am just trying to get you to see the point.

THINE OWN EYE

It's easy to see the faults of other but stay blinded to your own defects. **And why beholdest thou the mote that is in thy brother's eye, but considerest not the beam that is in thine own eye? Or how wilt thou say to thy brother, Let me pull out the mote out of thine eye; and, behold, a beam is in thine own eye? Thou hypocrite, first cast out the beam out of thine own eye; and then shalt thou see clearly to cast out the mote out of thy brother's eye** (Matthew 7:3-5). When Nathan got to David, he was so fooled. David was thinking, "Who is this person who has done this great evil? He is going to die." But when Nathan told David he [David] was the one that is what opened up his eyes. David was a king so he had knowledge. God delivered that message right on his front porch. David, he had to humble himself. From harlot to bride.

TELL THEM BOY!

The Lord told Ezekiel to go down and tell His people about their abominations. Ezekiel was changed with "warning" people about who God is! **Son of man, I have made thee a watchman unto the house of Israel: therefore hear the word at my mouth, and give them warning from me. When I say unto the wicked, Thou shalt surely die; and thou givest him not warning, nor speakest to warn the wicked from his wicked way, to save his life; the same wicked man shall die in his iniquity; but his blood will I require at thine hand. Yet if thou warn the wicked, and he turn not from his wickedness, nor from his wicked way, he shall die in his iniquity; but thou delivered thy soul. Again, When a righteous man doth turn from his righteousness, and commit iniquity, and I lay a stumblingblock before him, he shall die: because thou hast not given him warning, he shall die in his sin, and his**

righteousness which he hath done shall not be remembered; but his blood will I require at thine hand (Ezekiel 3:17-20)**.**

We are not talking about strangers here. We are not talking about people who did not know about the goodness and the righteousness and the mercy of God. The Lord told Ezekiel to go and tell the people, who had been kept by the Lord all this time, how they had violated against Him. The Lord wanted them to know their abominations. This is a great example of when people continue doing wrong for so long that now they believe it is right. **And for this cause God shall send them strong delusion, that they should believe a lie: That they all might be damned who believed not the truth, but had pleasure in unrighteousness** (2 Thessalonians 2:11-12)**.** When you are finally presented with the truth, because your heart is in a place where you can accept it, you feel so ashamed. In that shame is your road to recovery – your road to reconciliation.

NONE EY PITIED THEE

And say, Thus saith the Lord God unto Jerusalem; Thy birth and thy nativity is of the land of Canaan; thy father was an Amorite, and thy mother a Hittite. And as for thy nativity, in the day thou wast born thy navel was not cut, neither wast thou washed in water to supple thee; thou wast not salted at all, nor swaddled at all. None eye pitied thee, to do any of these unto thee, to have compassion upon thee; but thou wast cast out in the open field. This is just as a baby who is thrown away or aborted. **To the loathing of thy person, in the day that thou wast born. And when I passed by thee, and saw thee polluted in thine own blood, I said unto thee when thou wast in thy own blood, Live; yea, I said unto thee when thou wast in thy blood, Live** (Ezekiel 16:3-6)**.**

DIFFERENT VIEWS

There are many writers who have different analysis on Ezekiel 16th chapter, but I like what this author says. When Jerusalem was born the Lord took care of them. The great Jerusalem. The Lord told Ezekiel to speak to the people in Jerusalem. He had to show them how bad they had been. This chapter is about Jerusalem but it includes Judah as well. Ezekiel writes about its history, so he knew how bad it had been. The one thing I really like about the Lord is that He is so patient and long suffering. He tries to get people to see themselves or "auto-correct." You may ask, "What is auto-correct?" It is when you hear the Word of the Lord and you recognize yourself. You then go humbly before God and work all things out with Him. People are so easily deceived about themselves. Have you ever have been in the midst of some folks and just can't see the point and you wonder why? The only thing you can finally say is, "They can't see it." My hope in preaching the Gospel is that I can preach to people in the simplicity of Jesus so that they will see and say, "Man that is me." How glorious it is to discover something wrong about yourself? In this instance, you feel like no one had to tell you that. However, that does not mean they couldn't tell you. I pray that people will auto-correct themselves.

POINT BLANK

The Bible teaches us first warning and then destruction. Oh, when God lays His hand on you. Some of you the Lord will tell you point blank stop doing this and stop saying that. You might even be out with your friends. In which, you should not be out socializing with worldly people anyway. People who are full of sin and you are trying to live for the Lord. That power will overtake you. You will be right back in the muck and the mire. A little prick or little sensation, something will happen in your heart and in your mind, in your thought process. Something in your mind or your heart lets you know that a connection has been made and you think, "I shouldn't be here." Ezekiel he showed how bad it has been. Jerusalem is like a wife who has not be loyal to her husband. You know neighbor, if I could just say anything about counseling today, one of the hardest things for couple to endure and overcome is unfaithfulness. It is one of the hardest trust to regain but it can be done.

A PROSTITUTE

In Ezekiel 16, we find out that the Lord is depicting the sins of Jerusalem. The Lord is depicting how bad they have fallen by comparing them to a prostitute. I do not know where you live neighbor, but where I live they are up early. Sometimes they might come across one-time wonders. But, many of them are clientele. The Lord compares Jerusalem to a wife who has been unfaithful to her husband. Why would you marry a person you can't trust? Think about that today. Why marry a person that you have to follow around? You have to drive and see where they have been? When your companion arrives at home, you feel the need to check their cell phone? Now think about the great God of the Universe having to endure such a thing from a people who call themselves children of God. The accusation from God was that His people, had gone after foreign Gods. The Amorites and the Hittites were general names for the people of Canaan before the time of Abraham. These people built the city that later became Jerusalem. They lived in a country that became Judah. At first, the Israelites were weak and few in number. They had no strength and they could not defend themselves. The picture in words were as if they were a weak baby. That baby depends on the mother for everything. If you are a skillful mom, you can tell the difference in the cries. When it is an "I need my diaper changed cry, or I need something to eat cry. Or a sick cry." You recognize the difference in those cries. The Lord here is doing such a profound job in bringing us from the beginning all the way up to this point so that we will understand how the people came to such degradation. Sometimes you have to take a little time with yourself and the Lord, not with me, but between you and your Lord. If you are in a pitfall, you should ask the Lord to show you how and when this all started in your life. Ask Him when the very first particle of deceit regarding a certain matter appeared in your mind. From harlot to bride. It's deceitful to think you can make a person love you. Neighbor, you should not marry anyone outside your faith. You will be asking for trouble. You should not marry before talking about sex, money and your beliefs. Yes, before you get married, you must talk about if you are going to have children or not, especially in the very serious times that we now find ourselves. These are the things which married couples fight about. Money, sex and what God. If you are devoted to your church, and it's a good church or ministry, you have got to get that settled.

WE GETTING MARRIED

When I marry couples here in the ministry, I want to know certain things up front. A good example is my sister-in-law, who married a man who came from the mountains [Colorado]. I told him that she was not leaving the ministry. I said, "You can stay here with her, but she is not going to Colorado to the mountains." You know I thank the God of heaven that they are both still here today. He is here today. I reasoned with him and said, "You can marry her on one condition; she can't leave this church." And of course, I could not have said that if that was not her desire. I would not overruled what she wanted. Some people, when they get married, lose their minds. They let their mate talk them right out of church. Count on it. I've seen it over and over again. They let them talk them out of the ministry. That new husband or wife will talk and talk and then they are gone. This is important. The Lord wants people to understand

Him and how He works. The Lord knows all about you. It is just something to think about. The Children of Israel had no strength. They could not defend themselves. This is sort of like the picture of a weak baby. Nobody wanted that baby. In other words, the other people in the country hated them. They were in a country, just a few of them, and they were hated by those people. The custom in those days were to wash the new baby. The nurse would cut the umbilical cord. She would wipe the little one with salt and oil. Then she would wrap it and cloth it. She would repeat these steps until the baby was forty days old. But if the parents did not want the child, they would leave it at birth. They would not wash it. They would not clean it. They would not handle it or care for it. They would not cut the umbilical cord. They would throw it out into the field. Because they would neglect the baby, it would soon die. Jerusalem was like a baby that nobody wanted and nobody cared about. I know I can attest to that.

LIVE

Ezekiel 16:6 says, **And when I passed by thee, and saw thee polluted in thine own blood, I said unto thee when thou wast in thy blood, Live.** He says when you were in sin, degradation, pornography, homosexuality, angry, mean, hatred, variance, emulations, wrath; He said I spoke these words to you. **Live; yea, I said unto thee when thou wast in thy blood, Live. I have caused thee to multiply as the bud of the field, and thou hast increased** (Now He is building you up. Can you see it?) **and waxen great, and thou art to come excellent ornaments: thy breasts are fashioned, and thine hair is grown, whereas thou wast naked and bare** (Ezekiel 16:6-7)**.** So the Lord is talking about a lady who is no longer a bride. But, now she is becoming mature. Her breast has developed. Her hair is growing; whereas before she had no hair.

Now she is coming of age. But, it is because the Lord did it. The lady is growing and becoming beautiful because God did it. **Now when I passed by thee, and looked upon thee, behold thy time was the time of love; and I spread my skirt over thee, and covered thy nakedness; yea, I sware unto thee, and entered into a covenant with thee, saith the Lord God, and thou becamest mine** (Ezekiel 16:8). "It was just Me and you," the Lord said to us. "We left the world outside. It was Me loving you and you loving Me. You are all mines and I am yours." Our hearts melted with joy when we discovered the love we have been searching for. It was the Christ.

DOWN AT HIS FEET

The Book of Ruth, the third chapter has a wonderful example. Ruth was there and Naomi had given her some very important instructions regarding a great man. Naomi told Ruth to go in quietly and don't tell anyone where you are going. Because she was in such a situation, Naomi told her to lie down on the floor at his feet. Similarly, when you were tired, weary and the world had used you up and beat you down, you had no trouble praying. You had no trouble calling on God. Nobody would listen to you. I am talking about even your kids. You know the one that you have birth to. Nobody wanted to hear you. Your only hope was God. Naomi told Ruth to lay down quietly down at his feet, not loud and boisterous or voicing your opinion about things. She told her to study his likes and if he approved, he will take his skirt and lay it over you. The Bible tells in Ruth 3:8-9, **And it came to pass at midnight, that the man was afraid, and turned himself: and behold, a woman lay at his feet. And he said, Who art thou? And she answered, I am Ruth thine hand maid: spread therefore thy skirt over thine handmaid; for thou art a near kinsman**.

COVERED THY NAKEDNESS

Ezekiel 16:8 says, **And I spread my skirt over thee, and covered thy nakedness: yea, I sware unto thee, and entered into a covenant with thee.** The Christian jubilee has that covenant. Jesus bought each and every one of us with His blood. We are His. We are bound to Him with a blood covenant. **Ye are bought with a price; be not ye the servants of men** (1 Corinthians 7:23)**. What? Know ye not that your body is the temple of the Holy ghost which is in you, which ye have of God, and ye are not your own? For ye are bought with a price: therefore glorify god in your body, and in your spirit, which are God's** (1 Corinthians 6:19-20)**.** Just like a man and a woman who are married. They have entered a covenant. Now, if either party goes outside of that covenant. Whether it is with the same sex or opposite sex, and play some sex games, then the covenant is broken; *upstairs or downstairs*, the covenant will be broken. It is just like when you go outside of the will of the Lord and willfully sin, that covenant does not exist anymore – the blood is no longer on your soul. There is no such thing as "Once saved always saved." Oh, No! Neighbor that is doctrine of devils. Again he said, **And I spread my skirt over thee, and covered thy nakedness: yea, I sware unto thee.** Think about that for a moment. The Lord made an oath unto us**. And entered into a covenant with thee, saith the Lord God, and thou becamest mine. Then washed I thee with water** (Ezekiel 16:8-9)**.** Now see who is doing all the cleaning up. Notice this He said then I washed thee. You did not do it yourself. I will challenge you to underline this in your Bible if your Bible is a workbook. **Then washed I thee with water; yea, I thoroughly washed away thy blood from thee, and I anointed thee with oil.** All these things that they did according to the old testament for a baby; He said He did that for you. Ezekiel 16:10 says, **I clothed thee also with broidered work, and shod thee**

with badgers' skin, and I girded thee about with fine linen, and I covered thee with silk. I like this next verse. *I decked thee out*!

I DECKED THEE WITH ORNAMENTS

Ezekiel 16:11-13 say, **I decked thee also with ornaments, and I put bracelets upon thine hands, and a chain on thy neck. I put a jewel on thy forehead, and earrings in thine ears, and a beautiful crown upon thine head. Thus wast thou decked with gold and silver.** You were nothing when you started out; from harlot to bride. You were nothing when you started out. You were running around in the dark, up all night and you could not sleep. The thing about sin is you can never satisfy sin. It challenges you to go into deeper sin. So, when you reach a plateau, you go a little deeper. Then you reach a plateau and you go deeper into you fill yourself or someone fills you...for the moment. Sin is insatiable. *You will never satisfy it!* You cannot be satisfied. Sin was not created to be satisfying. But, it was created to continue to be lusted after. Did you know that? Only the Blood of Jesus can cure that! Yes! Notice this, in Ezekiel 16:13 **Thus was thy decked with gold and silver; and they raiment was of fine linen and silk, and broidered work**. The Lord did not just put us together any kind of way. Those of you who are saved, the Lord washed you and saved you from *all* sin. Our Lord has cleared up your skin, smoothed out your skin. He has healed you from some diseases and restored your memory. What a mighty God. He has brought your wife back and your wayward children. Now your children are looking at you right instead of cockeyed. Now you can have peaceful family dinners. The Lord is now allowed to prepare a table before you in the presence of your enemies. Even when you are at work, people are acting up but, they do not bother you anymore. He has made your enemies be at peace with you. Our great God has covered your head. What a work He has done in your life! Christ has brought you back to life. From a harlot to bride. Hallelujah!

EXCEEDING BEAUTIFUL

Thou didst eat fine flour, and honey, and oil: and thou wast exceeding beautiful (What made you beautiful? Lowliness, meekness, kindness, and humility.) **and thou didst prosper into a kingdom** (Ezekiel 16:13). Uh-Oh! People cannot handle prosperity. **And thy renown went forth among the heathen for thy beauty** (verse 14). People were amazed. People were amazed at how they could look and stay looking so young. They questioned, "How can you look so young?" They wondered, "Have you found the fountain of youth?" They may have commented, "You look so marvelous. Have you and your husband just gotten married?" In reality, you have the Lord's love guiding you and leading you. You have made His will your compass. People recognize when you are happy. They recognize when you have something going on with you. They may not say it. They may not point it out to you. People recognize harmony. They recognize unity. They recognize love. They recognize contentment. They recognize a beautiful woman; not a whorish woman. You do not need to recognize her because she is all out; she wants to be noticed. She showing off her "product." What a wonderful looking woman who has her chest covered; she dresses in moderation. Don't you know she gets more attention than a whore; who walks down the street prostituting herself with her breast exposed? Again Ezekiel 16:14 says, **And thy renown went forth among the heathen for thy beauty: for it was perfect through my comeliness, which I had put upon thee, saith the Lord God.** He says here, "You wanted to die, but I just wouldn't let you. You were on edge, but I pulled you back by My power of redemption. You wanted to give up, but I wouldn't let you give up." That is something to thank God for. Feel free to bow your head in thanks.

THE CHILD GREW UP

The author says that the Lord passed by the baby that would soon die. However, the Lord would not let the baby die. He rescued the child from certain death and gave it life. The child grew up and it was like a beautiful woman. Remember, we are talking about Jerusalem. But, she did not dress as a woman should. This article says the Israelites went to Egypt and there were not many of them. In Egypt, they increased in number. They were slaves there. They did not have the wealth or clothing that a young nation ought to have. The Lord saw that young woman was raised to be married. He spread a coat over the young woman which was a custom that held a special meaning. This was how a man proposed marriage to a woman. As in a marriage, the Lord made promises to Israel and Israel made promises to the Lord. Did you know this is where the marriage vows came from? It is a promise. They are making a promise to one another that is supposed to last them *in sickness and in health -- until death do us apart*. It is supposed to be the same way between you and the Lord. Same way between me and my Savior; and you and your Savior. It should be that covenant that nothing can break it not even death. If we live or if we die, we are the Lord's. Romans 14:7-8 says, **For none of us liveth to himself, and no man dieth to himself. For whether we live, we live unto the Lord; and whether we die, we die unto the Lord: whether we live therefore, or die, we are the Lord's.**

THE LORD RESCUED ISRAEL

Israel became special to the Lord. The Lord rescued Israel from Egypt. The Lord brought Israel through the water of the Red Sea. He gave the laws to Israel at the mount called Mount Sinai. Israel promised to obey the Lord and to worship Him only. Israel promised to obey the Lord. Israel, they promised. Isn't that what you did, those of you who have the Blood of Jesus on your soul? You said, "Lord, save my soul! Lord, save my soul! Lord, I believe thou art the Son of the living God. Lord, if you get me out of this, I will serve you. Lord, if you bring my husband back, I will serve you." You made a promise. You entered into a covenant relationship.

IF THOU WILL

And Jephthah vowed a vow unto the Lord, and said, If thou shall without fail deliver the children of Ammon into mine hands, Then it shall be, that whatsoever cometh forth of the doors of my house to meet me, when I return in peace from the children of Ammon, shall surely be the Lord's and I will offer it up for a burnt offering (Judges 11:30). The Lord honored Jephthah's vow and granted him a great victory. **And Jephthah came to Maspeth unto his house, and, behold, his daughter came out to meet him with timbrels and with dances: and she was his only child; beside her had neither son nor daughter. And it came to pass, when he saw her, that he rent his clothes, and said, Alas, my daughter! Thou hast brought me very low, and thou art one of them that trouble me: for I have opened my mouth unto the Lord, and I cannot go back** (verses 34-35). Jephthah had to keep his word and he did. The Bible teaches us that it is better not to make a promise than to make a promise to God and not keep it. Some of you have made promises to God that you have not kept. You have got to get that right. You promised that you would serve Him with your whole heart, soul and mind. You promised that if He gave you a good job you would be faithful in giving to His work. You have got to work it all out with God. You have got to work it out. Some of you cannot get your healing; the power of God will come upon you but God's hands are tied because you have not kept your word. Then you will go back to your old ways of cursing and hanging out and doing stuff that is wrong. People will be surprised at what keeps God from moving for them. So many tie the hands of God on a daily basis. Don't tie His hands in this final hour. There is much to do and you need His help for so much. Psalm 121:4 says, **Behold, he that keepeth Israel shall neither slumber nor sleep.** He is not on a sabbatical and our God is not taking a nap. Where would I be if He was on a nap when I was sick or when my dear mother was dying, those last few minutes? Where would I be if He was on sabbatical or away in another country when my baby boy was killed but He was with me and I praise Him for it. This is rich.

THE RED SEA

The Lord rescued Israel from Egypt. The Lord brought Israel through the water of the Red Sea. He gave the laws to Israel at the mount called Mount Sinai. Israel promised to obey Him and to worship Him. God led Israel to the Promised Land just like He promised. The Lord made Israel wealthy. A rich man gives gifts to his wife. Well, I know they use to. In present times, they are getting all the *goodies* before they marry; the man doesn't have much to wait for these days. The girl or young lady gives it right up so what does the husband-to-be need to prepare for or wait for? They no longer have to give the woman diamonds. They are getting the cubic zirconia. They have *tested* the products; tried them out. They believe they have to see, feel and touch what they are getting. What a mess. **But every man is tempted, when he is drawn away of his own lust, and enticed. Then when lust hath conceived, it bringeth forth sin: and sin, when it is finished, bringeth forth death. Do not err, my beloved brethren** (James 1:14-16). **For all that is in the world, the lust of the flesh, and the lust of the eyes, and the pride of life, is not of the Father, but is of the world** (I John 2:16). That's plain my brothers and sisters.

A RICH MAN GIVES MANY GIFTS

Again, a rich man gives so many gifts to his wife. In older times, they use to bring a dowry, money to the bride's family as they asked the father for the lady's hand in marriage. Some of these father's nowadays, when a man wants to come and marry the daughter, they are saying "Take them. Can I give you something?" Then people wonder why so many marriages are in the condition they are in today. So, the Lord was kind to Israel more than He was to any other nation. This shows the kindness and the love of God for Israel. Israel became a great nation in 1948 because the Lord made Israel great. Similarly, I am who I am today because of God's greatness in my life.

TWICE DELIVERED

Twice I had cancer. I had cancer once in my left breast. The pain was excruciating. When I would touch my breast liquid would ooze out. When I laid on something that pain would wake me up during the night. The last time, I had cancer; it was hard for me to walk. I had pain in my hip that radiated all the way down to my feet. I didn't know where it was coming from. I was diagnosed that I had a mass in my body that was the size of a quarter but no worries. God gave me a great miracle both times and I still carry His miracles in by body today. Not to mention all of the other great miracles, God has done for me. He has made me great. He has kept me. Neighbor, when there was no "keeping in me." When I was already down so low, I might have just given up. I was almost on the edge of giving up, but His great of hand of love came and pulled me back. He kept me when my son was suddenly shot down. Neighbor, if you have ever been through a sudden death, if God don't help you; you won't make it. I do not care what people say, it's a lie. Things never get better. But as Paul said that the Lord said to him, God's grace is sufficient. 2 Corinthians 12:9 **And he said unto me, My grace is**

sufficient for thee: for my strength is made perfect weakness.
He has kept me up until this appointed time. And neighbor, I was
the woman at the well, I was looking for love in all the wrong places.
It was because I was molested as a child, as a young teenage girl.
You know that molestation will manifest into depression. Then I had
chronic depression. I would have to go to the hospital. This was way
before clinics and mental health clinics and before people would
talk about it openly. I was in my own hell, with my own tunnel; with
my own rock pulled over me. But, because Jesus came out of the
grave. I was able to come out of the grave. Yes! Let's praise the Lord!
Give Him honor and glory!

CHAPTER 14

CAN ANYTHING GOOD
COME OUT OF NAZARETH?

I want you to clear your mind and let the Lord really bless you through this chapter. Can anything good come out of Nazareth?

BEHOLD THE LAMB OF GOD!

John 1:35-37 say, **Again the next day after John stood, and two of his disciples; And looking upon Jesus as he walked, he saith, Behold the Lamb of God! And the two disciples heard him speak, and they followed Jesus.** John was there. John had disciples but when Jesus came on the scene, you see when John announced Jesus, his [John's] disciples left being him and took up and became the disciples of Jesus Christ. It says in verse 38, **Then Jesus turns, and saw them following, and saith unto them, What seek ye?** Why are you following Me? What do you want? What is it about me? What do you know about Me at this point? Why are you following me? What is it? What is it about Me? Have you heared anything about me? Have you witnessed any of my miracles? Why are you following me? **They said unto him, Rabbi, (which is to say, being interpreted, Master,) where dwellest thou?** Where do you stay? Where do you hang out? Where do you live? He simply said unto them like He's saying to you today,

COME AND SEE

Come and see. So many times you isolate yourself, so many times you hold yourself back from being all that God wants you to be. God can't make you strong unless you will to be strong. God cannot heal you except you want to be healed. He cannot make you the man of your household except you want Him to make you (understand me) the man of your household. The Lord will not over rule your will, not now. I love the way Jesus preaches. He never preached over the people's head where they couldn't understand what He was saying. The Lord didn't use a lot of big words from theology school; He didn't use a lot of metaphors. He preached in such simplicity and was so plain because He wanted them to understand and to accept what He was saying. **Come and see.** That's what He's asking you to do today is to **come and see**. But in order for you to come and see that means you have to be bold enough, you have to be strong enough, you have to be hungry enough, you have to be sick and tired of being sick and tired enough to come and see what He has to offer you. Now we're talking about how your mama treated you, or how your daddy treated you. We're talking about how you hold yourself back. You let men say who you are, you let women say who you are, and you let your job dictate your possibilities. But Jesus is saying today **come and see.** Verse 39 again says, **They came and saw where he dwelt,** (they were following him) **and abode with him that day: for it was about the tenth hour. One of the two which heard John speak, and followed him, was Andrew, Simon Peter's brother. He first findeth his own brother Simon, and saith unto him, We have found the Messias.** Now when you find Christ, when you really find Him, you will let a whole lot of other stuff go!

A TEMPORARY FIX

A lot of things that is happening in your life is just a temporary fix *but you have a problem*! People get drunk, they go clubbing, but the next day not only do you have a hangover but *you still have the same problem.* You abuse your body; doing all kind of different things, different drugs, abusing your in so many ways. You hold on to anger, you hold on to pity, you hold on to regret! You are your own hindrance. The Lord is challenging you today to come and see what He is about. Can anything good come out of Nazareth? Nazareth is where you are at right now, Nazareth is where you lay your head at night. Nazareth is your crib. Nazareth is your mind. Nazareth is your physical being. Nazareth is the way you think about yourself. Can anything good come out of it? He's asking you today. The Lord is challenging you today to probe inside your own life. You're hindering yourself when there is power in the blood to make you strong. There's power in the blood to heal you. God can do for you what no other god can do! And if there is another god His word says, show Me; bring Him to me! But you won't find another one! Yes! It says **we found him being interpreted**, verse 41 **the Christ. And he brought him to Jesus. And when Jesus beheld him, he said, Thou art Simon the son of Jona: thou shalt be called Cephas, which is by interpretation, A stone.** Now notice that when they brought Peter to Jesus, Jesus knew all about Him. Jesus knows all about you. Peter came to Jesus, he proclaimed who He was. **Which is by interpretation, A stone;** verse 43 **The day following Jesus would go forth into Galilee, and findeth Philip, and saith unto him, Follow me. Now Phillip was of Bethsaida, the city of Andrew and Peter. Philip findeth Nathanael.** Each one can reach one! They had some history with one another, they had some rapport with one another, and they had some past with one another. When they met Jesus they wanted other people to have the same experience.

SPREAD THE WORD

When you find something good don't you tell people about it? Don't you want others to be blessed when you're blessed? When you find a way out of your problems, when the Lord blesses you in your body and your mind, don't you wish that for somebody else? If not, you should. Maybe your son was lost out in the world and finally he comes to himself. Don't you want to go and encourage another mother that's been sitting on that same bench crying like you were? You say, "Girl my son came back home. Surely if my son came back, yours can come back. There's still hope! It says **Philip findeth Nathanael,** (in verse 45) **and saith unto him.** Now if your Bible is a workbook, My Bible is a workbook. I underline, I have highlights, I look up words, I have numbers, I have phrases, and I'm hooking them up. Isn't that conjunction function? I'm hooking up phrases and making them work right. So I'm underlining stuff because this is my workbook this is what's going to get me through life. And if I mark it up where I can't see different things, I just go and buy me another one. This is my workbook. This is my reference manual. I depend on it deeply. This book helps me today so I can live tomorrow.

WE HAVE FOUND HIM – THE CHRIST

We have found him, of whom Moses in the law, and the prophets, did write, Jesus of Nazareth, the son of Joseph (John 1:45)**.** This is a magnificent verse! He found Nathanael. Philip is telling Nathanael something that he already knows about. He is reciting in the ears of Nathanael, "You know how we came up. We came up through the law. We came up studying about the books of Moses, we had the prophets, and the book of Moses, the law, the prophets they told us Jesus the son of Joseph would come and now we have found Him! You've heard about Jesus that He can make you new. You've heard about Him; that He can put your life back together again! You've heard of him no matter how low you are you can't be too low for him not reach down and help you! He's telling them that we have found this Christ that our fathers and our forefathers, and our father's fathers told us all about! In our lifetime, we have found the Christ!" And I bring you Jesus that same Christ today. Yes! **And Nathanael said unto him,** Who knows what he was thinking about. What could have possibly been on his mind? Had he been disappointed maybe by the Pharisees and the Sadducees which were church folks? Could he have put his trust in men? Could he have put his trust in some false prophet who said that everything was going to be all right, but everything was anything but all right? But notice Nathanael's spirit. Notice how he was feeling when he heard we have found the Christ. How many times did Nathanael hear the same old story about Christ but it wasn't the real thing?

YEAH, I HEARD THAT BEFORE?

How many times has somebody told you they loved you but they really didn't love you? How many times have people told you I'm going to stand by you but they didn't do that? And so Nathanael is a little apprehensive and somewhat perplexed. And he's saying here out loudly can any good thing come out of Nazareth? Nathanael was saying we've heard all the stories that a Deliverer would come. We've heard about a Christ that can heal me of cancer. We have heard that in the state that I am in, He can give me back my right mind; that I can be sober-minded again; that I can reason, that He can bring my husband back, that He can bring my wife back! And so, Nathanael was saying yeah I heard all of that! But can anything really good come out of Nazareth?

THEORIES

You're living on the theories, and the histories, and what people have said about you. You'll never be any good, you'll never do anything, you're down and you'll always be down. You're stupid you're ignorant, you'll never rise up! But they had the same spirit Nathanael had. But notice this Jesus didn't scold him. He met Nathanael right where he was because Nathanael was *sincere*. How many times have you been looking for the right answer and it just ended up being wrong? How many times have you confided in somebody and the first thing they said was I'm not going to tell anybody? They couldn't wait to get out of your sight to tell people your business. How many times have you confided in a brother -- you just wanted some strength about a situation that was going on in your marriage – just a man opening to another human being. That vulnerability and I'm not talking about homosexuality. But I'm talking about vulnerability. "I love my wife but I need some help. You are married, what did you do in the same situation? Man I just need to talk to somebody. I know its other men going through, I know its other women, I know there are other mothers, I know there are other people that have come to Christ but lack the knowledge and power to succeed. I just need somebody to identify with!" So many people are phony.

BLOODLESS. BLOODLESS. BLOODLESS

Many of our churches have failed to show people the correct way to serve God; that holiness is a way of life, not a denomination. They preach a gospel that is bloodless. The Bible doesn't support the teachings. The Bible is not a pedestal for the holding of their word. They preach a bloodless gospel when they say you cannot be made new. They preach a bloodless gospel when they say you cannot live free from sin when the Bible declares you must. It's a commandment. They preach a bloodless gospel when they say you can't come out of addictions. They preach a bloodless gospel but I invite you today come and see. **Philip saith unto him, Come and see.** Bring all your apprehension, bring all your doubt, bring your fears, bring your past failures, and bring how people have treated you in the past. But **come and see**! I know you've been hurt, I know you've been cast down, I know people have treated you bad, but still come and see! Be open-minded, think outside the box! Come on. Try.

WHAT DO YOU HAVE TO LOSE

People have said that you're not going to rise again but just come and see! You're not going to make it, you've been in that situation for so long; and you know that once you have been down for so long you get use to anything. You just get used to being a floor mat, you get used to being the back of somebody instead of the front, and you get used to being in the back instead of being a leader. You get used to following, you get used to accepting non name brand stuff but name brand items are available to you. Just come and see! You settle when the naysayers ask, "Can anything good come out of Nazareth?" You are not going to ever change; nothing good is going to happen for you. You're doing what you're doing now and you made your bed lie in it! But they have a bed and they're still laying in it. People are liars. They only tell you what it is they want you to know. People are just people. You need a power that's stronger than yourself. You need somebody who has had experience in what you are trying to deal with. You need somebody who knows what it's like to be betrayed. It says that when Jesus was on the cross, all the disciples fled even though John *the beloved* came back. Every man left Him.

HE KNOWS

You need somebody who understands you. Jesus knows about that. One week He was going in and they were throwing psalms down saying, "Hallelujah hail is the king!" The following week they were saying give us a murderer and a thief but kill Jesus! He knows! He knows what you are going through! He knows! He knows! In the one of the Old Testament chapters it talks about Jesus and how when we get to heaven we're going to have glorified bodies, we're not going to have any scars, we're not going to have any bruises. My dear, dear mom who is in heaven today; she had a mastectomy but when I see her again, she's going to be a whole woman! She's going to have perfect health! She's going to have perfect strength! She's not going to have Alzheimer's anymore! She's going to have a crystal clear mind! Yes! She will know me and I know her instantly when I see her. Come and see. Come and see. Come and see. Come and see. What do you have to lose? What do you have to lose? John 1:47 says, **Jesus saw Nathanael coming to him.** Don't you do cross referencing when you're studying the Bible? You should. I want you to write this scripture down. Right next to Jesus saw Nathanael coming to Him.

FROM THE FIRST DAY

Daniel was praying about what was going on in his life. He was fasting. Daniel was on a twenty-one day fast. He was seeking the Lord not about himself but the condition of his people. **Then said he unto me, Fear not, Daniel: for from the first day that thou didst set thine heart to understand and to chasten thyself before thy God** (Daniel 10:12). From the very beginning you started seeking God, and the angel said I have been on my way to see about you. Why not try Christ? Why not try Christ? You call the Lord with your whole heart, soul, and mind and He will be on His way to see about you. He wants you healthy and strong. He wants you to prosper. Can any good thing come out of Nazareth?

JESUS SAW NATHANAEL

Jesus saw Nathanael coming to him, Jesus saw Nathanael coming to him (John 1:47)**.** The Lord sees you. Draw nigh to God and He will draw nigh to you. Resist the devil and he will flee from you! If you call on the name of the Lord you shall you shall be saved! Not might not might shall; but with the mouth confession is made but the heart believes. You just can't say anything out of your mouth. He told us about that in the Old Testament. He said My people they talk about Me with their mouth but their heart is so far away. But when you really have been born again you confess with your mouth something and happens in your heart. You're transformed, you're renewed, and you're not the same old person you used to be. And so even though the naysayers say can any good thing come out of Nazareth? You see the Lord calling you because it says that before Nathanael came to Jesus that Jesus saw him and said, **behold an Israelite indeed in whom is no guile** (verse47)**!** Not looking on your past; The Lord said He will never leave you nor forsake you. He said Lo; I am with you all the way even until the end of the world. Are you so hopeless or you so helpless is life over for you? Are you throwing in the towel? Are you giving up? Keep reading. **Nathanael saith unto him, Whence knowest thou me?** How do you know me? How is it that you have come to know me? **Jesus answered and said unto him, Before that Philip called thee, when thou wast under the fig tree, I saw thee** (verse 48)**.** Underline that *I saw you*! Didn't we just read that in Daniel 10? He said from the first time you called out to God, the first time that you set your heart right, the first time that you chastened yourself *I have been on my way*!

ONE THAT FEARED GOD

A devout man, and one that feared God with all his house, which gave much alms to the people, and prayed to God always (Acts 10:2). Your whole house is in order and the people are not following you because they have to. They're following you because they are in awe that even in the day and time that you are living in that you show such love! Your prayers have come up before the throne as a memorial. Read more about Acts. Cornelius was devout and his whole house followed him as he followed God. Now if you can get your house in order things might turn out a little bit better for you! You get in your place, your wife gets in het place, you get your place, the husband gets in his place, and then you can set your house in order; not because you're going to die but because you're going to finally start living. Some of you all are just existing, you're existing, you're existing, you're existing! You're not happy! You don't have any peace! You don't have any joy! You don't have any love! You dread every other day that comes. You're not looking for tomorrow you're not expecting a miracle! You don't have hope! You're living in pity's valley. Get your house in order! Get your house in order!

THE KING OF ISRAEL

John 1:48-49 say, **I saw thee. Nathanael answered and saith unto him, Rabbi, thou art the Son of God; thou art the King of Israel.** Now you just must pause at this scripture because when you go back to verse 45 when Philip found Nathanael. Nathanael, in his heart and in my mind's eye; again, as I mentioned before Nathanael had to be saying within himself, oh here we go again!

WE HAVE TO LOVE THEM IN

How many people have we had come to this church? We have to love them in! We have to build them up with love they have been so hurt. They have been so rejected and disappointed by other ministries. The pastors, deacons, and the Levites were trying to hit on them. They are trying to find God! The ministry is nothing but a sex pool; they are not talking about nothing but money, money. Now don't get me wrong we need money to run a ministry but we're concerned about souls. We want to present you Christ. Some leaders say that they can heal. nobody can heal! No man can forgive sins! No man can heal! No man can forgive sins! Don't you know that's why they killed Jesus? Because He said He was the Son of God and that He could heal sin and sickness; that he could make alive again, that which people have cast down that He could rebuild and bring back up again! That's why they killed Him because He's the Savior of the world! Yes! So notice this this is magnificent. Nathanael had that hope in his heart but he never saw it in living reality. He heard about the Savior, he heard about being able to change his life, he never saw it! It's one thing to hear about you can live free from sin but have you seen it? It's one thing to hear about oh my God you can be healed of cancer. But have you seen it? Have you seen the manifestations of what people preach about in the church you go to?

SIN = DEATH

They say you can't live free from sin but there's no Bible for it! The soul that sinneth shall die! **Behold, all souls are mine; as the soul of the father, so also the soul of the son is mine: the soul that sinneth, it shall die** (Ezekiel 18:4). There isn't a smoking Christian. There is no such thing as a whoring Christian. it is no Bible for it! It's no Bible for it! There is no Bible for you trying to make it and God not willing to help you, it's no Bible for it! There's no Bible for you leaving the whole wide and Christ not helping you. It's no Bible for it! *He said if you will then I will*. You do the very best job you can and he'll I do the rest. But you have to come clean! So he's asking Nathanael here in verse 50, **Jesus answered and said unto him, Because I said unto thee, I saw thee under the fig tree, believest thou?** Nathanael had a good heart he just hadn't seen him. He heard about the Christ but he never met Him. He knew that it was a potential that he was around but he never saw Him. You have heard people say that they have been healed of cancer. But you haven't ran into anybody, you have heard men talking about they are the man of their homes but in Christ's eyes you haven't seen it! You have heard people talk about the different things that have happened in your life and you have gotten hope in it; but you never saw it! God wants to heal families but you never saw it, and that's why you don't believe it. You never saw it. You never saw it that's why you can't believe it. You've been told so many lies; you're not going to be better just settle the way your life is. You don't have to settle for anything! If you don't like the way your life is do something about it! If you don't like the way things are happening in your life do something about it! But start at that cross; you're not happy why? Start at the cross; the joy of the Lord is your strength. He promised you peace, He promised to build you up, He promised to keep you in your youth, He promised to give you a sober mind and to keep your mind sober! The Bible says that when Moses went up to the mountain to die the Bible says that his mind was still strong! But you haven't seen it. People prophesying over you prophesying lies; a prophet doesn't curse! The Lord doesn't use a cursing person to give out a prophecy. A prophet doesn't go to the boat he doesn't use people like that. A prophet isn't married with a whore in the congregation. He doesn't use people like that; Christ doesn't use homosexuals to perform his great works through. They said Christ was a homosexual so don't you fret. Some people have tendencies but if you don't act it out you're all right. God can help you with that too. We're living in a sin filled world.

A SIN-FILLED WORLD

I have had cancer two times not because I'm a sinner, but because cancer was cursed upon to the world when Adam let us down! But because I love God he healed me not one time but two times of cancer! Yes! Can any good thing come out of Nazareth? Can any good thing come out of your life? Can you change? Can you be new? Can you be different? Can you rise up and come out of that deadened state? Nathanael, he heard about it but he never saw it. What is Jesus telling you? Come and see. Go with me to Jeremiah the 1st chapter. Jeremiah 1:4 says, **Then the word of the Lord came unto me, saying, Before I formed thee in the belly I knew thee; and before thou camest forth out of the womb I sanctified thee, and I ordained thee a prophet unto the nations. Then said I, Ah, Lord God! behold, I cannot speak: for I am a child.** He said don't say to me that you are a child. God wants to use you but you must get in a place where he can use you. He can change your life he can make things better. I was suicidal, taking pills, going to see psychologists, and psychiatrists. But I wanted I willed myself will thou be made whole? I willed myself to be free! I wanted to be free more than I wanted to live, I wanted to be free more than I wanted water, I wanted to be free more than I wanted to eat! I wanted to let the Lord know, Lord if you set my mind free I'll serve you for the rest of my life! You have to will it; will thou will you will thou will you will thou will you will you will you let the Lord help you? Will you let him make you whole? Will you stay long enough for him not only to get the foundation done but to put on the roof? Will you? Will you? Will you? Will thou be made whole? Will you? It's up to you! Lord if you can do anything he threw that anything right back in his face. Can you believe it? Then he can do it; it's just one thing that God cannot do. It's only one thing that he cannot do. He CANNOT fail. Now you want to write this down you should read this scripture every day this week. Those of you that have low self-esteem, people saying that you can't, people saying you won't, your family telling you don't try.

THOUGHTS OF PEACE

Jeremiah 29:11, **For I know the thoughts that I think toward you, saith the Lord, thoughts of peace.** This is God talking to you today. He wants you to have peace, he wants you to be strong, he wants you to stop worrying, you are ruining your nervous system. He wants you to be calm and at peace. He said they're thoughts of what? Peace! God is not trying to kill you! God does not have to try and kill you he can just kill you. He can just think and you'll be dead. So don't let the devil deceive you. God is after you! If God is after you, he's chasing you. he knows where you are. Come on somebody. Some of this stuff you don't have to go to theological school. God is after me no I'm here. God is trying to track me down. God is trying to kill me. He does not have to try he can kill you. He can stop your breath and that's it. It will be over with. God is merciful, God is long-suffering, but his long-suffering does come to an end. What are you saying Reverend Thomas? Respond today; **Thoughts of peace, and not of evil, to give you an expected end;** here it is if your Bible is a workbook here it is. Here is the ten million dollar scripture. **Then shall ye call upon me,** there it is. Can any good thing come out of Nazareth? **Then shall ye call upon me, and ye shall go and pray unto me, and I will hearken unto you.** I'm not moved but you have my attention. Notice that. **Then shall ye call upon me,** (in verse 12) **and ye shall go and pray unto me, and I will hearken unto you.** Uh-oh you have my attention but I'm not moving yet. I'm listening, I've noticed you bit you need to do a little bit more work for me to move. I've noticed you, I've perceive because I am God, I perceive because I'm the son of God, I perceive because I'm the Spirit of God that moved around the whole world; when God the Father spoke. The Holy Spirit is saying I move, I perceive but you have to do a little bit more. **I will hearken unto you** verse 12. **And ye shall seek me, and find me,** Now I challenge you to look up those two words seek and find. **When ye shall search for me with all your heart;** Not just seeking Him on a Sunday, not just seeking Him when you're in trouble, not just paying your tithes every other month, but doing everything you need to do that's right; that's seeking the Lord.

GO AFTER HIM! RUN...

In Joshua the 3rd chapter, the Lord said when you see the Ark of the Covenant, leave your stuff and run after it! Can any good thing come out of Nazareth? Can you change your life? Can you be different? I say yes. Will you? That's up to you. Can you? Sure you can! Will you? It's up to you. Can God? Of course! Will he? It's up to you. He throws it all back off on you. We always want to blame everybody else. Oh you're the reason why you're the reason why; No you're the reason why! You're the reason why. No more excuses. You can't blame your mama for something that didn't happen in your life you're grown now. Paul said when I was a child I spake as a child but he said when I became a man I put away all that other stuff. When I was growing up, man we had one pair of shoes that we wore with everything. But now that I've became an adult I can get a shoe here and there that matches what I have on. Do I blame my mama? I thank them that they kept shoes on my feet! I thank them that they kept a roof over my head and a coat on my back and a hat on my head! It did not matter the condition of it but when I got older and I was able to bring in my own substance; and you know my kids which they're all grown! God is a good God yes he is! And they were in private school and we had to buy books I still had those shoes that had to match every outfit. But see now they're grown I can get myself a shoe with some names on it other than Payless. Why pay more when you can payless? But I can get myself a good pair of shoes. See how it works? When I was growing up I always had bad teeth and I started having my children real early. Do I blame my mama for that? No I'm glad my mama didn't kick me and the baby out. She had to raise him while she was still raising me until I was able to get grown and realize that I was a parent. Come on somebody and I thank her for that. My daddy didn't put me out. It's always a way to look at stuff. Oh when we were growing up oh God it was like three of us in the room. You're thinking about getting a boarder now you can't pay all that rent yourself. So let's not start acting like a fool that's what I'm really saying. So he says what? With your whole heart God wants your heart. **I will be found of you, saith the Lord: and I will turn away your captivity.** I will change things for you I will change what's going on in your life! I'll get rid of that depression and oppression! I can fix it! I can turn your life around! Can anything good come out of Nazareth? You need to rise up and say I came out of Nazareth! I'm not going back that way! I'm different, I'm new, he saved me, he healed me! Yes! Can anything good come out of Nazareth? You must rise and say Yea! I'm coming out of Nazareth today that's what you have to jump up and say. But some of you, you are just so happy in church, God moves, you cry and those songs you just be singing; and then you go back home and then you be recaptured and you go back into captivity. Even before you get to the door you don't even have your key out you just put your handcuffs back on. You put your stuff around your ankle and then you go back in. Some of you all are only happy in church. Man you just you have to take that joy with you right. In Mark the 5th chapter a man there was possessed with devils, and you can read it at your leisure. He had about two-thousand devils in him. Think about how is family must have felt. Is he going to ever change? Is this is? Is this what we have to look forward to? People ask about him oh we don't know where he is at. We don't even talk about him anymore. Some of our children have so many bad things; Some of our companions have done so many bad things. So Jesus finds himself here and the demons say that their name is Legion. But we find out as we go along that Jesus was able to heal the man; and the man when he was healed he wanted to go and be with Jesus. Let me find that verse I want to read that.

GO HOME

Mark 5:18 says, **And when he was come into the ship, he that had been possessed with the devil prayed him.** He said I want to go with you! Think about maybe how is family was treating him. But what did Jesus tell him to do? He said go back to your family. Go back and let them see life is not over! Go back to your family; to those who have been praying for you and let them see I have all power! Go back to your family and let them know that all hope is not lost; that all was not in vain! That's what he wants to do with you; you're in a situation today bit you don't have to stay that way! Things are not going right in your life today but something can change. Prayer can change the order of things. You can be different, you can be new. In John, the 8th chapter verse 3 and 4 we find a woman that was caught in adultery and they were ready to stone her, she knew for certain. I'm going to die today. But she lived. How do you speak to yourself? How do you talk to yourself? How do you speak over yourself? "I'm not any good." "No boy is going to ever want me but this boy". Now if he wants you another wants you too. He's just telling you that so he can get the goods for free. But you better get a contract (Referring to wedding ring). now Reverend Thomas I'm trying to tell you about these contracts.

WHERE ARE YOU TODAY?

Your life and your situation; where do you find yourself today? It's you! If you don't like what is going on in your life change it. I don't see one person in here today that God won't help. You don't have to stay in the shape you're in. You can be different. Mental illness is the worse illness because if you break your arm at least they can put it in a cast. But they can't get in the mind and put a cast on it. It took the power of God to deliver me to set me free! Stuff has happened to you too. But you have to ask yourself a question today can anything good come out of Nazareth? You're the only one that can answer that. I took a longtime for the Lord to help me. I had to be courageous, I had to face some things about my past. I was depressed because I had been molested when I was a young girl. And I went to see a psychiatrist they told me they couldn't do anything for me. Now I'm for good doctors I'm for taking medicine but sometimes they can't help you. Sometimes the help you need is beyond man. You know I have so many nurses in my family. Sometimes it's just it's beyond. It's beyond. They can't do it for me! But I know a man, He's healing sin-sick folks today. He's healing the lame, the halt, the deaf, the blind, people with cancer, people bound from being molested, people that's have addictions. I know a man that can set you free today! The only thing it costs you is a holy life. You went and did everything else. What do you have to lose? Why don't you just come to Jesus? He's calling he's calling. Just come to Jesus. Why don't you just come right now? Can anything good come out of Nazareth? Why don't you give the Lord a chance? You've let people use you men and women. Some of you let your kids seduce you. I don't care how big my kids got I still punched them with my fist. You're in my house; I'm so glad I don't have to raise another child. My poor little dog, Cyrus, I feel sorry for him sometimes but he has learned how to even take care of himself until I get home. But see now my children, who are all grown, they are realizing man wow what mamma was saying was right. Some of them have their own kids now.

GOD WANTS TO HELP YOU

God wants to help you today. Are you going to let Him help you? Come on he wants to help you today. Can anything good come out of Nazareth? That's you that's you. Nathanael, He had that hope in his heart but he hadn't seen it. And if you believe it today you will see you will see the greatness of God. If you believe it today He'll move for you! If you believe it today He will move for you today! He will move for you this day. The Bible says where two or more are gathered together in my name I am there in the midst. He is ready to show up today. Christ is here, I bring you the Christ; Not myself because I can't heal you and I can't forgive sins but I bring you Jesus the Christ; the spotless lamb. He can fix it for you today. And if you want to be free of what's going in your life, if you're going to live your life right I want you to lift those hands and say the sinner's prayer with me.

The Sinner's Prayer:

Oh God! Oh God! Oh God! Please help me! Please forgive me for sinning against you. But I have come home never to leave you again. Oh Lord I know there are many false Christ'. Oh Lord I know the Antichrist is in the world now, and if he's in the world now I know my only way out is to make it to Rapture ground; is to make it to Rapture ground. And by faith in the blood save my soul! Save my soul! Wash me in your blood! Cleanse me and make me whole! Save my soul! Save my soul! Come on in Jesus! And if you meant that neighbor He is there. Stay with God and He will stay with you. Are you ready? Let's go!

NOTES

DJG

NOTES

DJG

NOTES

DJG

NOTES

DJG

PART 6

FINAL EXAM

CHAPTER 15

FINALLY, REAL LOVE

John 15:12-13 say, **This is my commandment, That ye love one another, as I have loved you. Greater love hath no man than this, that a man lay down his life for his friends.**

THERE WILL BE SEARCHING

Finally, real love. Finally, real love. If you have ever been in love or infatuated with something or someone, you were searching, looking for something --- looking for someone. You were looking for love; you were looking for someone to accept you "Just as you are." A façade came in the beginning when you tried to live up to the expectation of others. Some have gone from relationship to relationship, whether it was a man and a woman, sisters, brothers or co-workers, it doesn't matter. Wherever there is a lack of love, there will be *searching, hunting* – looking finally for real love.

LET US LOVE ONE ANOTHER

I John 4:7-8 say, **Beloved, let us love one another: for love is of God; and everyone that loveth is born of God, and knoweth God. He that loveth not knoweth not God; for God is love.** What's is real love? Real love is being loved *without stipulation*; no *ifs, ands* or *buts*. There are no conditions tied to it. It is "unconditional." There exists no prenuptial agreement, saying that I will love you "If. I'll love you today but not tomorrow. I'll love you today just as long as it pleases me. I'll love you until it becomes inconvenient for me." Real love is not like that. Real love has nothing to do with how well you look and how well you speak or present yourself before others; how well you fit into an outfit, your status or how much money you make. Real love, the Word teaches us, is strong as death (Song of Solomon 8:6). Real love covers a multitude of sins (Proverbs 10:12).

LOVE IS

Real love, as recorded in the love chapter [I Corinthians 13th chapter], **suffereth long, and is kind; charity** [love] **envieth not; charity vaunteth not itself, is not puffed up, Doth not behave itself unseemly, seeketh not her own, is not easily provoked, thinketh no evil; Rejoiceth not in iniquity, but rejoiceth in the truth; Beareth all things, believeth all things, hopeth all things, endureth all things. Charity** [love] **never faileth (I Corinthians 13:4-8(a)).** Whether you want to face truth today or not, that's the love we [me and you], are looking for; the love we are longing for; the love this *whole world groaneth for. Real love*. All the love that we will ever need can be found in Jesus Christ. **For God so loved the world, that he gave his only begotten Son, that whosoever believeth in him should not perish, but have everlasting life** (John 3:16). Christ loved us so much that He gave His life for us. What love is that? It's divine love of course. **And being found in fashion as a man, he humbled himself, and became obedient unto death, even the death of the cross** (Philippians 2:8).

LO, I COME

For it is not possible that the blood of bulls and of goats should take away sins. Wherefore when he cometh into the world, he saith, Sacrifice and offering thou wouldest not, but a body hast thou prepared me: In burnt offerings and sacrifices for sin thou hast had no pleasure. Then said I, Lo, I come (in the volume of

the book it is written of me,) to do thy will, O God (Hebrews 10:3-7). Jesus was born to die for all of our sins, once and for all. **Now is my soul troubled; and what shall I say? Father, save me from this hour: but for this cause came I unto this hour** (John 12:27). Yes, Jesus paid it all! What love He showed to each and every one of us. **Wherefore, as by one man sin entered into the world, and death by sin; and so death passed upon all men, for that all have sinned. For it by one man's offence** [Adam] **death reigned by one; much more they which receive abundance of grace of the gift of righteousness shall reign in life by one, Jesus Christ** (Romans 5:12, 17). Adam loved himself which caused the curse to come on the entire human race. Christ loved us all which, through His shed blood, brought redemption, salvation and healing for soul, mind and body. Through Christ's death we have the hope of eternal life in Him. That's real love, my friend.

GOD REMEMBERS

And God heard their groaning, and God remembered his covenant with Abraham, with Isaac, and with Jacob (Exodus 2:24). God hears and He delivers. *Everyone* is looking for love. *Everyone* **needs** love; some recognize their need for love while others do not. **For we know that the whole creation groaneth and travaileth in pain together until now** (Romans 8:22). That's what we have been searching for. Real love or a lack of it controls us – that need for love. That's what motivates or does not motivate us – the desire for that love. Everyone wants love. Real love.

A STATE OF CONFUSION

James 1:8 says, **A double minded man is unstable in all his ways**. For a number of years, many year ago, before starting this work, I lived in a state of confusion. I was unable to discern between love and lust. My mind was filled with weeds of deceit, leeches and hurt, all of which lead to destructive behavior. Boy, what a mess those years proved to be. I was truly in search of the love that could only come from my Maker. My soul travaileth in me for Him but I lacked direction; I didn't know where to start.

MY THINKING WAS ALL WRONG

Many times I thought that if I gave myself to someone physically and emotionally, surely that individual would love me. My thinking was all wrong. In a large number of cases, women and men view love slightly different. A woman, she looks for the time, and the effort. She looks for that little extra something. It doesn't have to be grand. It doesn't have to be much but she looks for the consideration; the compassion; the time; the thought. Yes, it's the thought that counts. A woman looks forward to flowers; the rose. The little notes left around the house. Not much. Not much else. To a man, some men like flowers too. Men as well as women need encouragement, support and love. They need to know that they are wanted, cared for and appreciated. Of course, they know this without hearing it – having it affirmed through the passionate, considerate voice of a loved one brings great joy and contentment in the worst of times. "You did such a wonderful job. I missed you today. I am very proud of you." Those words may seem so insignificant to some but those few, simple words carried with great love, mean more than the wealth of this world.

MOMMA'S HOME

Our children, yes, our children, they need love and encouragement as well. They need to hear "How was your day? Here, momma has something special for you in this bag." I remember when I was growing up. I couldn't wait to hear that doorbell ring from the living room. I knew it was momma. She always brought home something good from work. Oh, it didn't matter that it was the remainder of her cold lunch; it was my momma and I wanted it. She knew it too. Automatically, we each headed for that bag. So it is with my children when they were growing up. They are all grown now and some even have their own families. When they young, they would stand waiting for momma [me] to come in the front door. They were so helpful with all the bags – to see what I had brought for them, of course. When I got home from the day's journey, I knew what to expect. It was like clockwork. I knew that my family would need "their" few minutes with me and rightly so. After they had gotten their fill of me, after they had each received a bit of my attention – a bit of my love, they would gladly go on their way to resume whatever it was that held their attention before I walked through that door. I *had to learn* and had to realize what a great treat and honor it was to be wanted, missed and loved; to have someone waiting to hear of the my day's events; to even care about what happened to me. I am truly grateful for my family and good friends. I love family. So many people go and come without anyone giving them a thought. Some people don't see their immediate family members but once or twice a year. There are houses today, not homes, where loved ones come and go and no one cares and even notices if they don't arrive back for hours and even days. I am blessed. I am blessed. So many people come and go from their various destinations without one word of love uttered, either upon entering the house or leaving the house. I am grateful. It makes a huge difference to know that someone cares. It makes a big difference. If use to complain and fuss about all the attention and demand required of me. "Don't these kids know… blah, blah, blah." I had to learn what a blessing the "blah, blah, blah" was. I have learned that, even as a mom in this world, the Lord has given me such magnetism – people are drawn to me automatically and most of the time I don't even know it initially. I thank God for the love that He has put into the hearts of others for this "preacher gurl." I am thankful for real love and the ability to give that same real love to others. I John 3:1(a) says, **Behold, what manner of love the Father hath bestowed upon us, that we should be called the sons of God.**

I WANTED SOMETHING TO LOVE

When I was very young, I was so depressed; I would have plants all over my home. I wanted something to love. So, I would buy plants and more plants. I would buy them tall. I would buy the real small ones, and I would nurture them and cultivate them. I got such joy in transplanting them and watching them grow. But what I was doing was looking for love. It couldn't fight me back, couldn't retaliate. I was quick to cut those dead leaves off and prune them. I was watching over them. At the time, I didn't realize that was something I picked that I could love. They wouldn't negate me, wouldn't cast me down, wouldn't push me aside, and wouldn't prejudge me, just me, the plants and the sun. I didn't realize it at the time, but that's what I was doing. I had plants all over my house, big ones and small ones. As I began to recognize the love of God, I stopped buying plants. And if they died, ok, it wasn't a big deal. My kids will tell you, I didn't want a brown leaf to come up. Don't plant them. I'll water them, because you might overwater them. Don't bump into my plants! But that was my little way of wanting to love something. But I didn't want that false love that attacks, hits, kicks and talks about. And words...ooh. I would rather you put a knot on my head than to say something mean and cruel to me. As I began to recognize the love of God, I didn't feel the need of the plants any more. I began to let the love of God heal me. I didn't feel the need any more for those plants.

DANNY BOY

When I adopted by son, Daniel, he was about eight months when he came into my home. I was talking to my father one day about him. I went over there to where Daniel was living at the time. He was at a relative's house where they had him in a back room. He was in a little playpen, and nobody was paying attention to him. I thought, "My God, his mom can't be here." He was just as cute as he could be, laying there. He was small for his age. I just wanted to love him. I just wanted to love Daniel. I would talk to my father about him, and my father said, "You know what? You needed that love. You needed him." I think back on that now, and my Dad was right. To love, change those diapers, and watch him grow, to know he needed me. But that was because I didn't and couldn't recognize love. I didn't see it around in my home. I knew my father loved my mother, even though I didn't *see* the love. Maybe that was the way they expressed love toward one another. But then, when it came around to me being with somebody who was emotional, I would be like, "Are you crazy, touching me out in the street? Get back off of me." Listen to what I'm telling you today. You can't give something you don't have. You can't do it. It's impossible. And loving somebody is more than having a child, people. Listen to me. It's more than intimacy. If all you can do is show love in the bedroom, that's not love [sex is not love]. Most couples that do not get along in the bedroom will not get along outside the bedroom. Count on it. It's a strong form of a communication in marriage. That's the way the Lord planned.

UNABLE TO GIVE LOVE

I use to struggle so hard with being love and wanting love. Outside of God's great love umbrella, I was unable to receive love from others nor was I able to give love to others. John 15:5 says, **For without me ye can do nothing.** I just wanted to be accepted for who I was. That proved to be a problem at first because I didn't know who that was. Therefore, I attempted to fit into some protocol of others. If long hair and red nails called attention my way, that's what I did. On the inside, however, I was still stuck in the "lost and found," waiting to be collected by my owner. I was still malnourished from a gross need of love. I love deficient. I was dying from malnutrition. I was so baffled about life and love – real love, not realizing that having all that was needed, it was hard. My parents did a wonderful job with us kids. I lacked the reality of God's love and that created many problems in my life. I am grateful for the seed that my parents planted in my life of fearing God and going to His house. They taught us how to conduct ourselves in the House of the Lord. **The fear of the Lord is the beginning of wisdom** (Psalm 111:10).

CRYING FROM WITHIN

Train up a child in the way he should go: and when he is old, he will not depart from it (Proverbs 22:6). The Lord was able to hold on to me because of the seed that was planted in me by my parents. I found my way home. Thank you momma. I found my way home. I cried, without knowing how hard I was crying, **I will arise and go to my father, and will say unto him, Father, I have sinned against heaven, and before thee, and am no more worthy to be called thy son: make me as one of thy hired servants** (Luke 15:18-19). Crying from within, Precious Jesus met me. I reached out and the Lord reached toward me and pulled me up. Oh Hallelujah! **Then I said, I am cast out of thy sight: yet I will look again toward thy holy temple. The waters compassed me about, even to the soul: the depth closed me round about, the weeds were wrapped about my head. I went down to the bottoms of the mountains; the earth with her bars was about me for ever: yet hast thou brought up my life from corruption, O Lord my God. When my soul fainted within me I remembered the Lord** [that seed that had been planted in me by my parents]**: and my prayer came in unto thee, into thine holy temple** (Jonah 2:4-7)**.**

RIGHT IN THE MIDDLE OF A DESERT – OASIS

Before I met you, my life was standing still
I had a one-way ticket to nowhere.
My heart was filled with fear and it was very clear
That I was going down for the third time.
You brought an oasis right in the middle of a desert
You brought an oasis right in the middle of a desert
Oasis, oasis,
Oasis, oasis[27]

This is the testimony of my life. I knew that I was "Going down for the last time." Jesus, I love you. Thank you for saving my life.

I DIDN'T KNOW

Having different relationships in the world, I really never understood my responsibility in marriage before coming into the knowledge of the truth. I didn't know what I was getting into. I heard a lot of things but I was not properly trained according to the Word of God but that lack of knowledge didn't lessen my accountability or responsibility to the Word of God regarding the holiness and sacredness of marriage. I didn't know. I was ignorant.

---

[27]   Baylor, Helen. *"Oasis."* Look A Little Closer. Word 1991.

I STRUGGLED SO HARD

Acts 2:21 says, **And it shall come to pass, that whosoever shall call on the name of the Lord shall be saved.** I struggled so hard with someone loving me for me. Then I began to build up fences, doors, bridges and gates around my heart. I was double minded. Finally, I just shut down. I decided that "nobody is going to hurt me again. I am going to put up a front. No one is ever going to hurt me again. I understand now." I understood all too late. Take the time to show love to each other. Most of the troubles, trials and problems that emerge from various relationships stem from a lack of love in the home; a lack of love from the "nest." We are 80-90 percent of what we were taught as children. That is profound yet true. You can trace most emotional, physical, physiology troubles back to childhood. Count on it. Take time to be kind. Take time to show love. Take time to give love. A lack of love can be generated from a missing family altar – no family prayer. People don't sit down to dinner anymore; don't pray together. Communication has been swapped for texting and face time. We have lost so much in transition and modernization. You have to keep the line of communication open between one another. We can't be *too busy*. It will cost us down the road. We must become good stewards of God's love. It is our most vital possession and our most vital responsibility – the use of God's love. That's the only way we will be able to capture the multitudes in this last and final hour. God's great love for mankind must be and will be demonstrated and then the end will come.

A LABOR OF LOVE

When you have God's love, you don't mind laboring with someone. Romans 15:1, 3 says, **We then that are strong ought to bear the infirmities of the weak, and note to please ourselves. For even Christ pleased not himself; but, as it is written, The reproaches**

of them that reproached thee feel on me. You don't mind being longsuffering with your neighbor, friend, co-worker, companion and others. I told the Lord so many years ago, before He delivered me, "I don't like myself." A lack of real love often shows up as low self-esteem. [The woman at the well] and [the woman caught in adultery] who does that but a person who doesn't know or are confused about their worth? When you lack real love, you try to fit the images of others. The false images that are often presented on television. There is a great amount of distortment outside of God's love but in God's love, there is completeness and wholeness, contentment and peace of mind. Your voice, appearance, height, weight; your color, the enemy can and will use it against you if you one speck of self-doubt. He will ride you and grind you down. You have to come out of that bed every morning ready. Ready to get things done. Push the faith button. Your life can be a living hell, right here on earth because there is no peace in your mind. Isaiah 26:3 says, **Thou will keep him in perfect peace, whose mind is stayed on thee: because he trusteth in thee.** Without peace in your mind, it becomes a battlefield for the devil and he will continue(th) to drop bombs of depression, despair and fear. Blow those bombs up before they land anywhere in your mind. How long can you keep going down such a destructive path? The love of god is full of endurance, courage, peace and contentment. The blessed Savior will give you strength for *every* need.

Genuine love. "Just love me for whom I am. Don't try to make me into something 'you' want. Don't try and make me be somebody different; somebody old, somebody new, but just me. Just love – the way that I am." *The only person I know that has that much love* is Jesus Christ. He is the only one that is willing and qualified to spend the kind of time, energy and effort to fix you – to put you back together again, ever so gently, ever so kindly, ever so patiently.

This is a great time to begin again. Please repeat this simple prayer with me, asking for complete restoration and deliverance. The Lord is ready and willing. This is a time for love.

And when I passed by thee, and saw thee polluted in thine own blood, I said unto thee when thou wast in thy own blood, Live; yea, I said unto thee when thou wast in thy blood, Live (Ezekiel 16:6)**.**

The Sinner's Prayer:

Oh God! Oh God! Oh God! Please help me! Please forgive me for sinning against you. But I have come home never to leave you again. Oh Lord I know there are many false Christ'. Oh Lord I know the Antichrist is in the world now, and if he's in the world now I know my only way out is to make it to Rapture ground; is to make it to Rapture ground. And by faith in the blood save my soul! Save my soul! Wash me in your blood! Cleanse me and make me whole! Save my soul! Save my soul! Come on in Jesus! And if you meant that neighbor He is there. Stay with God and He will stay with you. Are you ready? Let's go!

NOTES

DJG

NOTES

NOTES

NOTES

NOTES

DJG

NOTES

DJG

NOTES

DJG

NOTES

DJG